IMAGES
of America

ATCHISON COUNTY

ON THE COVER: The interior of Westboro Harness and Hardware Store, owned and operated by Oscar S. and Emma A. (Peck) Uttvits, is seen here. The general store had just about any item a homeowner needed and was always looking for anything else customers might want. These stores had to be a "one-stop shop" to keep customers from going to competitors, so they carried everything from cooking stoves, warming stoves, washing machines, and push lawn mowers to smaller items such as buckets and lanterns. These shop owners also provided services for their customers, such as repairing harnesses, bridles, shoes, and belts. Store hours were long, with many open from 6:00 a.m. until 9:00 p.m. (Courtesy of Marcia L. Frede.)

IMAGES
of America

ATCHISON COUNTY

Kim A. Evans

ARCADIA
PUBLISHING

ISBN 978-0-7385-9082-0

Published by Arcadia Publishing
Charleston, South Carolina

Printed in the United States of America

Library of Congress Control Number: 2012943533

For all general information, please contact Arcadia Publishing:
Telephone 843-853-2070
Fax 843-853-0044
E-mail sales@arcadiapublishing.com
For customer service and orders:
Toll-Free 1-888-313-2665

Visit us on the Internet at www.arcadiapublishing.com

To my wife, Myra

Contents

ACKNOWLEDGMENTS

Many people have assisted me in the preparation of this book, including those who took these photographs years ago and saved them with a brief history, which made my job so much easier. To the memory of those who have gone before us, a great debt of gratitude is owed. When these photographs were taken, it was not known that these people were creating a historical record of Atchison County that would be available for years to come. Even events that seemed trivial at the time help future generations recall the local people, the economic situation of the era, the happy and the tragic times, and so much more.

One special historian in our area who is no longer with us but to whom I am greatly indebted is Harry Broerman, who was a walking encyclopedia of Atchison County lore. Also, Harry and Mary Combs, Betty Wennihan, Megan McAdams, Hon. Corey K. Herron, Dorothine Woolsey, Marcia L. Frede, Kay Gibson, Lyllis Vette, Phil and Meta Hull, Maxine Staples, Sheridan Mires, George and Patty Laur, Anna Belle Johnson, Delores Harrington, and Ken Kolodzie all opened their homes to me and were extremely cooperative and happy to share their historical photographs. Billie Schneider, Charleen Spencer, Kevin Evans, and Casey Martin also assisted me, and many thanks are due to them. Thanks also go out to the *Atchison County Mail*, the *Tarkio Avalanche*, Bob Alldredge of the Fairfax Exchange Bank, and the Atchison County Historical Society and all of their staff.

A big thank you goes to my editor, Liz Gurley, for her encouragement and the nudge I needed to stay within the deadline.

If I have omitted anyone, I beg your forgiveness for my forgetfulness and will thank you personally.

INTRODUCTION

Atchison County is only one small part of the Platte Purchase of 1803. Prior to that time, this far-reaching area was inhabited by Native Americans and British, French, and Spanish fur trappers. After the Platte Purchase was made, white settlers began their trek west into the new territory to find a place to call home and make a living from the land. While the white man believed in ownership of the land and began to section off their claims, this was a completely new concept to Native Americans, who believed that the land belonged to all and should be left to the next generations unchanged. Indian culture is memorialized in the area with local names like Tarkio, "where walnuts grow," and Nishnabotna, "where canoes are made," among others.

The influx of white settlers caused friction, and the settlers asked their government for protection. Several army posts sprang up in places like Fort Osage, near Independence, Missouri; Fort Leavenworth, in Kansas; Fort Atkinson, 20 miles north of Omaha; and Fort Kearney, in Nebraska City. The influence of the forts was felt in Atchison County, as the supply lines helped create the north-south stagecoach routes in those early days. This road was on the east side of Tarkio River Valley and crossed the Tarkio River going north, close to where St. John's Lutheran Church stands today. It was referred to as the "Drover's Trail." According to an account researched and written by Harry Broerman, "This overland route was pretty much adopted by the operators of stage coach lines who entered our county near Irish Grove (later called Milton), went to Fugitt Mill (north of present day Rock Port), through Linden, Mckissick's Grove and Pleasant Grove settlements to present day Sidney, Iowa."

The Missouri River had a major impact on the earliest settlements in Atchison County, as the river was used as a natural transportation waterway. It was a geographic influence, as it forms the western border of Atchison County, but it was also used by Indians and fur trappers, who canoed up and down its banks, and later by steamboats that brought new settlers as far north as their shallow hulls would allow. Timber was plentiful near the river and its smaller tributaries, especially the Nishnabotna and the Tarkio Rivers. The first settlers made their homes close to water sources and timber, which they built homes out of and used to keep warm in the cold months. Many early community names reflected the importance of groves of trees of that area, including Oak Grove, Elm Grove, Maple, Hickory, and Locust Grove.

Atchison County was originally a part of Platte County, along with the present-day counties of Andrew, Buchanan, Holt, Nodaway, and Platte. After Buchanan County was authorized on February 10, 1839, the area north of it was known as Neatawah for a short time before becoming Holt County, which stretched all the way to the Iowa border.

On February 14, 1845, Atchison County was officially organized and split from Holt County. The first meeting of Atchison County representatives occurred on that date at the home of Conrad Cloepfil, and Elijah Needles, David Hunsaker, and Alexander McElroy acted as the first commissioners of the county court.

These men divided up the county into five townships: Clark, Polk, Bluff, Nishnabotna, and Tarkio. Most of Bluff Township was deeded back to Iowa after the Honey War, when the US Supreme Court decided once and for all the location of the state border between Missouri and Iowa.

One early notable and prosperous resident was David Rankin, who had many titles but is best remembered for his agricultural pursuits. Although Rankin had large landholdings in Illinois as well, by 1876 he was moving his center of operations to Tarkio. He did not formally live in Tarkio until 1885, building his home there two years later and purchasing large parcels of land in the area. While many farmers and ranchers preferred land closer to water or timber, Rankin bought land that was considered less desirable at a much lower price. Over time, the value of the land only increased as modes of transportation became more modern and more people moved into the area. At the height of his success, Rankin owned 1.42 million acres in Nebraska alone. He also completed three terms in the Illinois Legislature and had holdings and investments in at least seven banks.

Many of the early towns of Atchison County are no longer found on the map, including Grove, Dotham, Linden, Milton, and Sonora. It is the hope that, by printing this book, the families who lived in the many towns of Atchison County will never be forgotten.

One
Mobility

From about 1815 to 1915, horses provided the main mode of transportation in the United States. Horses were able to maneuver the most difficult terrain, and later, when roads were smoothed and mud was not too deep, they could pull buggies. When horses were not transporting their owners, they could be hooked up to farm implements to turn soil or cultivate weeds.

All this time, owners spent time with their horses, sharing food and water and getting to know each other's temperaments. Owners knew it was in their best interest to keep their animals in peak health; if an animal came up lame, farmers would have to find a replacement, costing them money they may not have had, or work 10 times harder doing it alone. Over time, horses and owners had a bond that ran deep. The animals often lived to be 25 or 30, with about 20 of those years being its most productive.

When automobiles became more affordable and more farmers purchased them, many horse owners resisted the change, choosing instead to do as their parents had done. For long distances, train travel was readily available in most thriving towns, negating the need to purchase a car. Also, roads in the early 1900s were still dirt and turned to mud in poor weather. Automobiles became stuck easily in winter and spring, while a horse could get through the terrain if need be. Train travel was inexpensive and dependable, usually coming through town twice a day.

By 1909, though, Henry Ford's reliable Model T was available for only $850, while most of his competitors' automobiles cost between $2,000 and $3,000. Over time, the Model T became even more affordable; by 1916, a standard touring model cost only $360. In the city, the automobile made more sense, as roads were much better and salaries more dependable. But eventually, automobiles came to the rural towns and villages as well. After all, a car never tired, did not need to be fed, and did not get sick or come up lame.

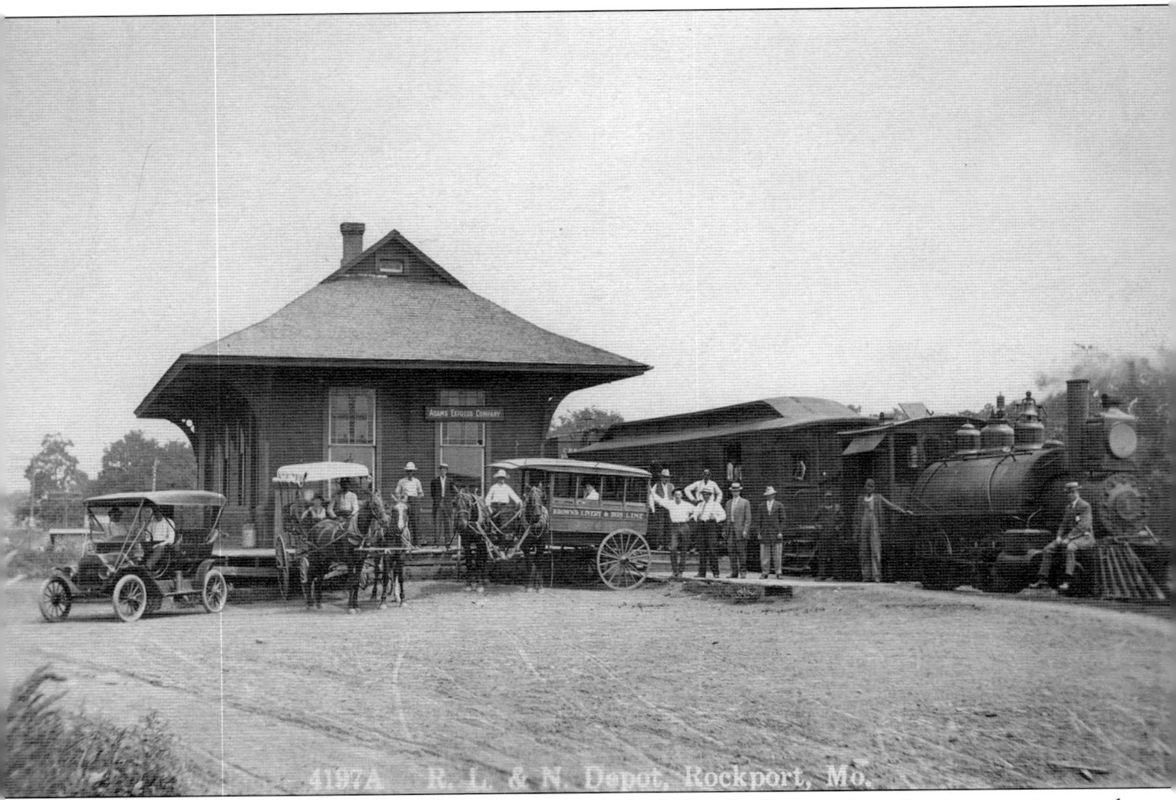

The Tarkio train depot is seen in this image, which shows all three modes of transportation used at the time. Horse-drawn wagons were on the way out, trains were about 60 years old and relied upon heavily for travel between towns, and automobiles were just beginning their cultural ascent. The sign on the window reads, "Adams Express Company," and the taxi belonged to the Brown Livery and Bus Line. (Courtesy of the Atchison County Historical Society.)

When the train came to Watson, the population shot up rapidly, as many people in the area knew they could now travel to surrounding towns and receive shipments much more quickly. Trains still come through Watson, but being mostly coal or freight trains, they no longer stop. (Courtesy of Kay Gibson.)

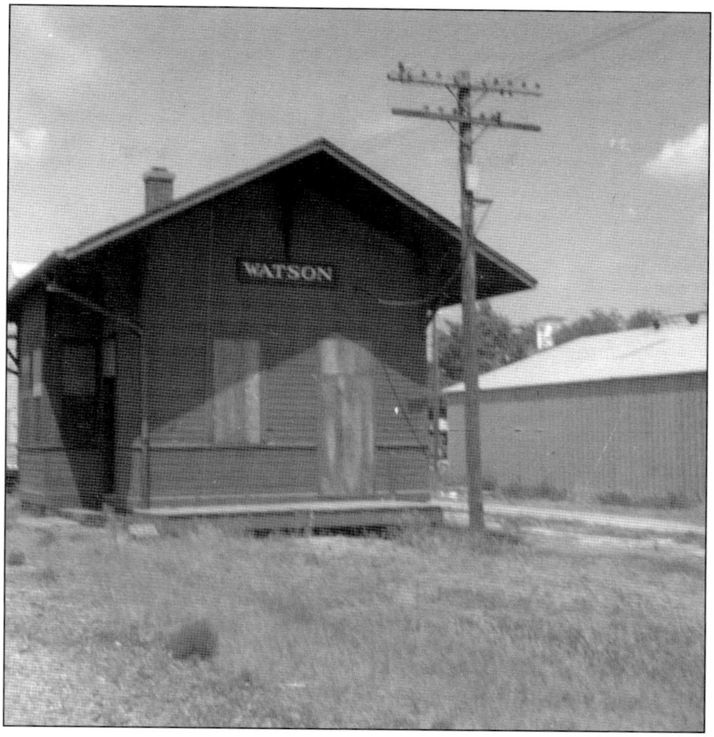

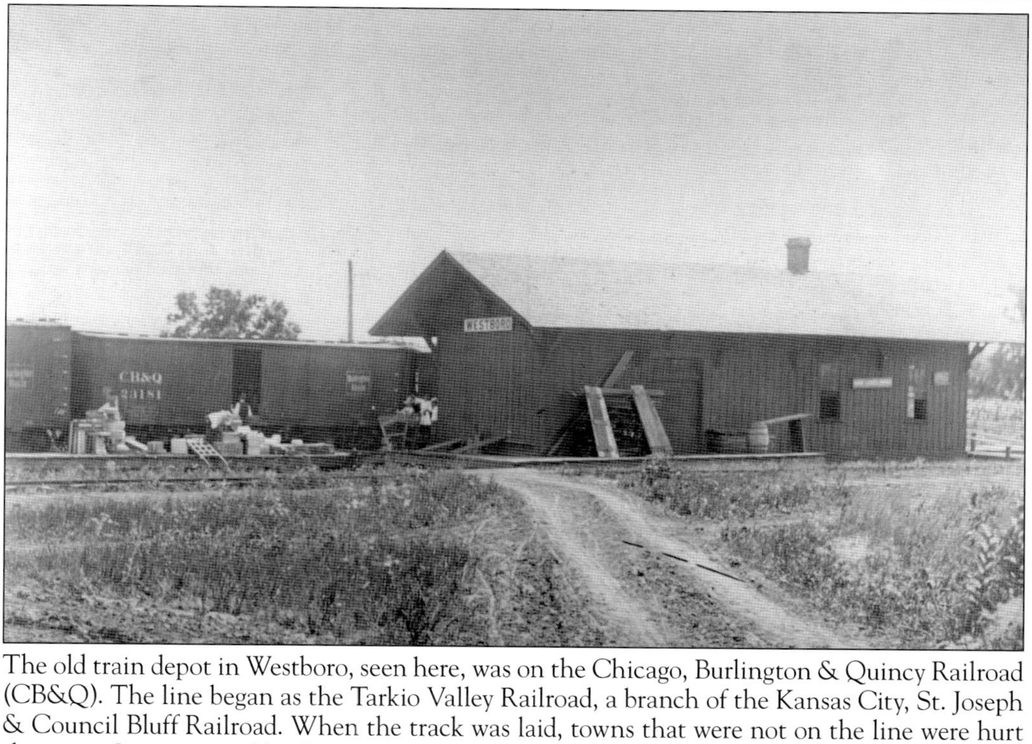

The old train depot in Westboro, seen here, was on the Chicago, Burlington & Quincy Railroad (CB&Q). The line began as the Tarkio Valley Railroad, a branch of the Kansas City, St. Joseph & Council Bluff Railroad. When the track was laid, towns that were not on the line were hurt the most. Some towns like Center Point, about halfway between Tarkio and Westboro, packed up, with residents moving to the new railroad towns. When they moved, some people even took buildings with them. (Courtesy of the Atchison County Historical Society.)

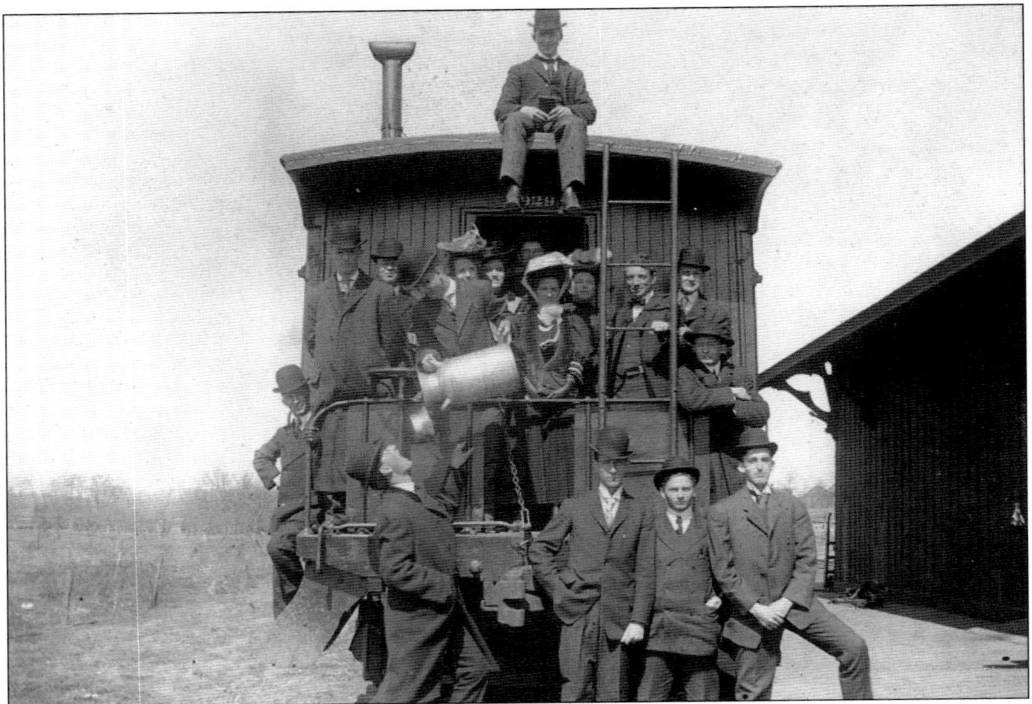

These Tarkio College students clown around on a CB&Q caboose in 1908. Student Katherine Gelvin is on the rear platform next to the ladder. While Tarkio College drew many local residents, it also attracted students from across the country. (Courtesy of the Atchison County Historical Society.)

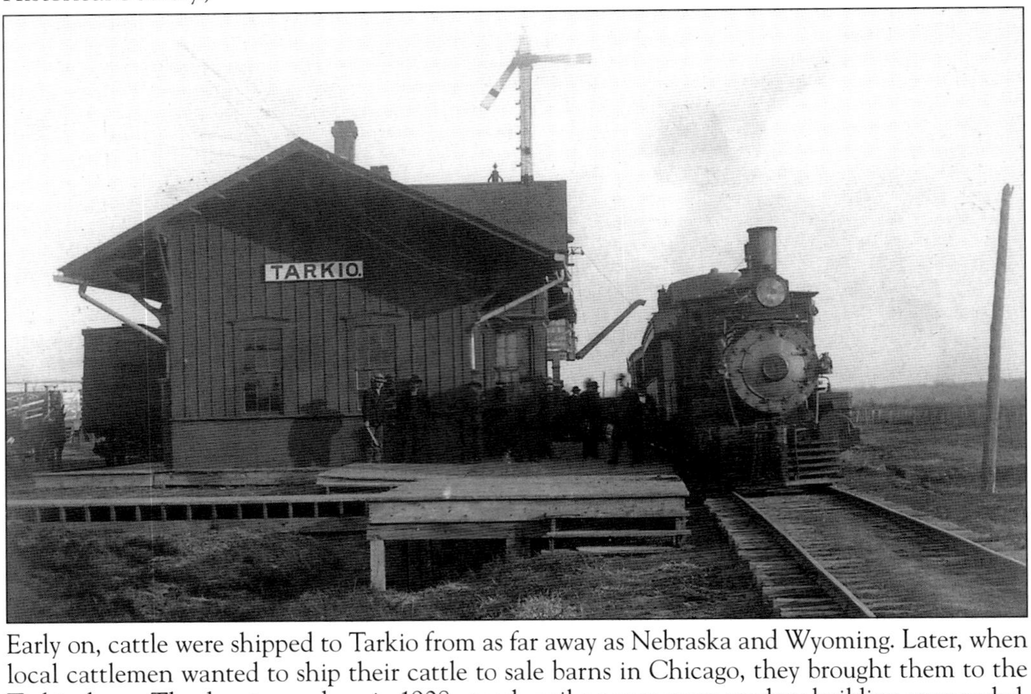

Early on, cattle were shipped to Tarkio from as far away as Nebraska and Wyoming. Later, when local cattlemen wanted to ship their cattle to sale barns in Chicago, they brought them to the Tarkio depot. The depot, seen here in 1908, stood until a newer, more modern building was needed, befitting a town of Tarkio's size. (Courtesy of the Atchison County Historical Society.)

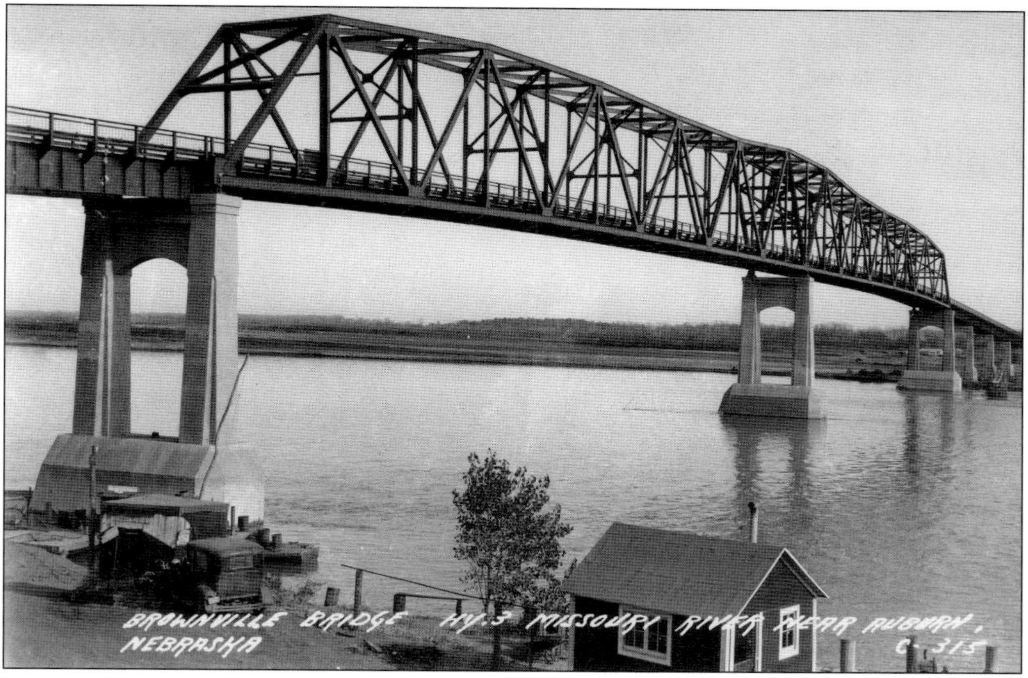

Leaders of Atchison County were partly responsible for acquiring this bridge on Highway 136 west of Rock Port. They claimed it was one of the quickest routes between Indianapolis and Denver. It was close to this site that Scott City was located for a short time before floodwaters washed it away. Another town, Kalamazoo, was located a half mile north but was also washed away by floodwaters. (Courtesy of the Atchison County Historical Society.)

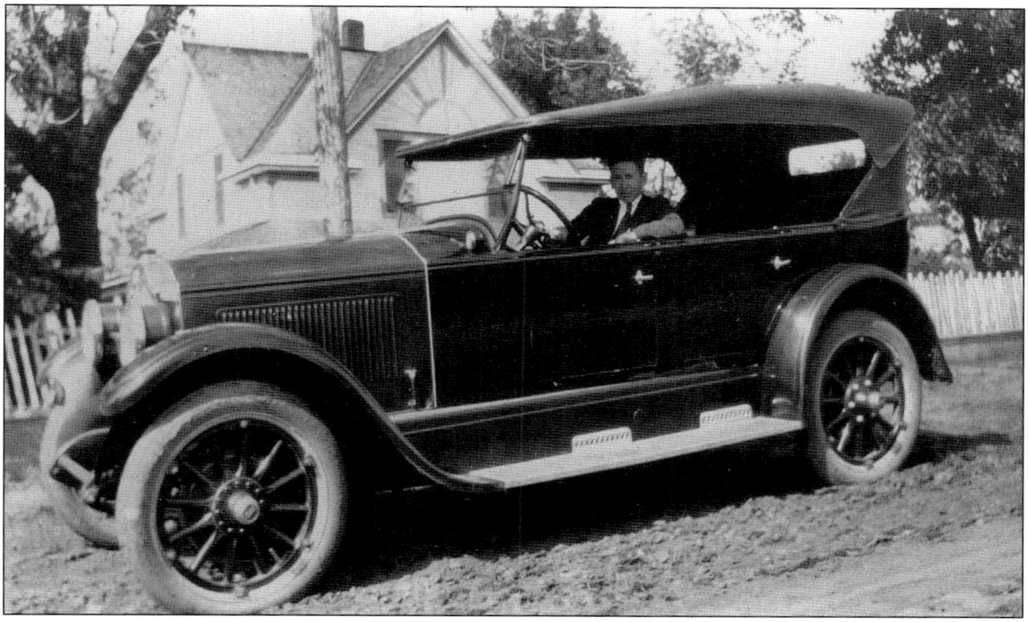

Glenn Alva Stevens of the Blanchard, Missouri, area is seen here in one of the Buicks he drove for most of his life. Stevens was born in 1908, the son of R.L. and Ora E. Stevens. He married Frieda Layden and had two sons, Roy and Max. The family lived on a farm previously owned by Emery Clark in the North Star School District. (Courtesy of Anna Belle Johnson.)

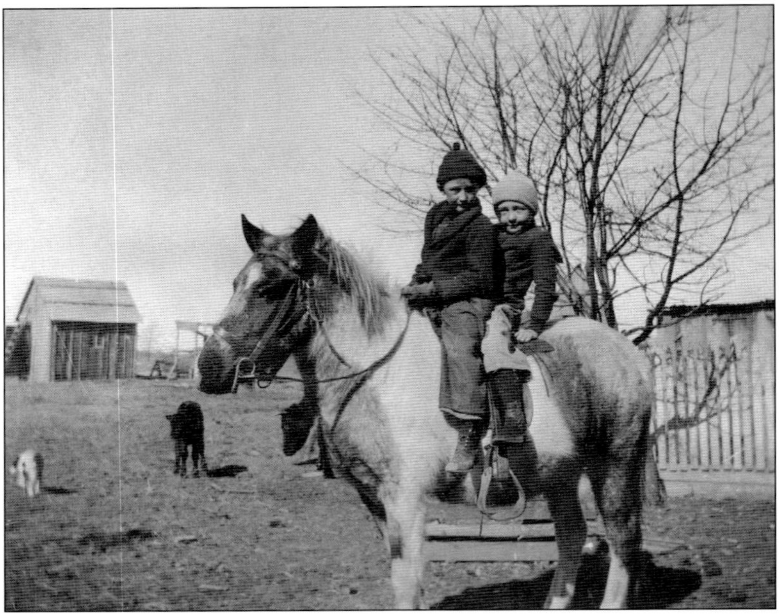

Horses were important to families because they made travel of more than a few miles much faster and easier. They could also be hooked up to a plow or a planter to help speed up farming activities. A third benefit was that younger members, like these children here, could proudly ride to school. (Courtesy of Maxine Staples.)

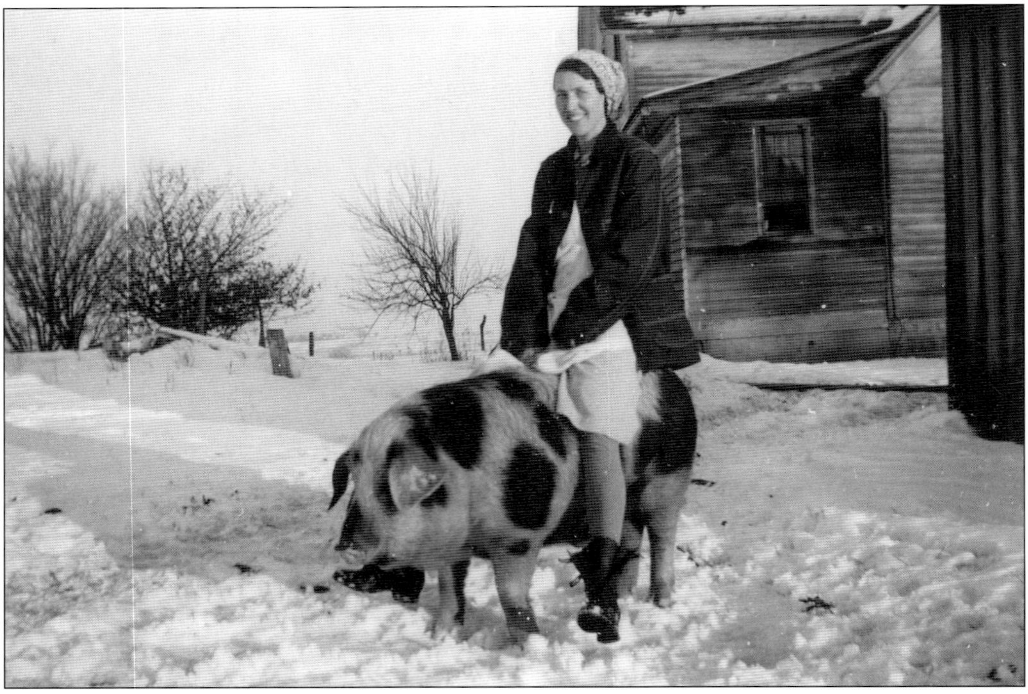

In the early 1900s, most farms had chickens, horses, hogs, cattle, row crops, and a garden. With all of these animals and crops, there were many chores for everyone in the family. By 1929, when the Great Depression hit, the experience was felt from coast to coast. Many farmers, however, at least had food on the table for their family. Here, Lena Combs McDaniel rides on her pet pig in 1923. (Courtesy of Maxine Staples.)

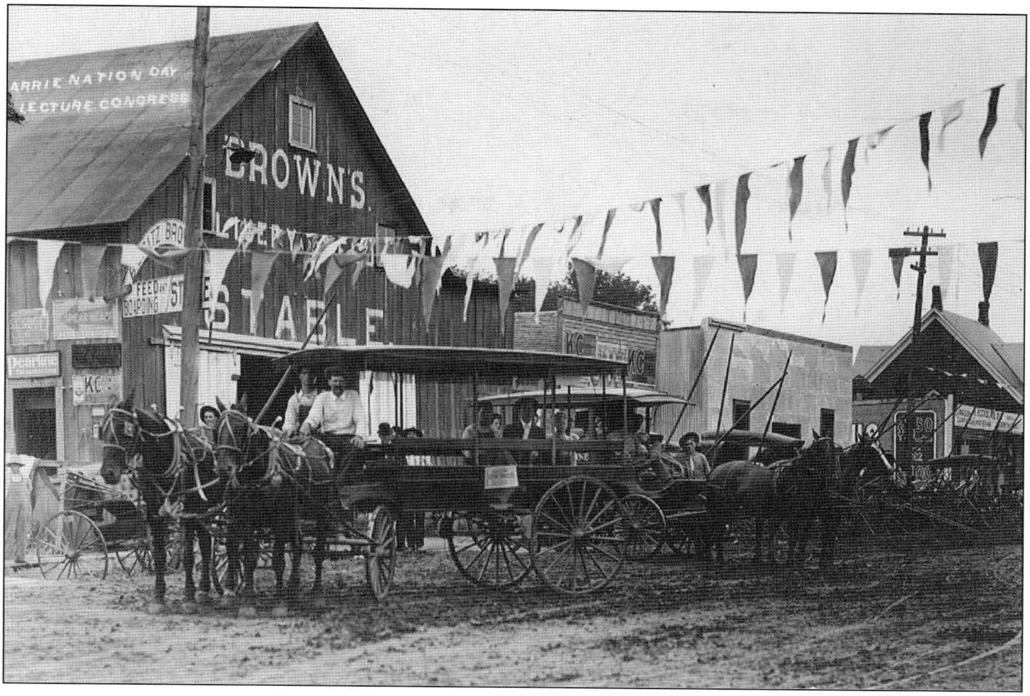

These two images are of livery stables in Atchison County, which were important places of business for all towns at this time. They provided care for horses but also supplied wood, coal, grain, and hay to the public. The photograph above shows Brown's Livery Stable in Rock Port, and it is noted that the picture was taken on Carrie Nation Day, which commemorated the work Carrie Nation performed in the name of the temperance movement. The photograph below is of Creed's Feed and Stable at the time when the United States was switching from horse-drawn vehicles to the self-propelled automobile. (Both, courtesy of the *Atchison County Mail.*)

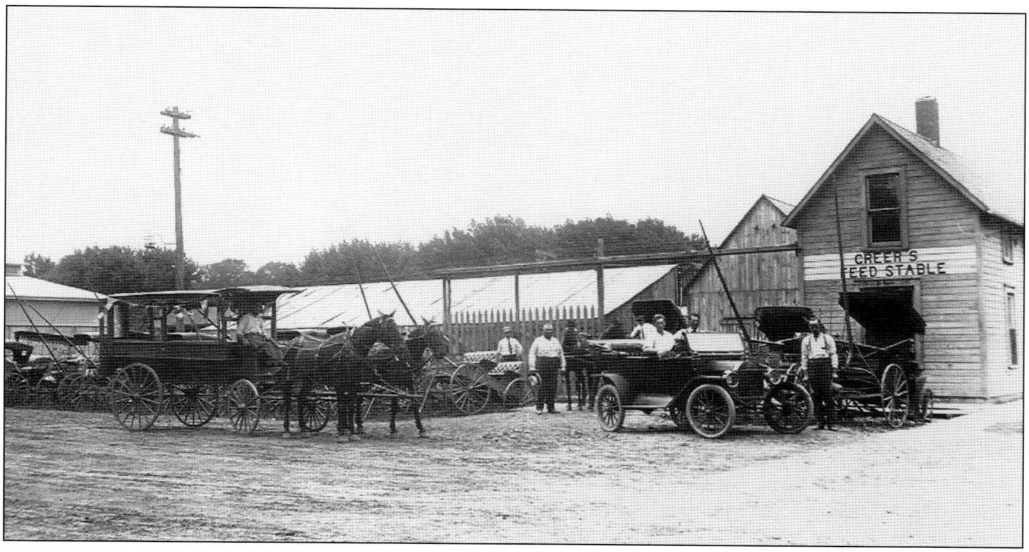

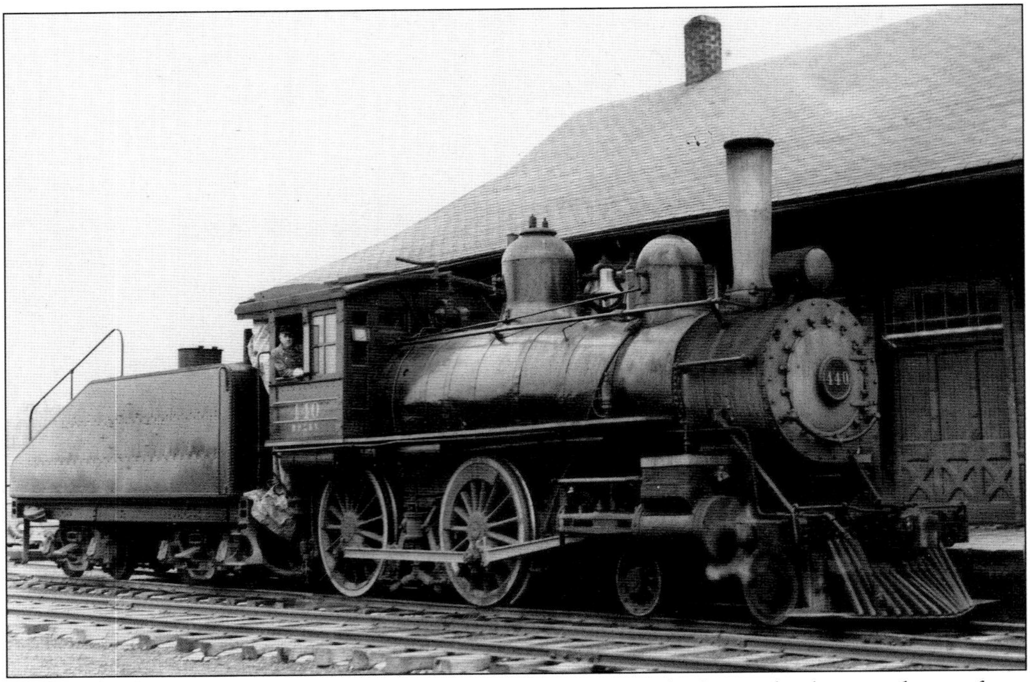

The Rock Port, Langdon & Northern (RPL&N) line is only five miles long and runs from Rock Port to Langdon (formerly Thompson's Switch), where it connects to the main line of the Burlington Railroad. The railroad line was incorporated in December 1889 and was vital to the area because it connected to the Chicago, Burlington & Quincy Railroad. James H. Hedgpeth operated the RPL&N, beginning in 1909, and was successful enough to purchase a new saddle-tank engine. (Courtesy of Hon. Corey Herron.)

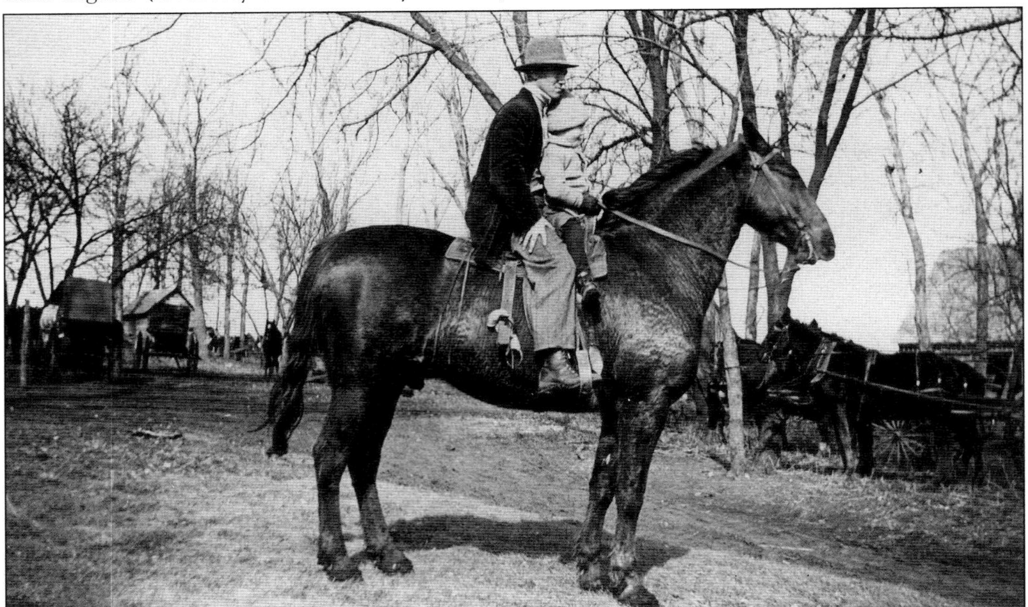

Brothers Clay (left) and Scottie Staples saddle up for another day of work on their farm about nine miles east of Tarkio. Their grandfather settled in Atchison County in 1872, and the farm is still in the family today. (Courtesy of Sheridan Mires.)

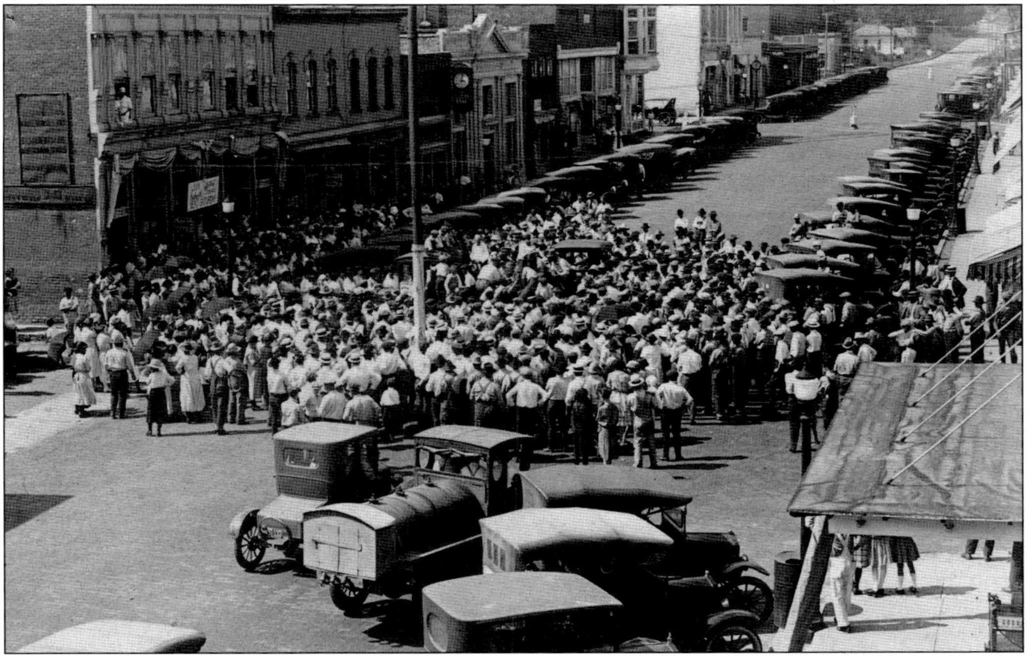

Speaking from the back of a pickup or a flatbed trailer was a good way for a candidate to reach as many voters as possible in the 1920s. Many of the Rock Port buildings in these two photographs, taken just minutes apart, are still in use today. (Both, courtesy of the *Atchison County Mail*.)

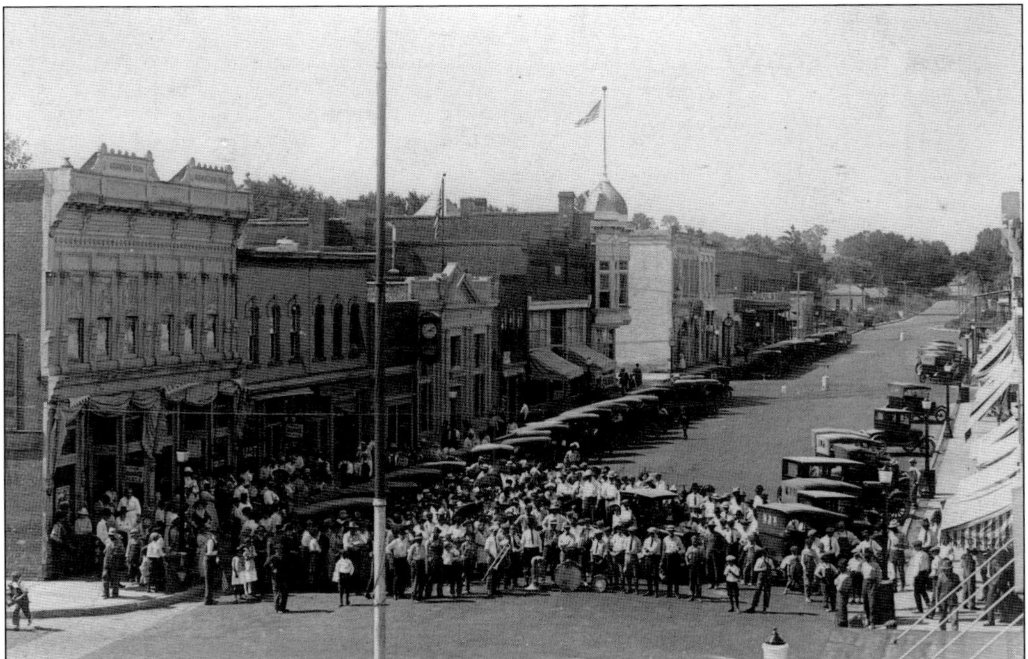

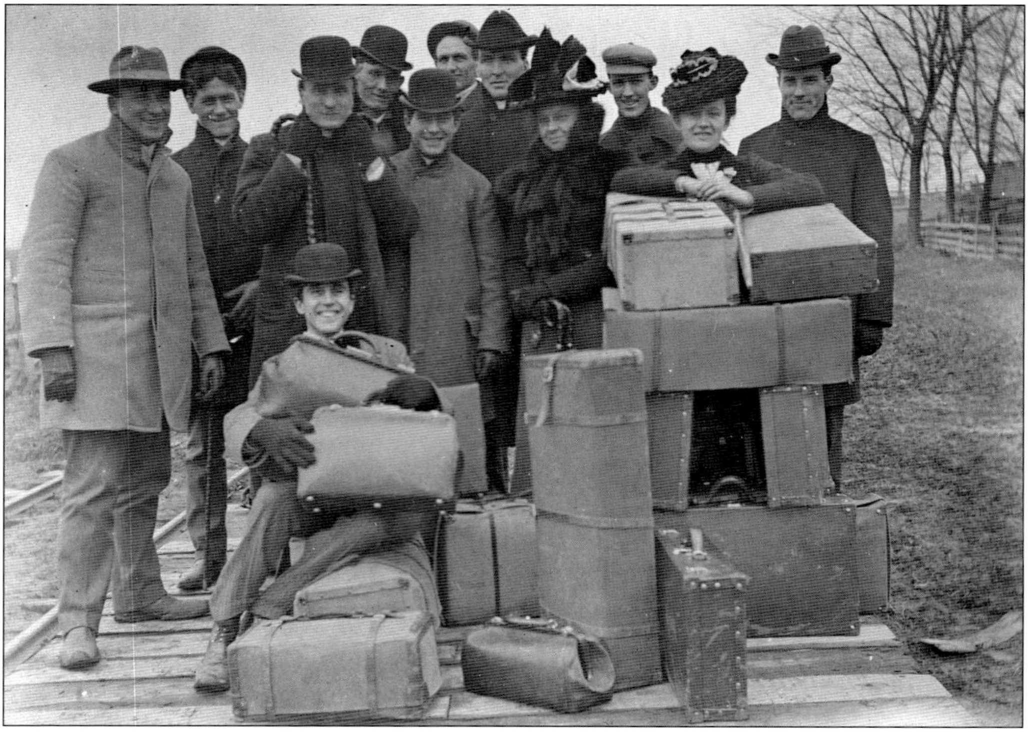

Back when trains were the predominant mode of transportation, even a trip from Tarkio to Maitland was a major undertaking, but these folks were happy to make the journey. The Tarkio Valley Railroad, a branch of the Kansas City, St. Joseph & Council Bluffs Railroad, was built through Atchison County in 1881. (Courtesy of George and Patty Laur.)

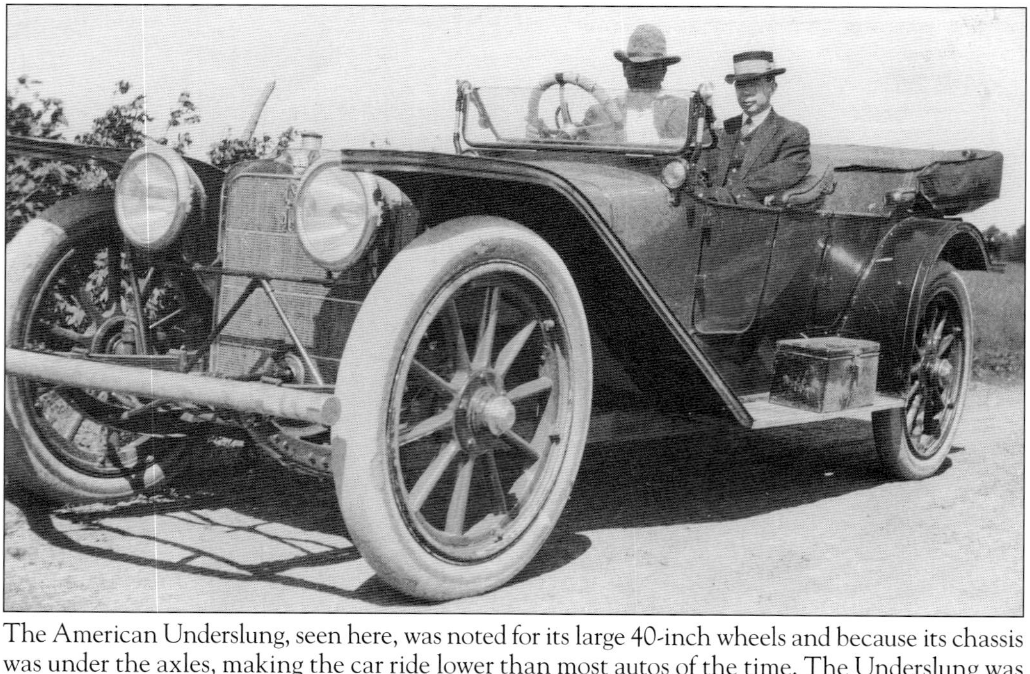

The American Underslung, seen here, was noted for its large 40-inch wheels and because its chassis was under the axles, making the car ride lower than most autos of the time. The Underslung was only produced from 1905 to 1914 in Indianapolis. (Courtesy of Maxine Staples.)

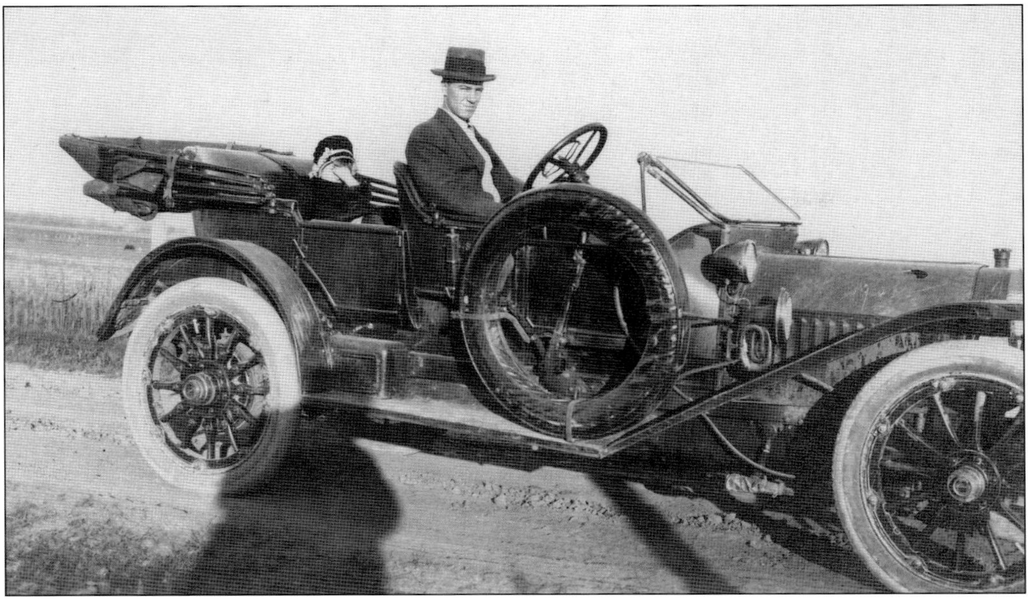

The Locomobile was made from 1899 until 1929 and was driven by steam until 1903, when it was changed to an internal-combustion engine. Here, Rodolph Staples sits proudly behind the wheel of his Locomobile. (Courtesy of Maxine Staples.)

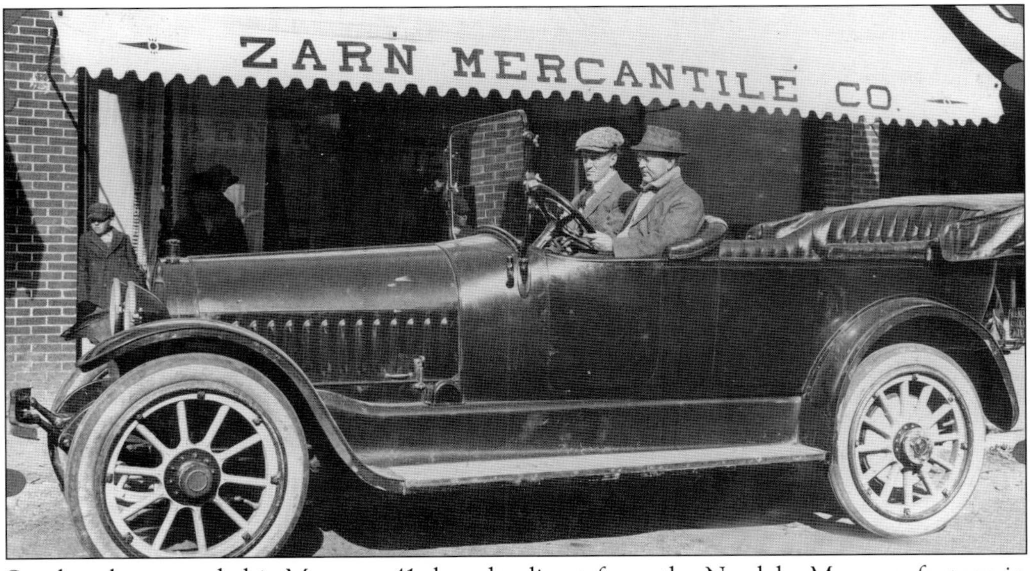

Staples also owned this Marmon 41, bought direct from the Nordyke-Marmon factory in Indianapolis. The company had its beginnings in 1851 as a manufacturer of milling equipment and mills. By around 1900, many felt that the US automobile market needed a better-quality luxury car. In 1902, Nordyke-Marmon began making this luxury auto to fill that need. (Courtesy of Sheridan Mires.)

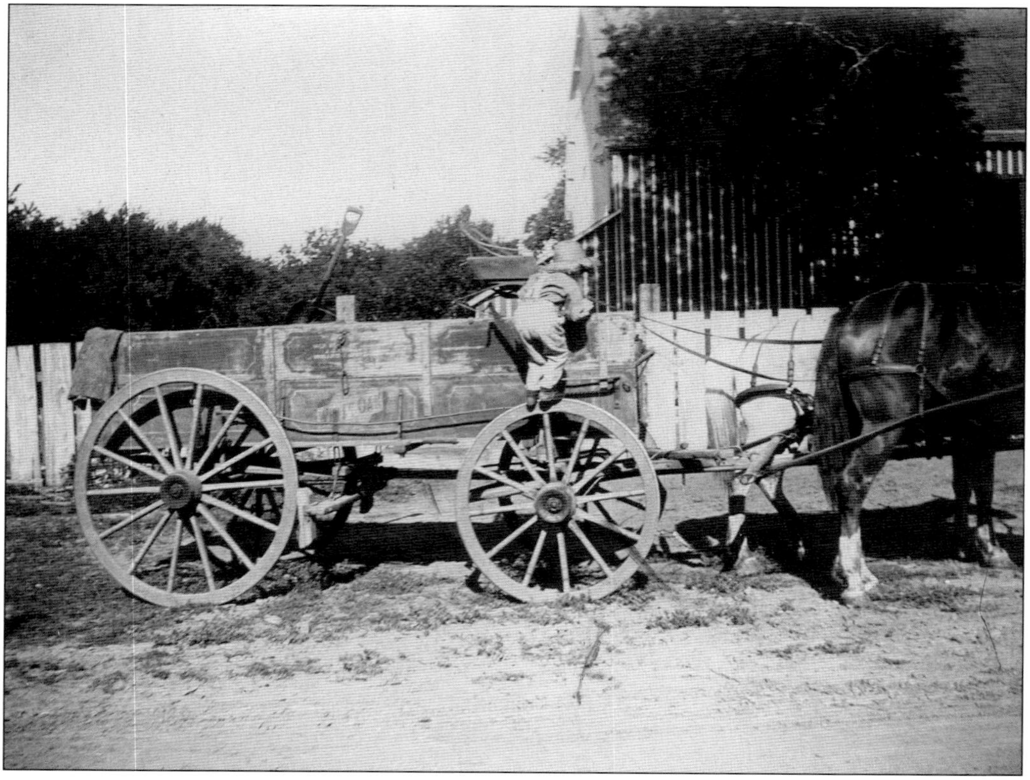

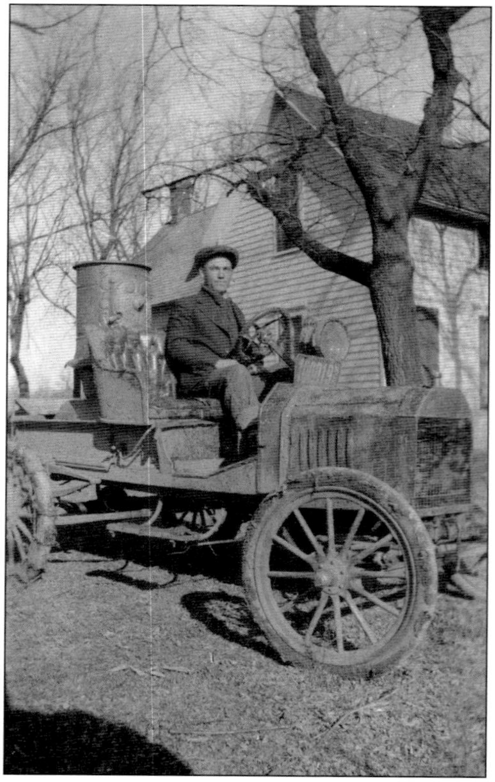

Long after the advent of the automobile, a buckboard wagon like the one above was still a popular piece of equipment for farmers. When hooked up to horses, farmers could get around easily with a load of seed to plant or feed for livestock. Scottie Staples, seen here, does not want to be left behind and climbs aboard the family wagon. There are still a few wagons of this type left in Atchison County. (Courtesy of Sheridan Mires.)

Model Ts were used and refitted for various purposes. This one was called the Dog Wagon; note the single headlamp in front of the steering wheel and the license plate underneath. Wike Harmes is behind the wheel, hauling a stove behind the mud-covered vehicle. (Courtesy of Betty Wennihan.)

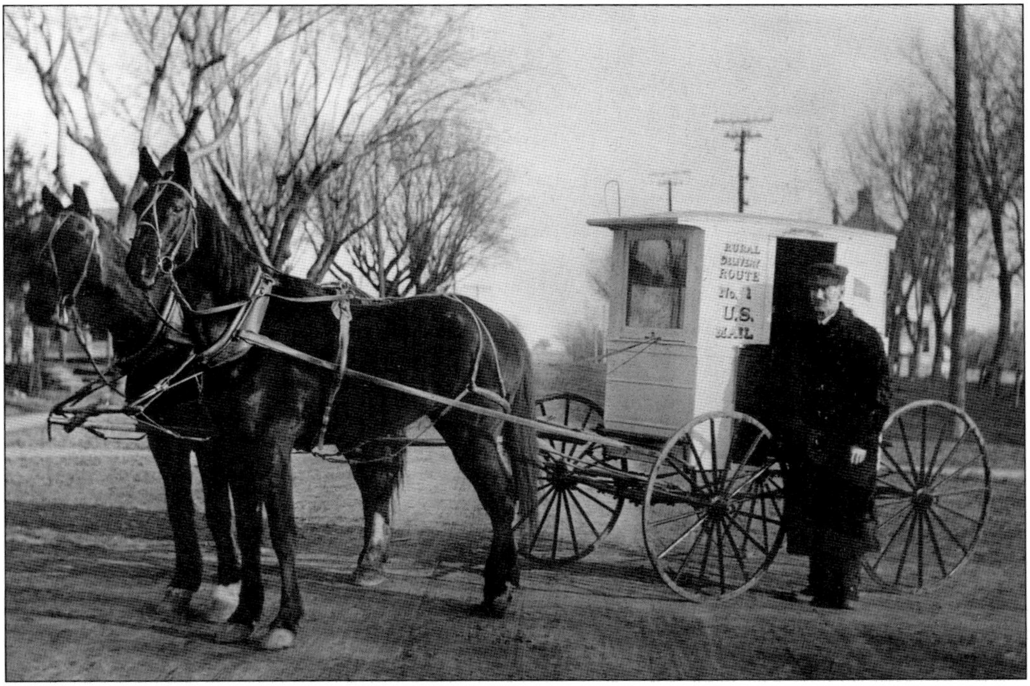

Experiments using rural free delivery began in 1891, and it was fully adopted in 1901. It caused a big jump in service for the post office. With the advent of parcel post, the post office received another boost in business. It allowed newspapers and magazines to be mailed, leading to the rapid growth of mail-order businesses. Pinkney W. Davenport, seen here around 1915, operated the route northwest of Tarkio. (Courtesy of the Atchison County Historical Society.)

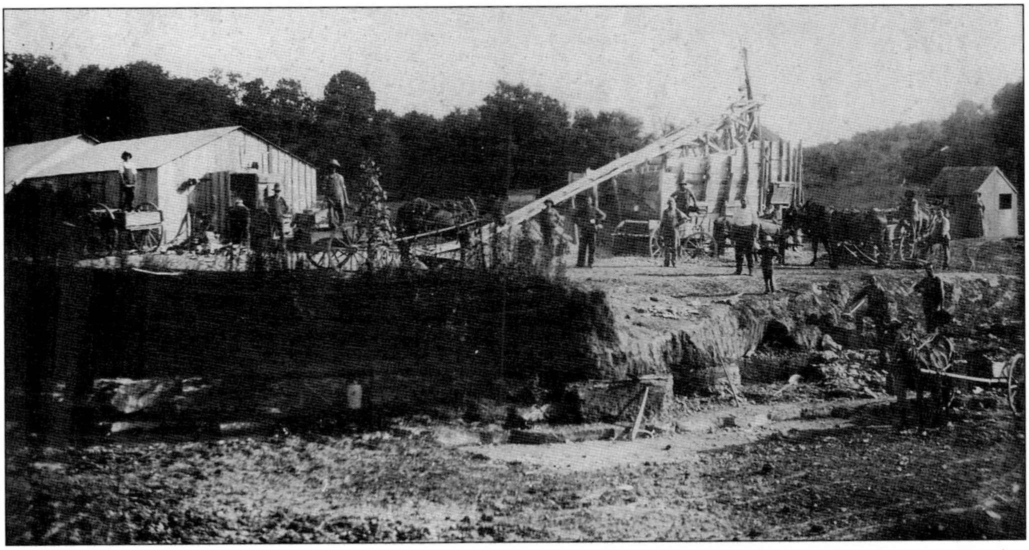

Wheat has to be grown, cut, shocked, bundled, threshed, and then hauled to the elevator. In the early days, each of these steps required many men and several machines. In addition, larger fields required moving and setting up the machinery several times. The name "combine" that is used today comes from the idea of combining the thresher and the wheat binder into one machine. Combines pulled by horses were used around 1910 and were later replaced by gas- and diesel-powered engines. (Courtesy of Kay Gibson.)

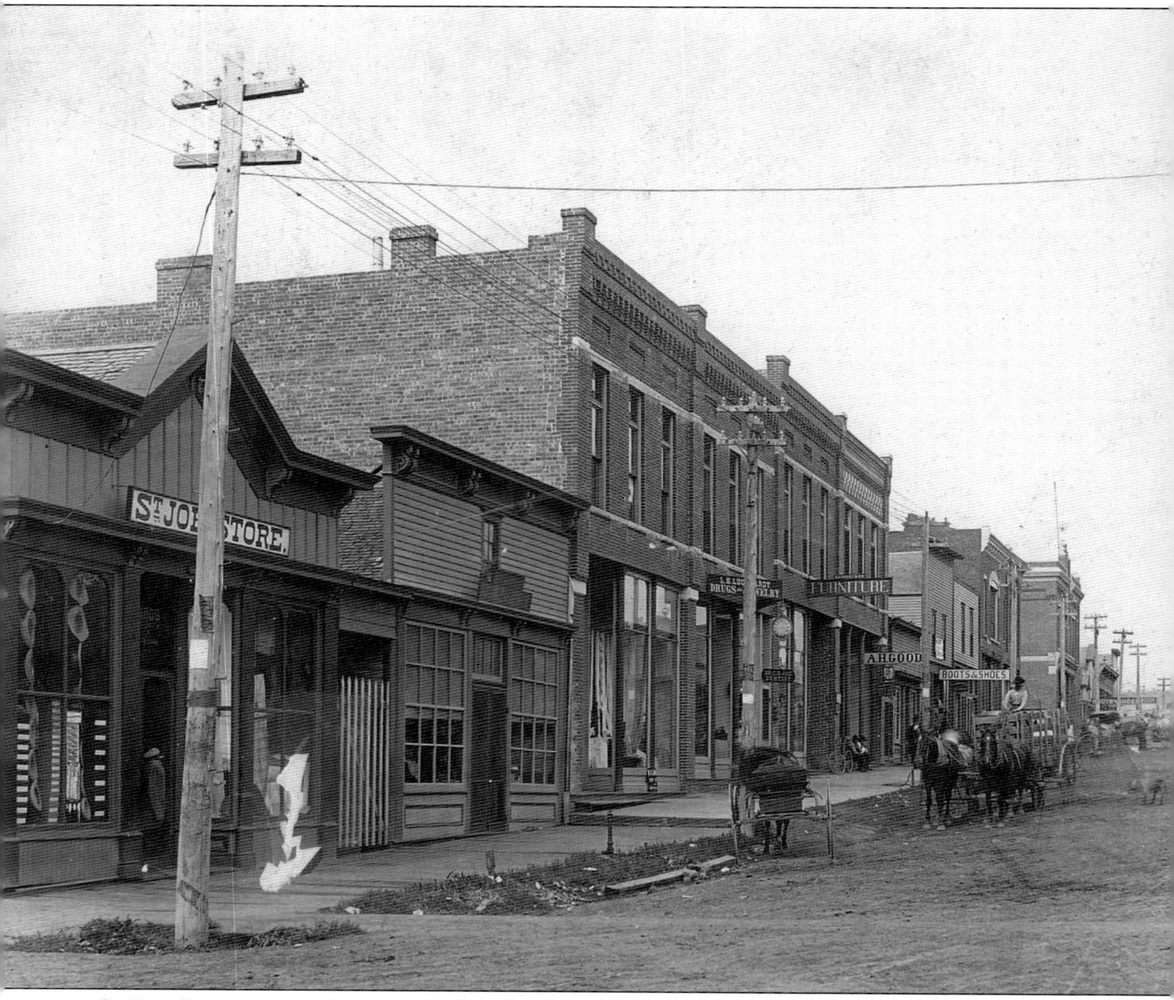

St. Joe Store, pictured on Main Street in Tarkio looking west, was torn down and replaced by the Hurst Brothers store in 1898. Up the street is a sign for L.H. Luckhardt's Drugs and Jewelry, dentist Dr. C.H. Coe, and N.C. Trout and Co. Furniture. (Courtesy of the Atchison County Historical Society.)

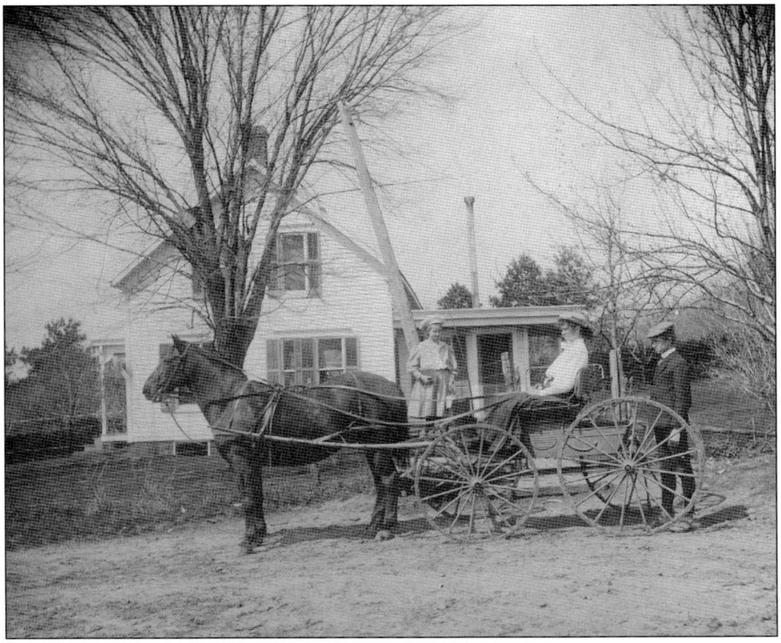

The children of John A. and Myrtle A. Rankin prepare to go to Homer School around 1905. They are, from left to right, Irene, Emma Louise, and Henry Rankin. Emma Louise died tragically at age 15 and Henry at 27 in Cairo, Egypt. They are both buried in Home Cemetery in Tarkio. (Courtesy of the Atchison County Historical Society.)

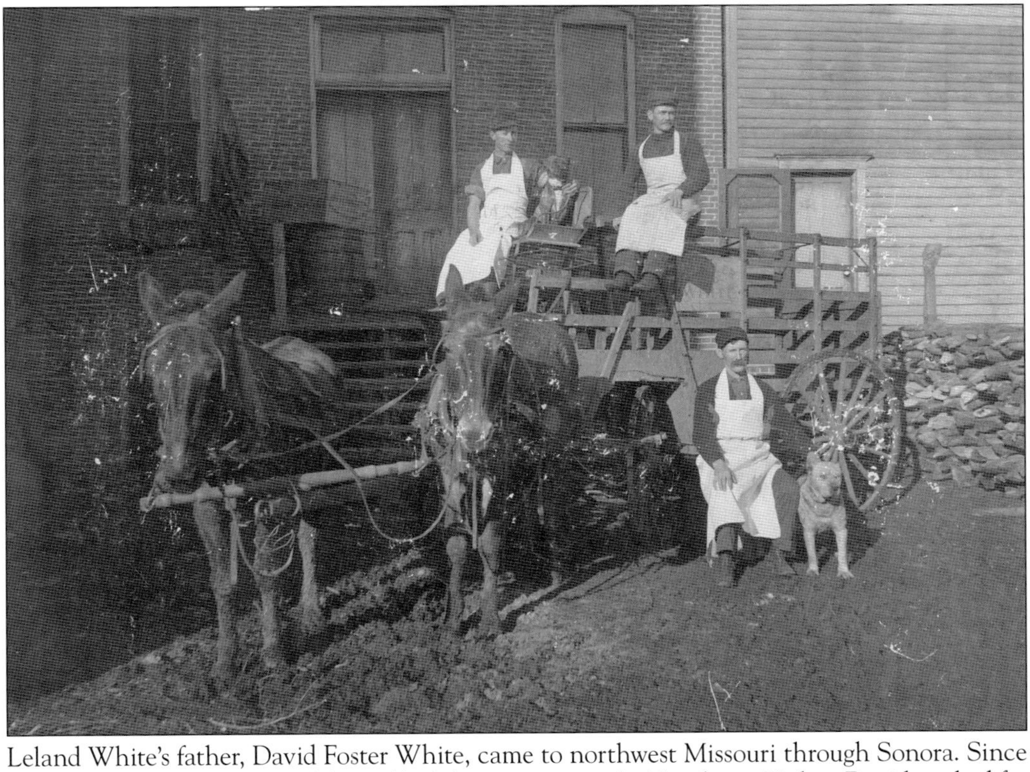

Leland White's father, David Foster White, came to northwest Missouri through Sonora. Since he had no other way to travel, he walked the approximately 15 miles to Tarkio. David worked for a butcher shop in Tarkio and then started his own successful shop. At an early age, Leland drove his pony and cart to deliver meat from his father's shop. He went on to graduate from Tarkio College and eventually farmed land that had belonged to his father. Leland's butcher shop is seen here in the early 1900s. (Courtesy of the Atchison County Historical Society.)

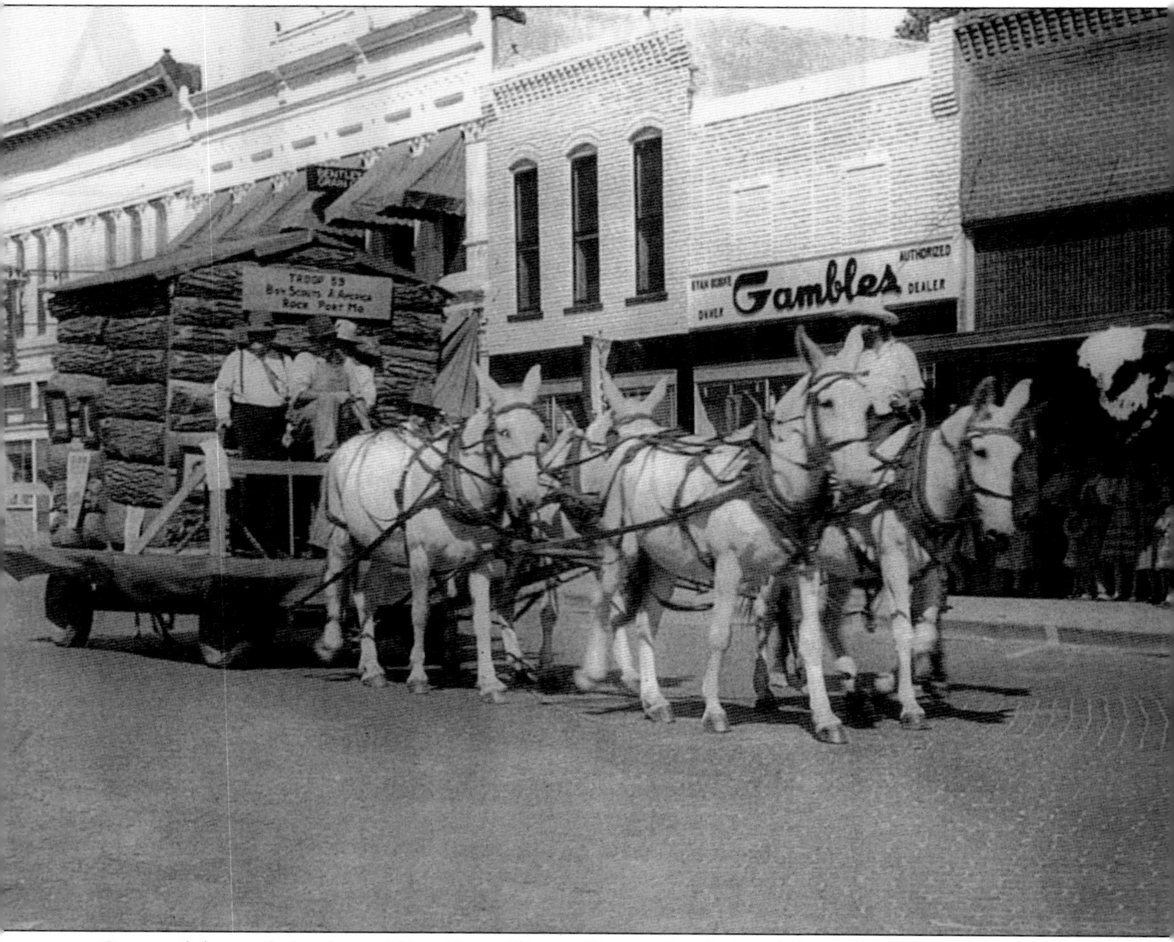

Some of the early leaders of Boy Scout Troop 59 were Les Jones, Morris Forbes, Bob Fay, and Jack Wilson. The Boy Scouts of America, incorporated in 1910 and chartered by the US Congress in 1916, sought to instill citizenship, personal fitness, and character in young boys. Troop 59 is still active today and has produced more than 40 Eagle Scouts. The troop parade float is seen here in a Rock Port parade. (Courtesy of the *Atchison County Mail.*)

Two
AGRICULTURE

So much of Atchison County's history and future depends on agriculture. When the farmer has a good year, so do the automobile salesman, the store owner, and the grocer. When times are lean for the farmer, everyone feels the cutbacks. Today, when the agricultural economy is down, donations to churches, cancer research, or updating equipment at local hospitals all take a hit.

Times were especially difficult during the Great Depression. Banks failed, family farms went under, and worst of all, people went hungry. At the same time, when the economy was at rock bottom, Mother Nature took its toll on the nation, creating one of the driest periods on record. Dust clouds that began on The Plains did not stop until they finally reached Washington, DC, and the rest of the East Coast. While unemployment in the cities reached 25 percent—today, it is troublesome when unemployment is at 10 percent—some people in rural areas at least had gardens, poultry, and livestock to keep themselves supplied with food. Rural families could even sometimes spare some food for those "just passing through," living up to the lessons taught in the Bible.

The images in this book show the ups and downs of life in Atchison County. In good times, photographs show new things acquired: automobiles, a new barn, or a house. In bad times, images show tattered clothing and houses in need of a new coat of paint. Even in bad times, however, families are together, and there is a special feeling because of the bonds of shared experience. Children smile because for them it has always been this way, while the parents hold out hope for better times ahead.

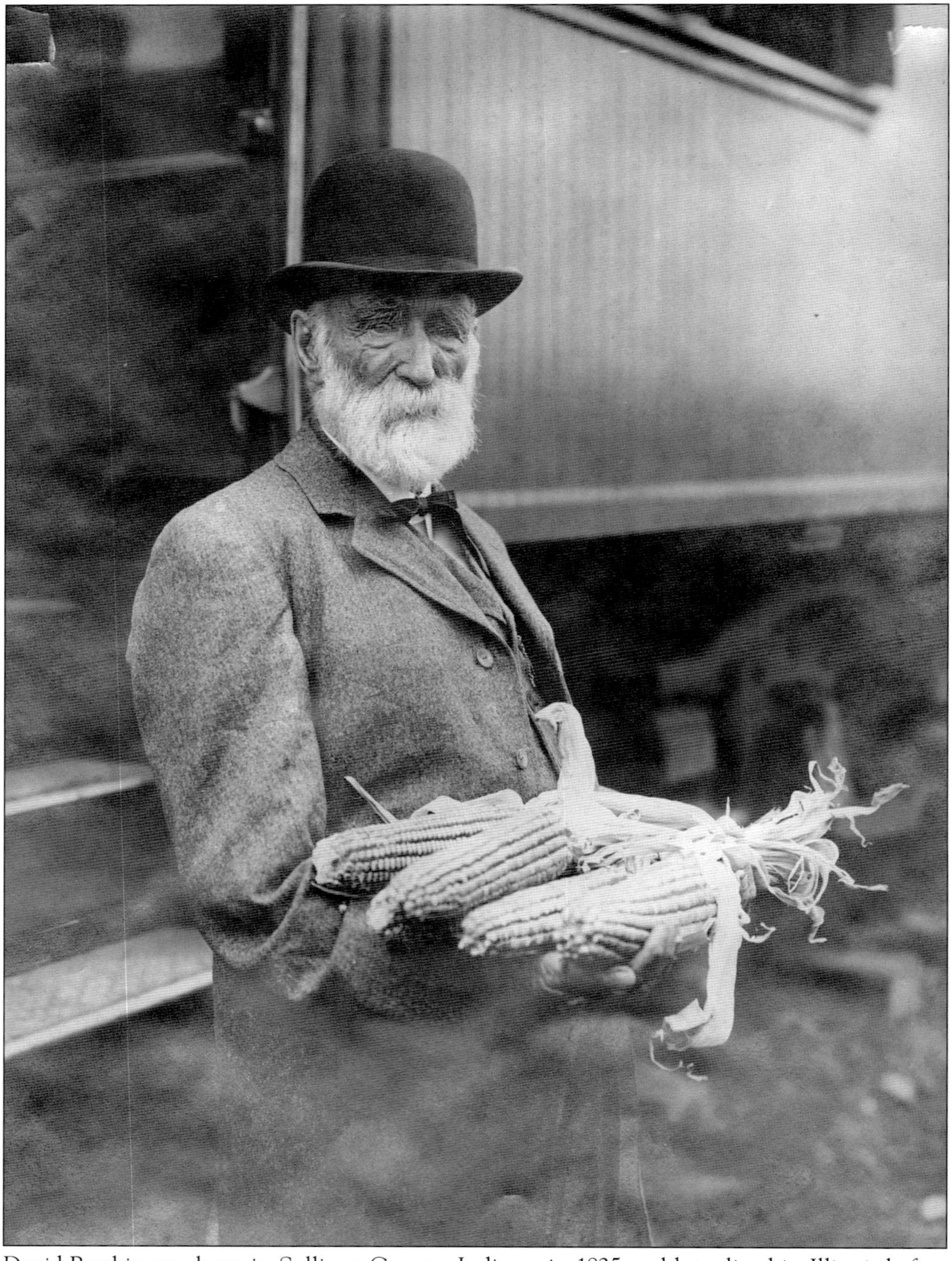

David Rankin was born in Sullivan County, Indiana, in 1825 and later lived in Illinois before moving west to Tarkio permanently in 1885. He served three terms in the Illinois Legislature, from 1874 to 1880. Remarkably, all the corn raised on his farms went to feed his cattle and hogs, with none of it going to grain elevators as is the custom today. Rankin built the opera house in Tarkio, the First National Bank, and Tarkio College, among other endeavors. (Courtesy of the Atchison County Historical Society.)

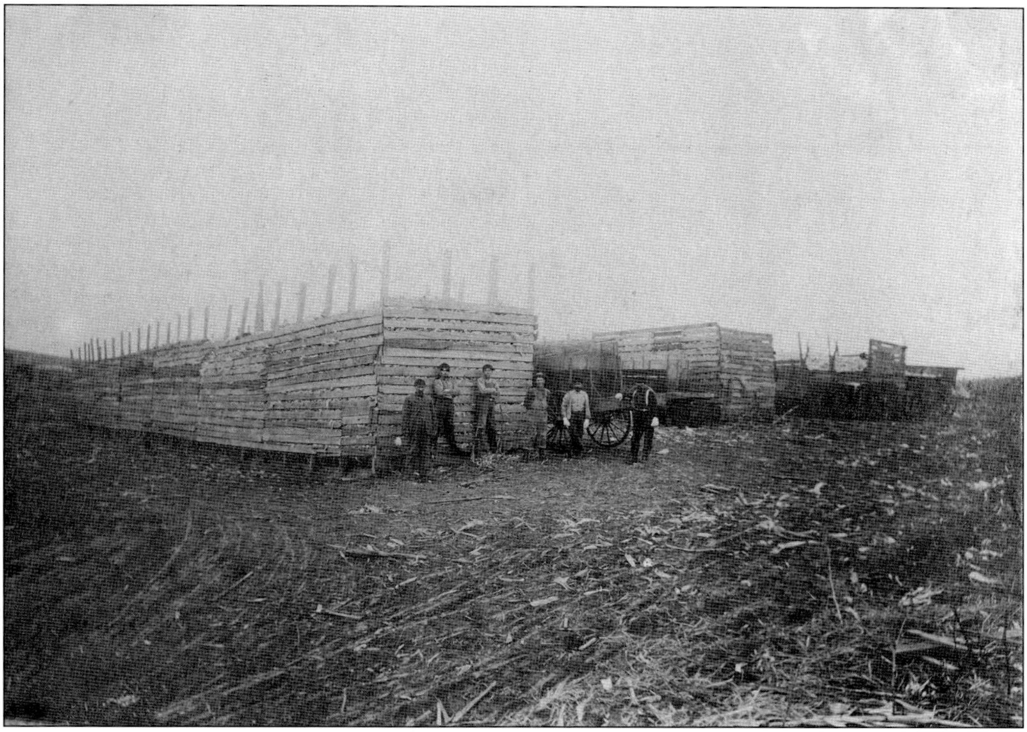

In the early 1900s, corncribs were the best way to store grain while it dried. These men are building several large corncribs for a local farmer who needed a lot of storage. David Rankin would have needed corncribs of this size, as he had workers farm 23,000 acres for him at one time, using all the corn to feed his livestock. (Courtesy of the Atchison County Historical Society.)

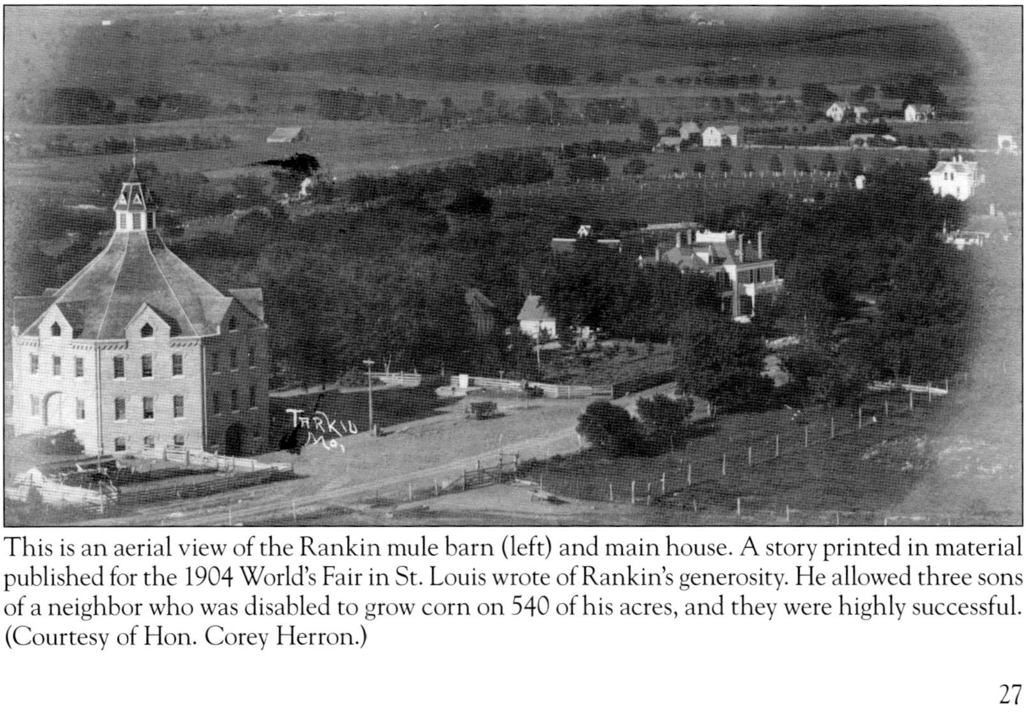

This is an aerial view of the Rankin mule barn (left) and main house. A story printed in material published for the 1904 World's Fair in St. Louis wrote of Rankin's generosity. He allowed three sons of a neighbor who was disabled to grow corn on 540 of his acres, and they were highly successful. (Courtesy of Hon. Corey Herron.)

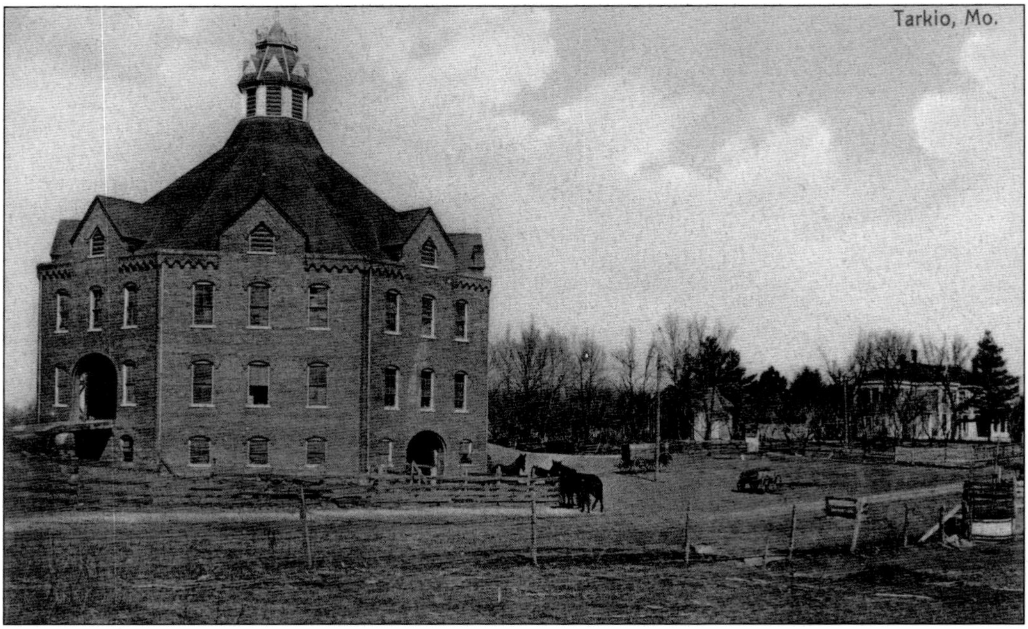

This barn was three stories high, and horses and mules could enter on the first two levels. The peaked roof and cupola seen here were lost when the barn burned the first time. In later photographs, it has a flatter roof. After serving its purpose for agriculture, the barn was given to the community and converted to a theater, becoming a valuable asset to residents. The barn caught fire again in 1989 and was beyond salvaging. (Courtesy of Hon. Corey Herron.)

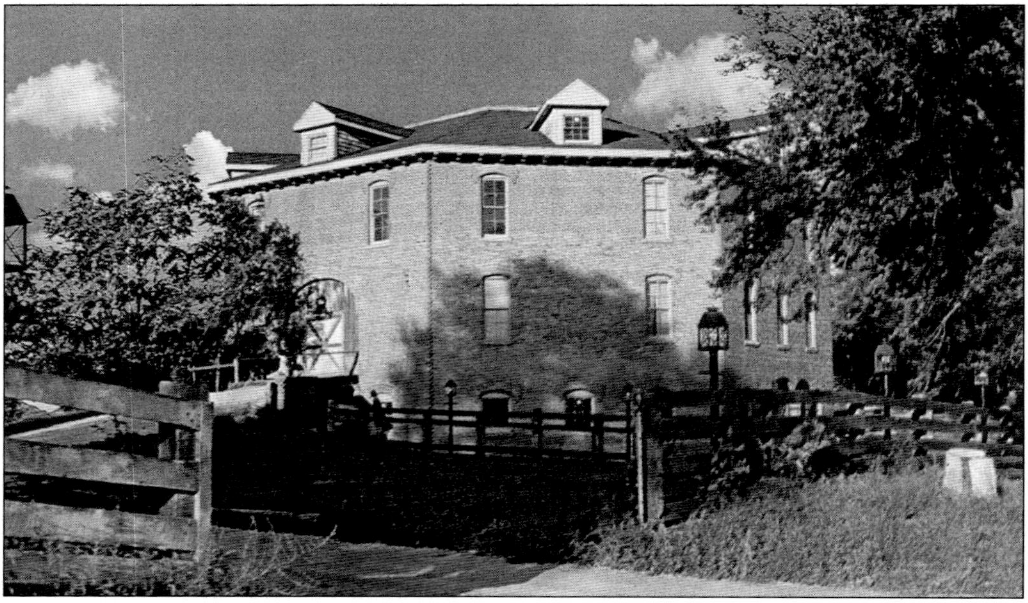

In the barn's last years, the Mule Barn Theatre Guild put on productions there after forming in 1975. Through its many members, who paid $7.50 per year to belong, many improvements were made to the building. Restrooms, a new roof, a drinking fountain, and air-conditioners were just some of the improvements made. Members were mainly from the four-state area, but a few were found across the nation. This postcard shows the mule barn in its later years with the lower, flat roof that was installed after the first fire. (Courtesy of the Atchison County Historical Society.)

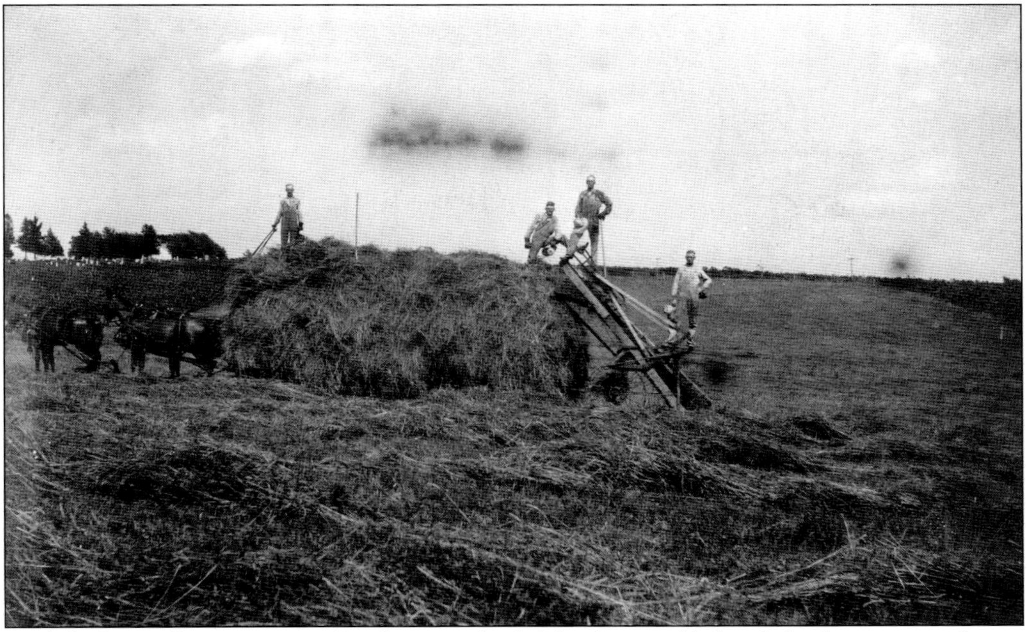

English Grove Cemetery near Fairfax is in the left background behind this hay crew with two teams pulling a hay wagon. English Grove gets its name from the early English settlers who came to the area before 1839. It was also a stagecoach stopover for Mormons en route from St. Joseph, Missouri, to Kanesville, Iowa (now Council Bluffs). (Courtesy of Betty Wennihan.)

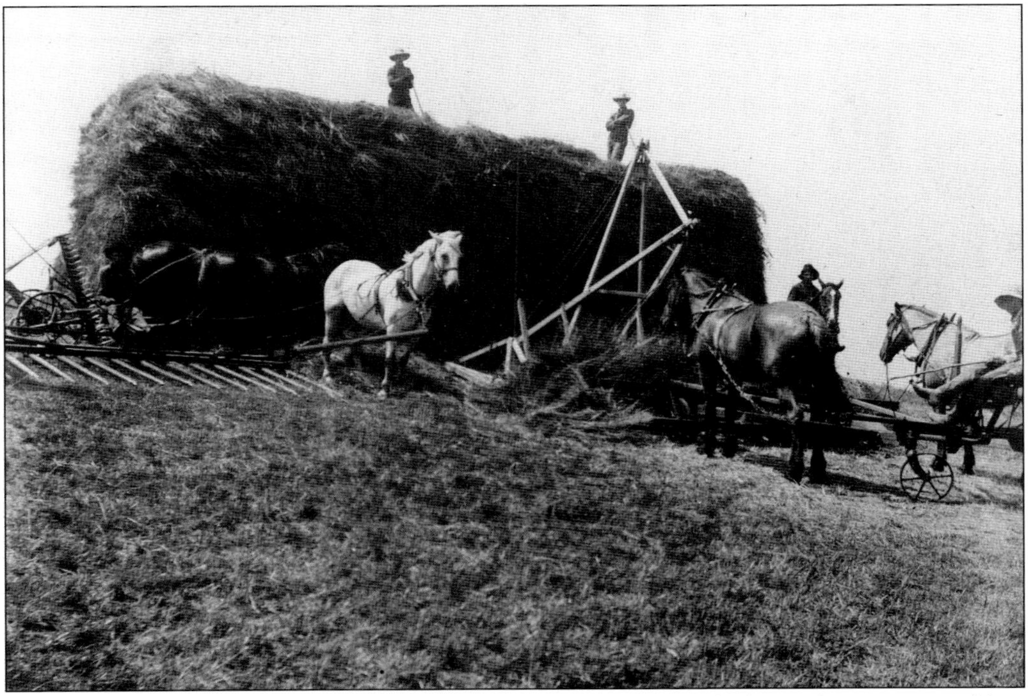

A hay crew near Westboro is seen here at a time when there was little mechanization and lots of manual labor. The ideal time to cut grass for hay has about a two-week window; hay cut too early will not cure properly and could be too moist, while hay cut too late could lose some of its nutrient content and will have a lower resale value. (Courtesy of Anna Belle Johnson.)

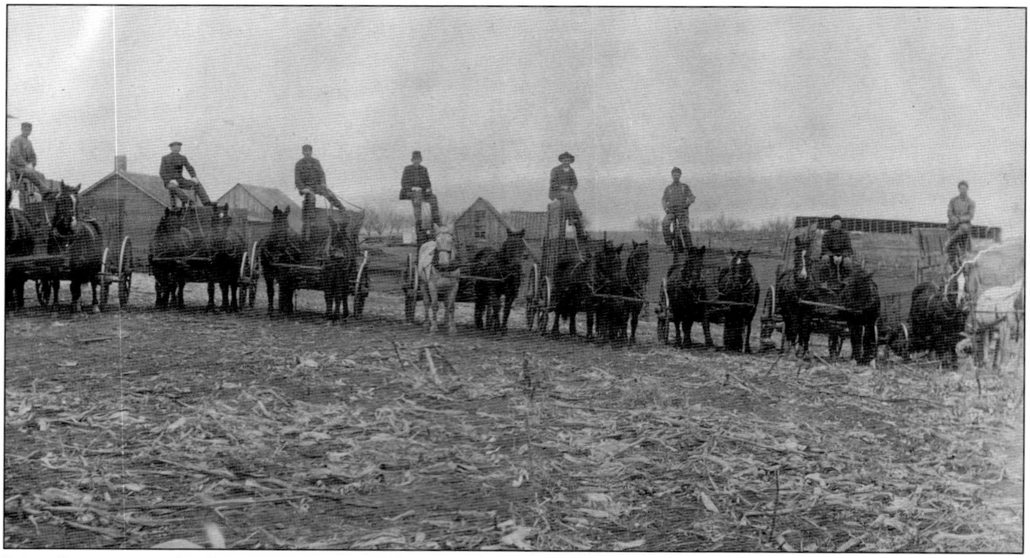

Men line up with their wagons and horses as they prepare for the day's corn harvest. The men walked alongside the horses and wagons and picked the corn by hand. Once the corn was picked, they tossed it toward the high board, also called a bang board, on the opposite side of the wagon until the wagon was full. Today's technology allows one combine to harvest approximately 40 acres per day. (Courtesy of George and Patty Laur.)

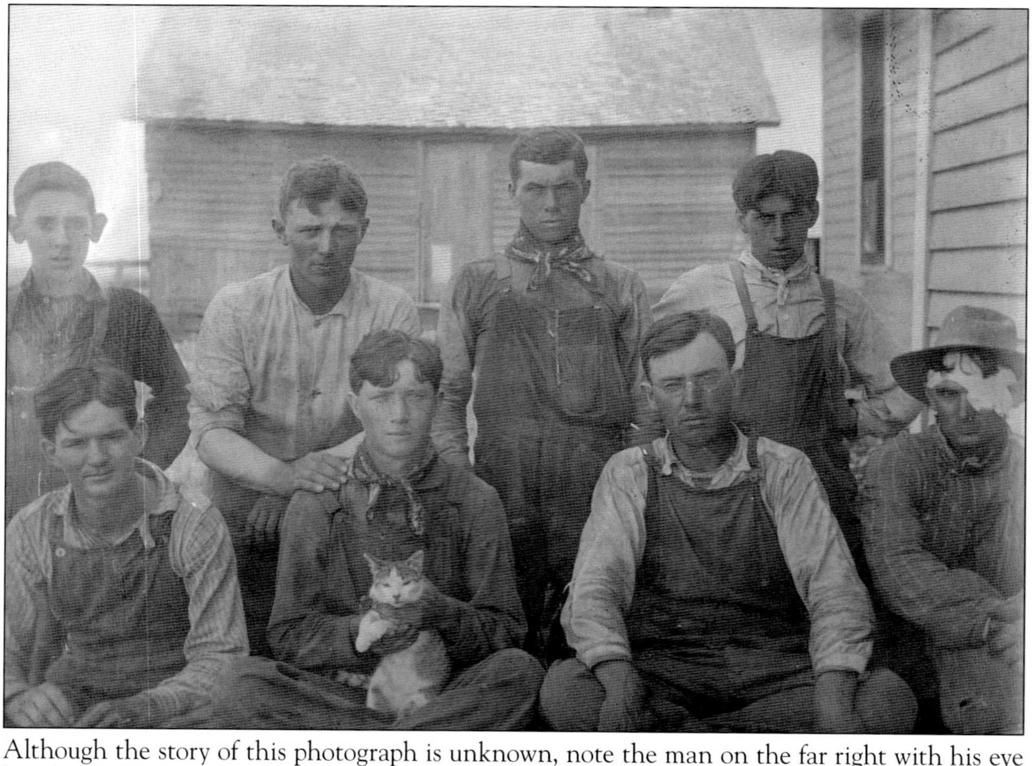

Although the story of this photograph is unknown, note the man on the far right with his eye bandaged, likely injured in a farm accident. In addition to farm accidents, mortality rates for women giving birth and infants in general were also high in the early days of Atchison County, largely due to the remoteness of the farms. (Courtesy of George and Patty Laur.)

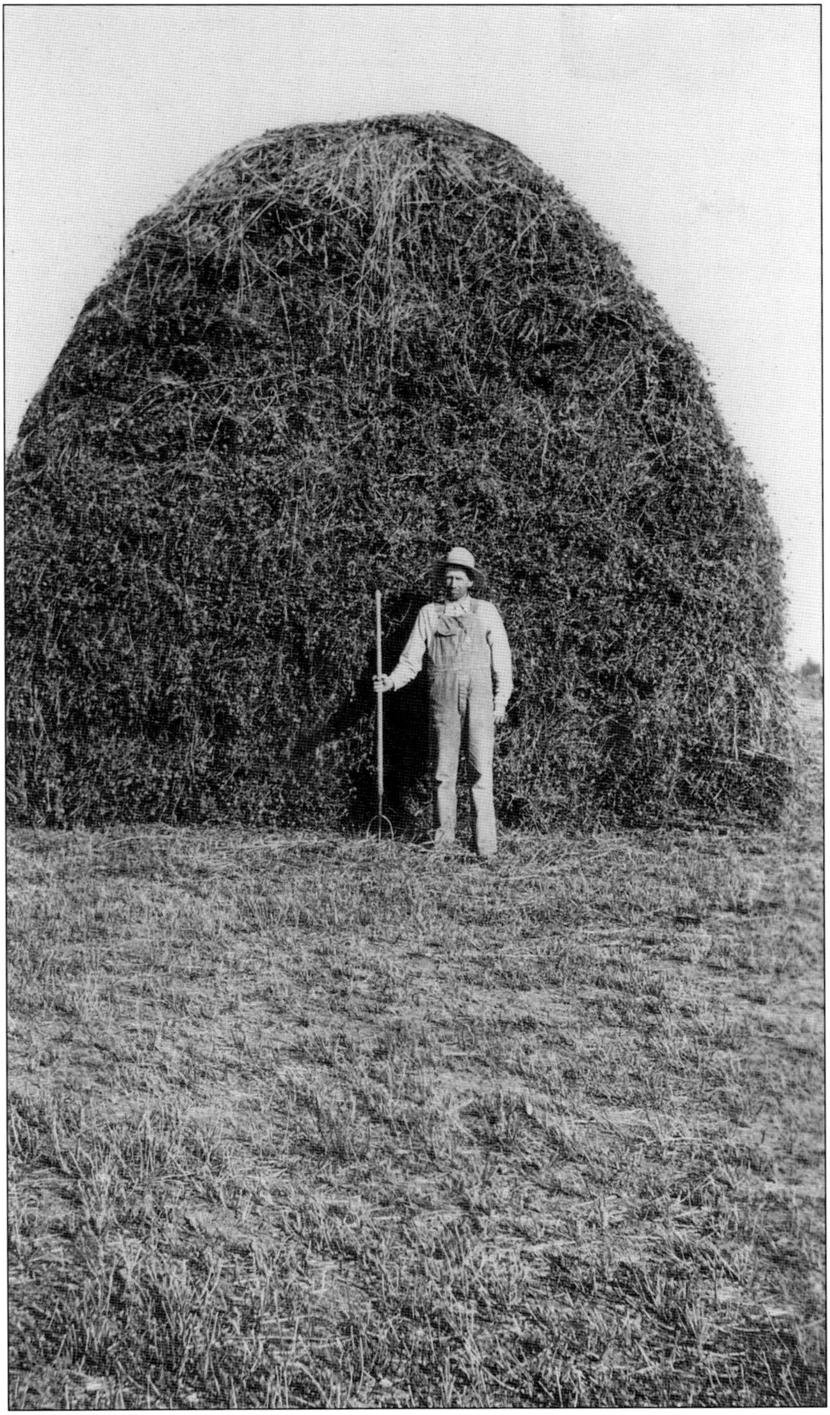

Glenn Stevens, who lived south of Blanchard, Missouri, stands with his three-pronged hayfork and the result of all his hard work: a large stack of hay that will feed his animals throughout the year. Blanchard is unique because half of the town is in Iowa and half is in Missouri. It lies on the Wabash Railroad line, which ran from St. Louis west to Omaha and east to Chicago and Detroit. (Courtesy of Anna Belle Johnson.)

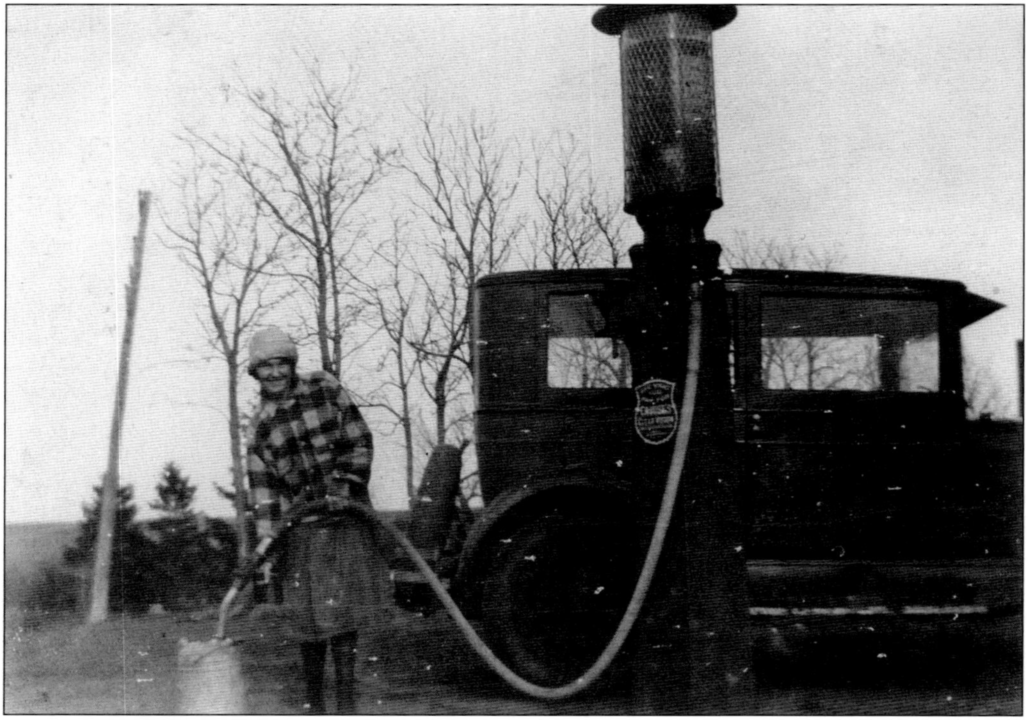

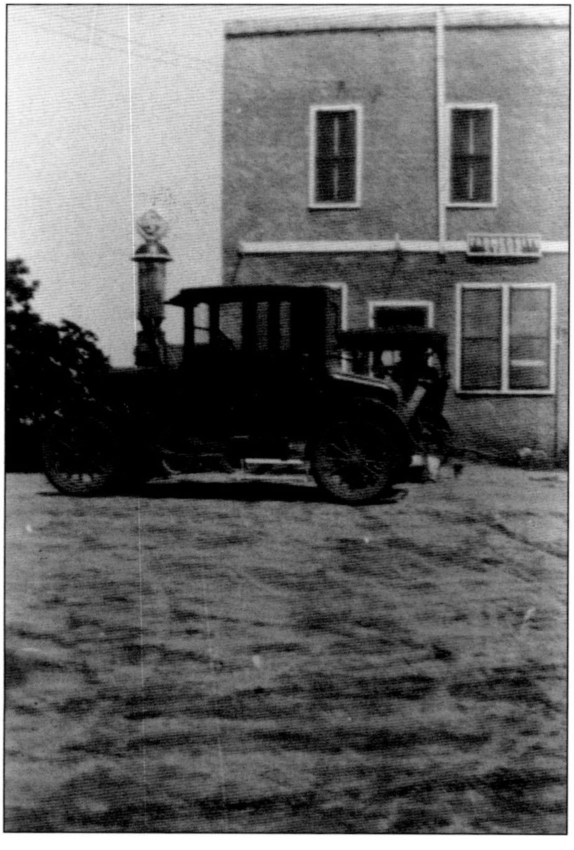

Above, in 1927, Dora Howard happily pumps gas at the Farmer's City Store. She went on to marry Lee Nelson on January 16, 1929, and raise eight children. Howard is remembered for breaking down 100 pounds of sugar into smaller bags that sold for 10¢. She also siphoned large jugs of vinegar into containers and sold them to the public. Wire, stockings, overalls, and ice from the icehouse were also sold at the store pictured to the left. When the store opened, it was 13 miles from Rock Port, 13 miles from Farragut, 14 miles from Hamburg, 8 miles from Westboro, and 10 miles from Tarkio, so it was considered strategically located. (Both, courtesy of Lyllis Vette.)

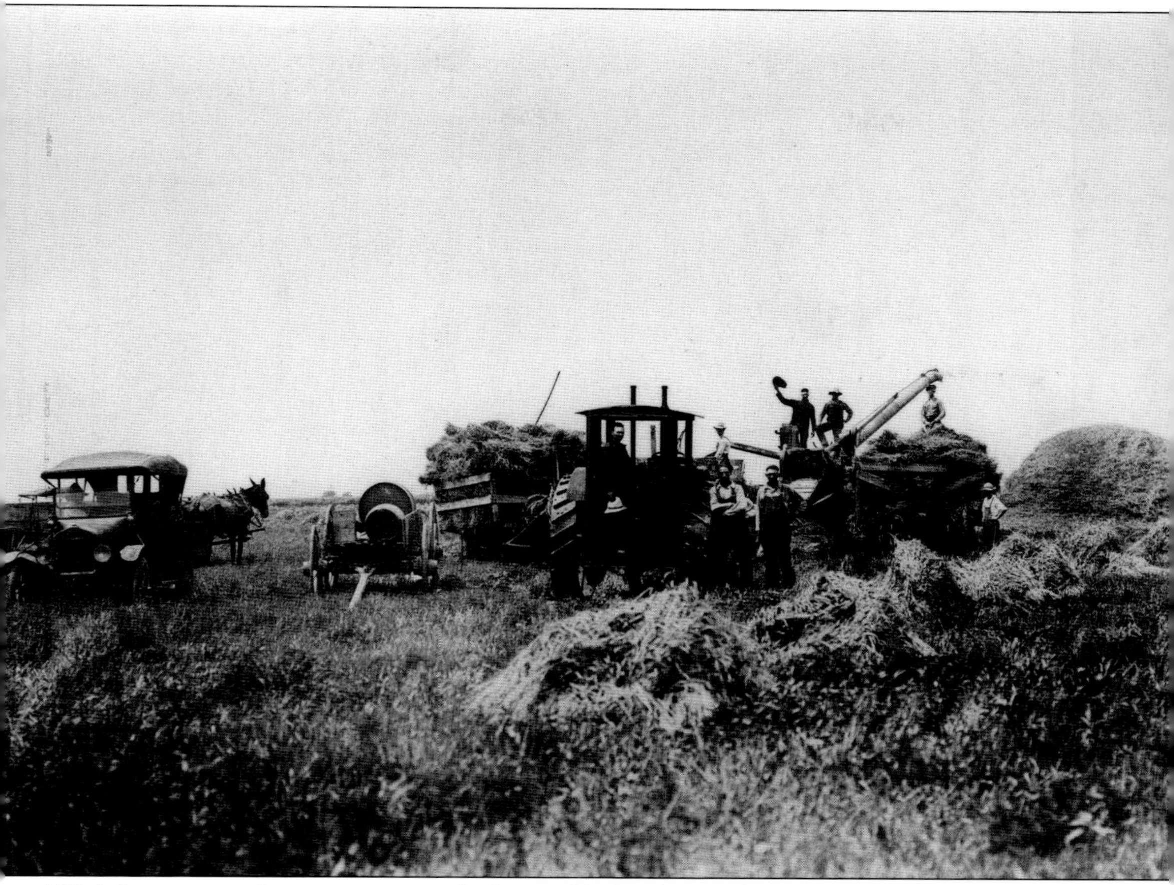

While harvesting wheat, a tractor needs plenty of fuel and water, hence the two different barrels on the wagon to the left of the tractor. The belts were hooked up to the threshing machine and the tractor at a good distance to prevent the belts from slipping. Because of this, it also made the job very dangerous, as one could get a sleeve or a pant leg caught in the belts very quickly. (Courtesy of Kay Gibson.)

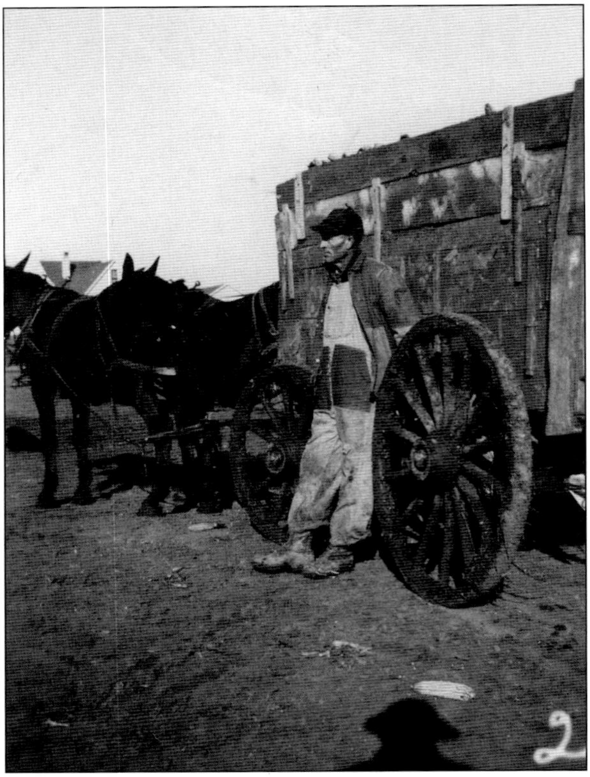

Clarence Hull takes a break from the corn harvest in 1939, when the US economy was still in the Depression. Clarence was born in December 1884 in Page County, Iowa, and married Mabelle Seaburg in February 1915. In 1943, the family moved to farmland a mile east of St. John's Lutheran Church, and in 1953 they moved to Westboro. Clarence and Mabelle had three children: Dale, Phillip, and Phillis. (Courtesy of Phil and Meta Hull.)

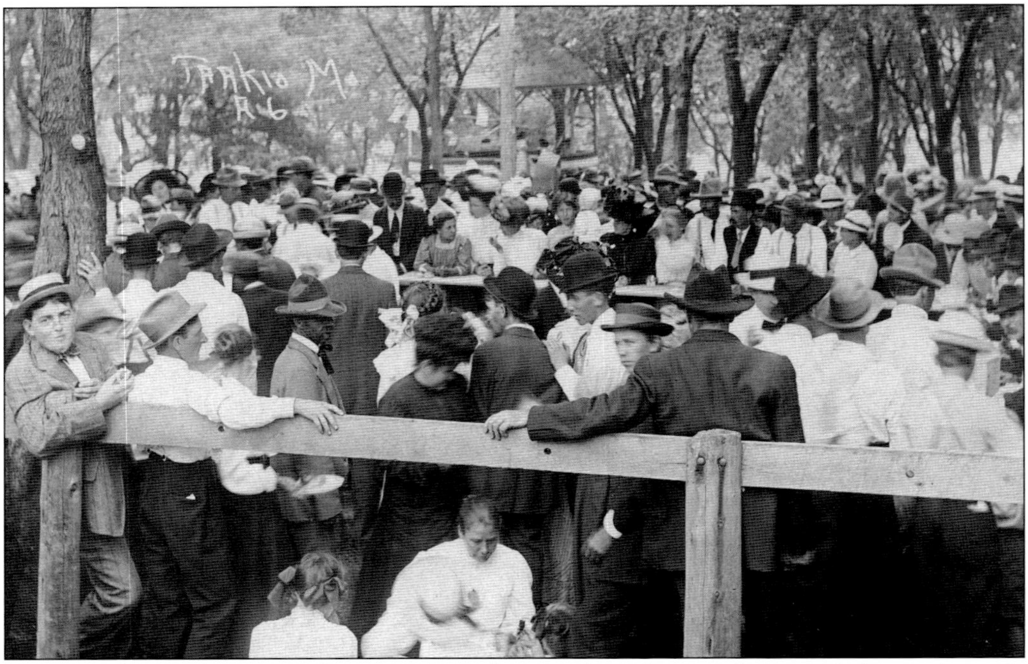

Even for a mule sale, men and women dressed up in white shirts and ties in Tarkio in the early 1900s. This was a major business and social event and drew people for miles around. This chosen location looks to be ideal for both man and mule, as there are plenty of shade trees to keep everyone cool. (Courtesy of the Atchison County Historical Society.)

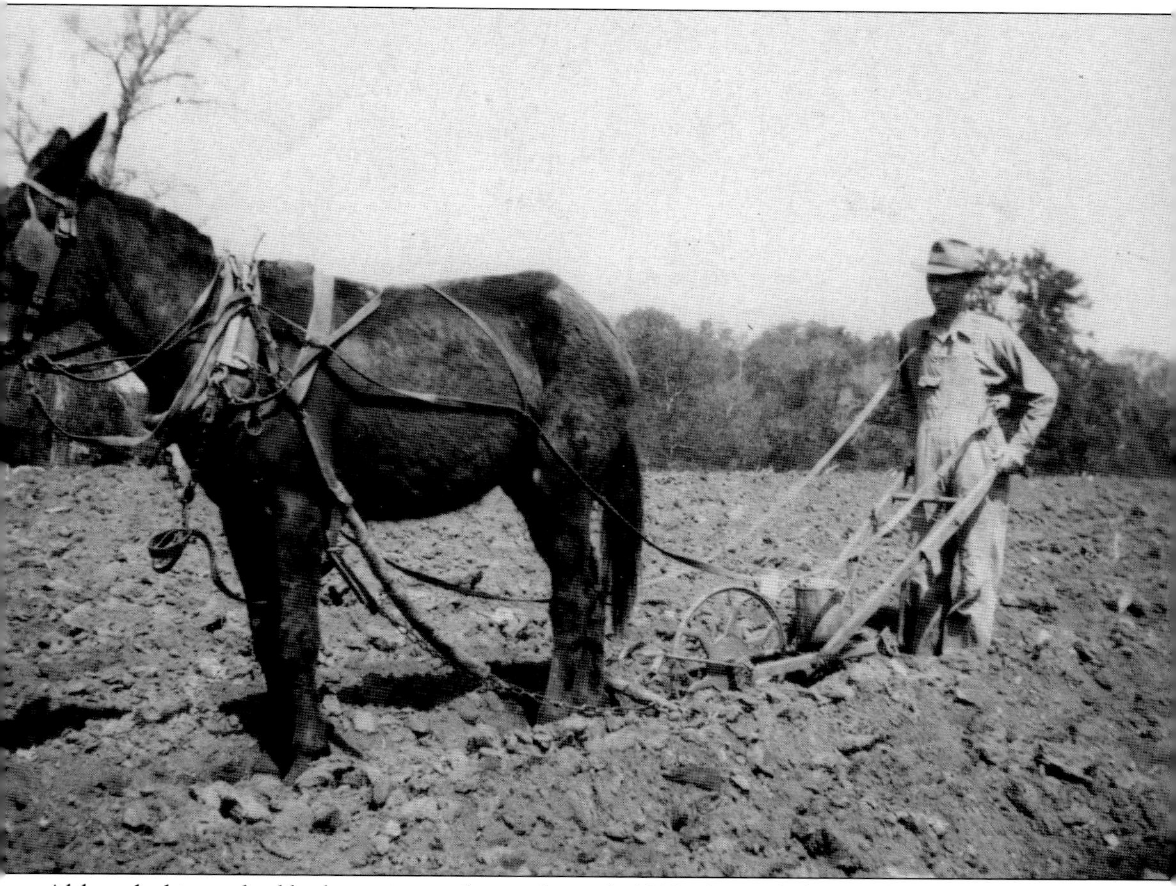

Although this method looks ancient today, in the early 1900s the steel plow made planting much easier. Prior to the plow, many farmers were still using a wooden moldboard and carried a paddle to clean off the dirt and mud. Farmers from that time reported that with a good team of oxen they could only plow one acre per day. Fred McDaniel of the English Grove area is seen here walking behind his one-row planter. (Courtesy of Maxine Staples.)

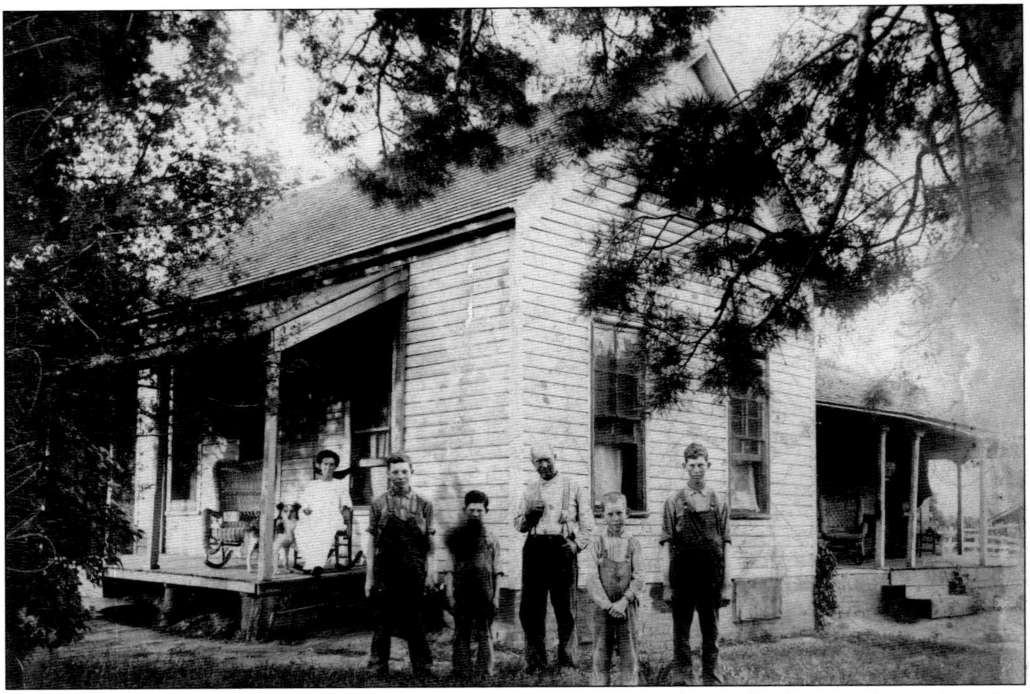

All children were a blessing, but having four healthy boys to help on the farm in the early 1900s was something a father could be especially proud of. This farm has been in the same family for more than 100 years. Here, the proud parents, Michael Roberts (third from right) and Stella (Layden) Roberts (sitting on porch), pose with their four boys. They are, from left to right, Ralph, Guy, George, and Alfred. (Courtesy of JMR Farms.)

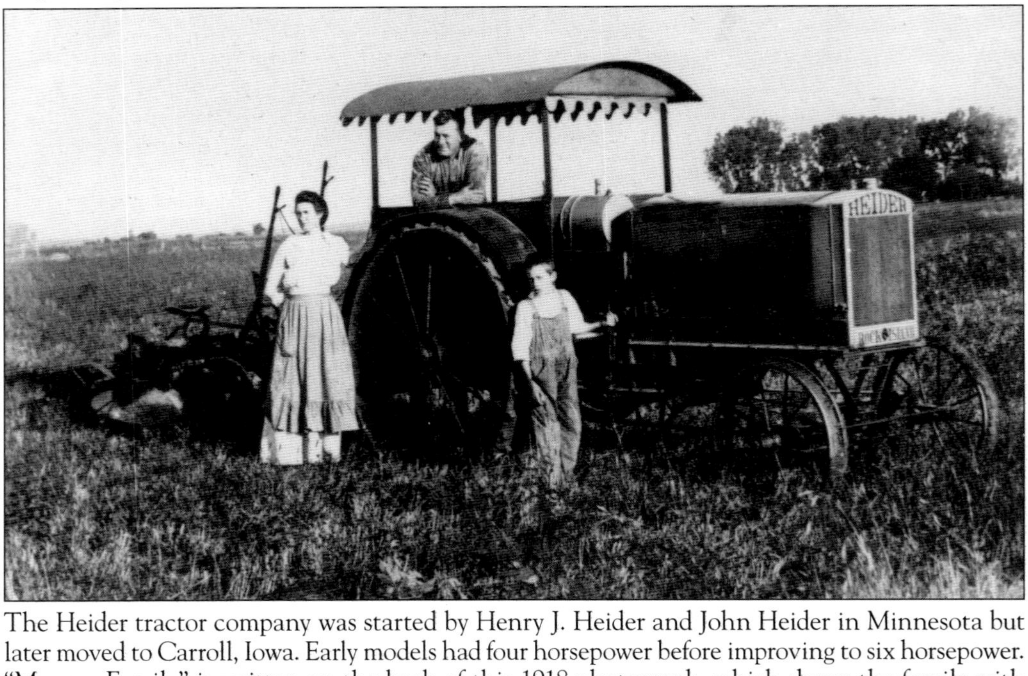

The Heider tractor company was started by Henry J. Heider and John Heider in Minnesota but later moved to Carroll, Iowa. Early models had four horsepower before improving to six horsepower. "Morgan Family" is written on the back of this 1918 photograph, which shows the family with their Heider tractor in the Watson area. (Courtesy of Kay Gibson.)

James R. Freeman is seen here with his best mules, Tom and Jerry, in 1928. Freeman came to Tarkio from Faucett, Missouri, the year before. This barn was cut into the side of the hill on the Culbertson farm. Freeman raised four boys and five girls after settling in Tarkio. He farmed until 1943, when he and his wife moved to town. (Courtesy of Dorothine Woolsey.)

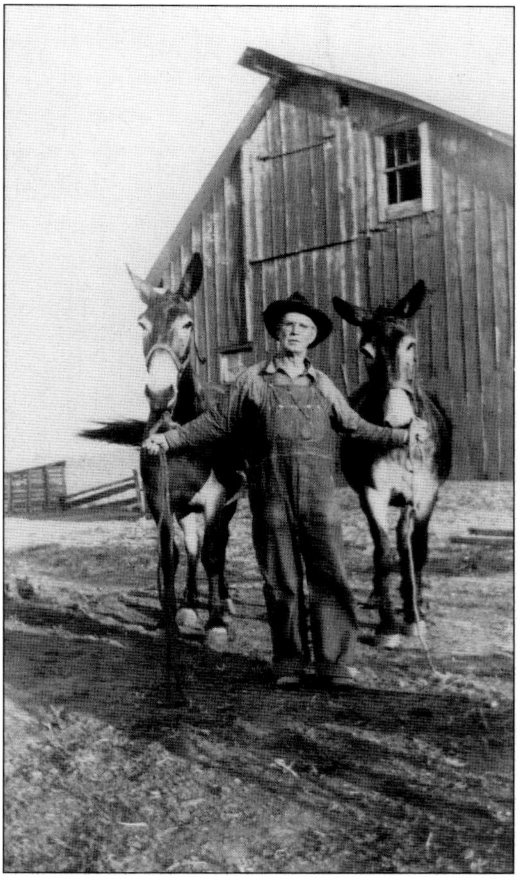

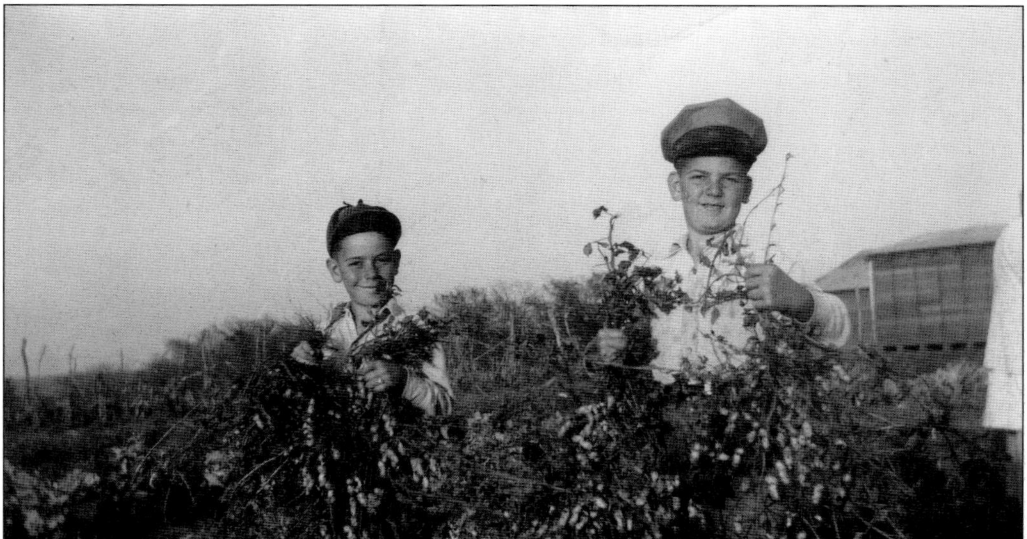

LeRoy (left) and Charles William Smith hold peanuts grown on the North Culbertson farm outside of Tarkio. Successful farmers tried anything to get ahead: raising hogs, chickens, cattle, and many row crops. (Courtesy Dorothine Woolsey.)

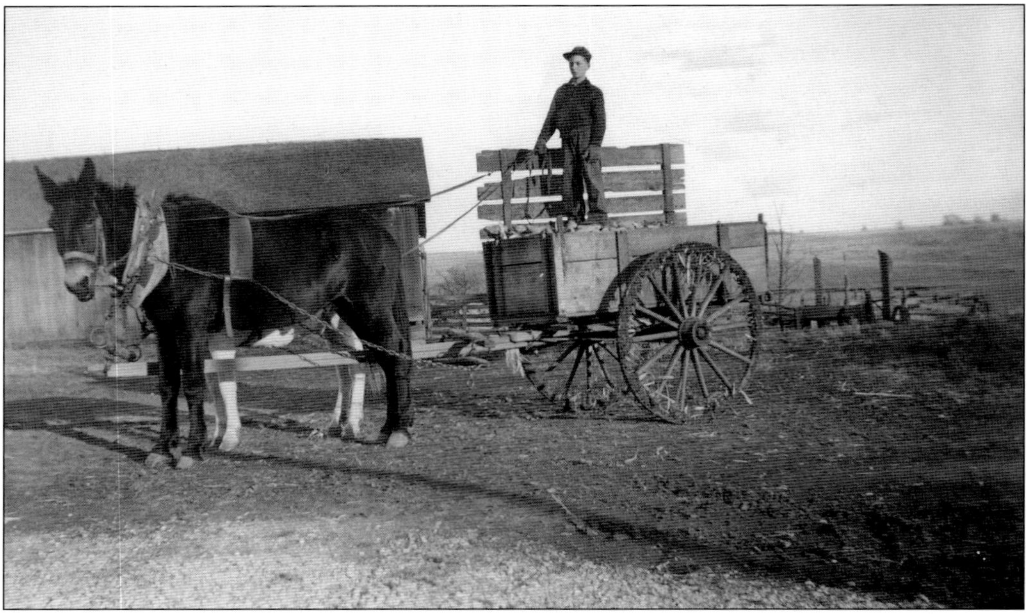

A match set of horses was a prized possession for many farmers, but some had to work with what was available. Although a young boy in this photograph, Scottie Staples was doing man's work, coming in with a wagon full of corn and wheels covered with mud during the fall harvest. (Courtesy of Maxine Staples.)

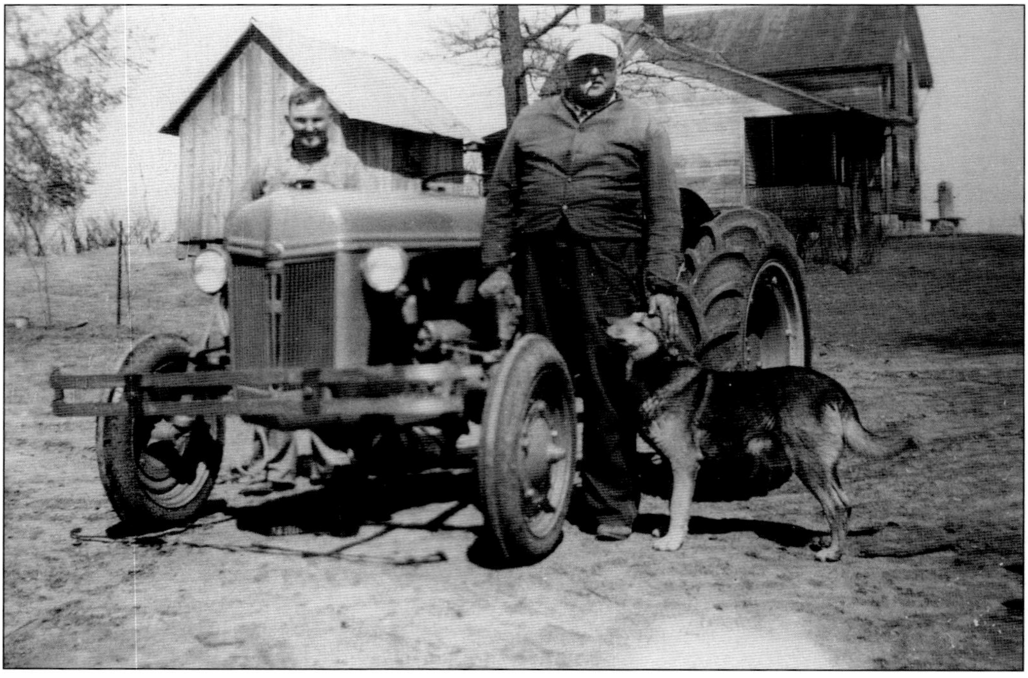

The Ford 9N-series was a breakthrough in tractors, especially for smaller farms. This was the first tractor to come out with rear power take-off and a three-point hitch, which is still used on most tractors today. The tractor made its debut in Dearborn, Michigan, in 1939, hence the "9" in its name. Here, Gene (left) and Otto McDaniel pose in front of their home with their tractor and their dog. (Courtesy of Maxine Staples.)

Poultry provided many things for the rural homeowner, including eggs and meat for the family. Excess food could be taken to town and sold to help purchase other necessities. Here, a startled Mary Graves tends her flock in common attire of the time. (Courtesy of Betty Wennihan.)

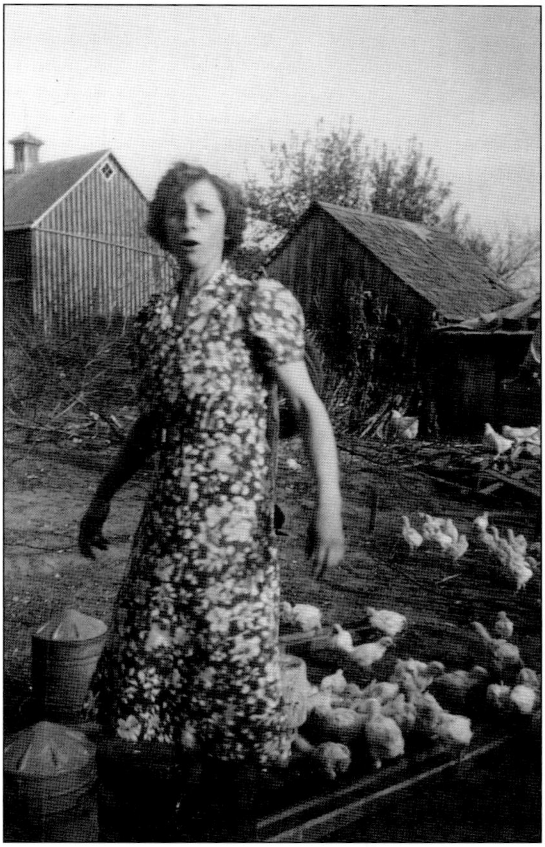

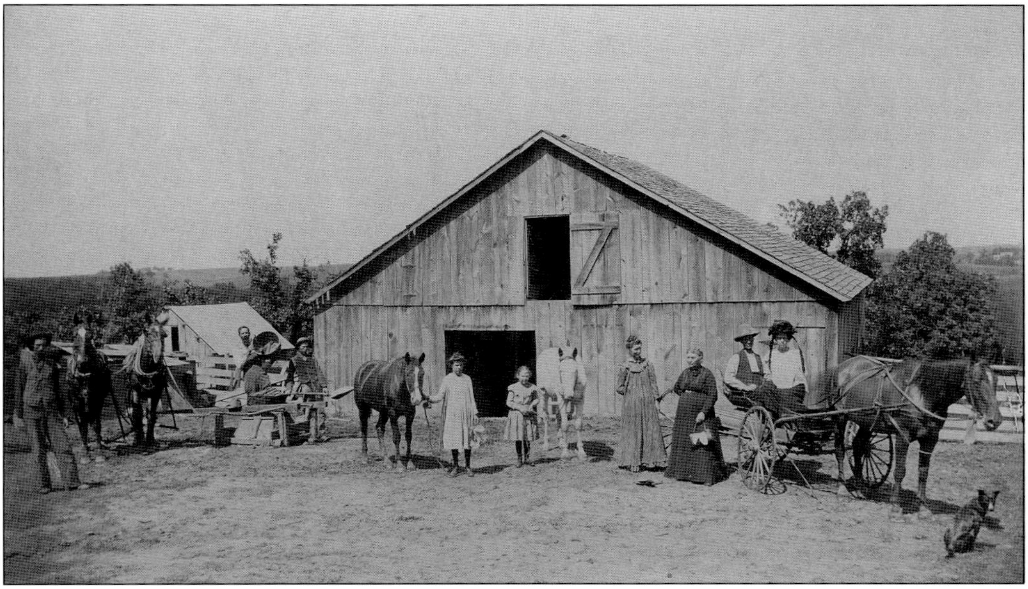

Horses, buggies, and the family dog are assembled as the family puts on their Sunday best for this photograph. Notice the hired hands holding up produce and a shovel. The family may not have had much compared to the barons of Wall Street, but they earned everything they owned and were proud of it. (Courtesy of George and Patty Laur.)

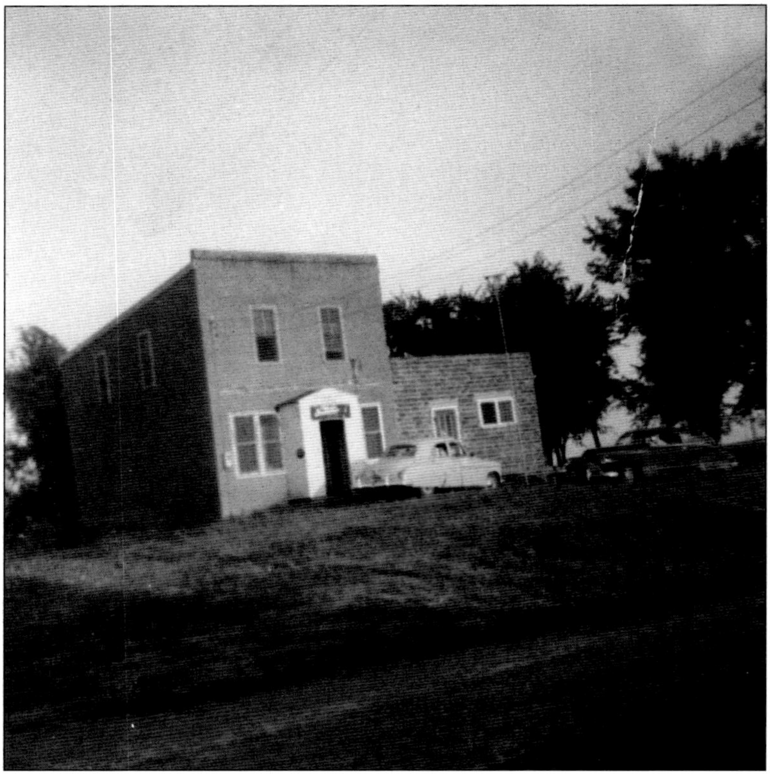

The Farmer's City store, three miles west and seven miles north of Tarkio, near present-day St. John's Lutheran Church, was a hub of activity in the German community. The lease for the land from Henry Vette began in 1924 and was for 99 years. It was signed by J.H. Meier, A.F. Tieman, John Wessler, and Henry Vette. Farmers brought their produce, eggs, and dairy products and sold them to the store, which supplied much-needed income for farm families. (Courtesy of Lyllis Vette.)

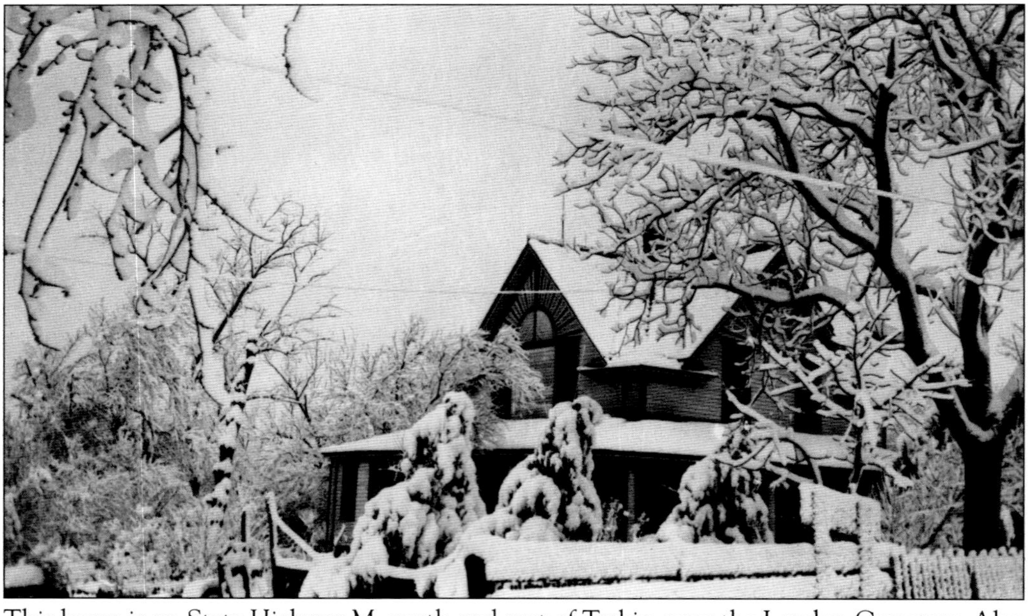

This home is on State Highway M, north and east of Tarkio, near the London Cemetery. Alva Stevens built it, and it still stands today with its distinct "sunrise" design near the roofline. Stevens's son Robert "R.L." Stevens married Ora Bevard and raised nine children in this home. With the help of his family, R.L. was a successful livestock and grain farmer who raised feeding cattle and purebred Hampshire hogs. (Courtesy of Anna Belle Johnson.)

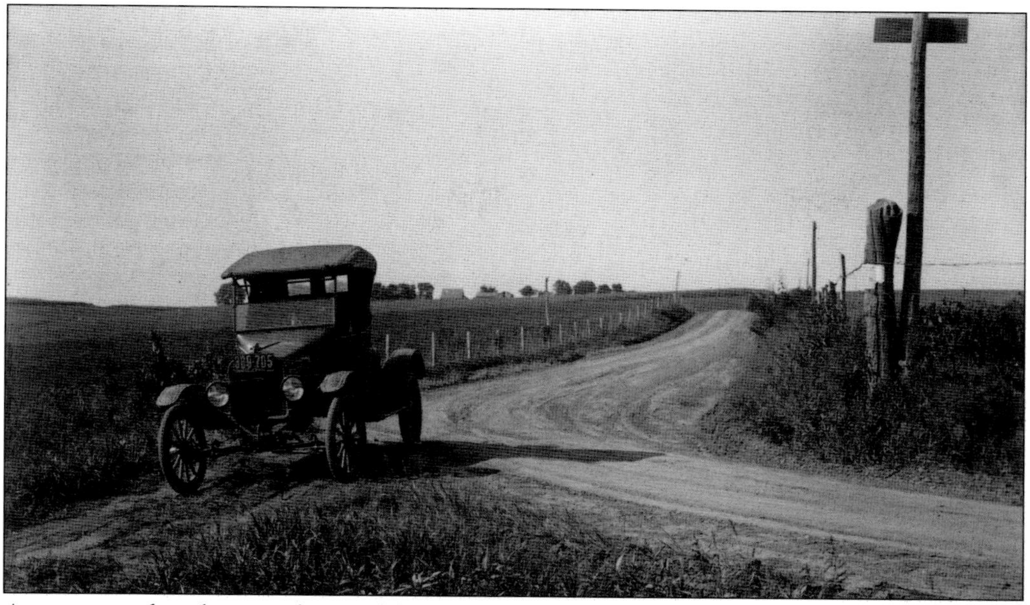

At a crossroads in history, this Model T Ford came to wary rural customers at a time when they were very attached to their horses. The automobile did not have to be fed or cleaned up after; it also did not need to be hitched or unhitched. Yet, with unpaved roads and the unpredictability of the weather, cars could easily get stuck in the mud. As automobile prices came down and people realized their reliability, horses were used less and less. (Courtesy of the Atchison County Historical Society.)

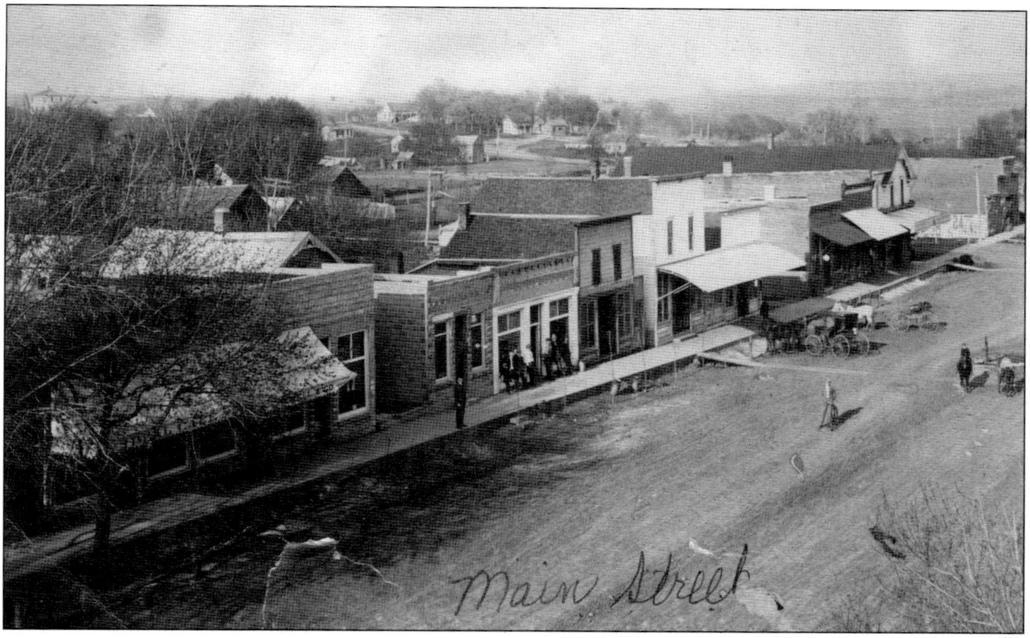

While this view of the north side of Main Street of Westboro in 1914 does not show any automobiles, there were some in the area by that time. Note the raised wooden sidewalk in front of the stores. The raised walkways made it much easier to load and unload a buckboard wagon, and although they are concrete paths today, they still line Westboro's streets. (Courtesy of the Atchison County Historical Society.)

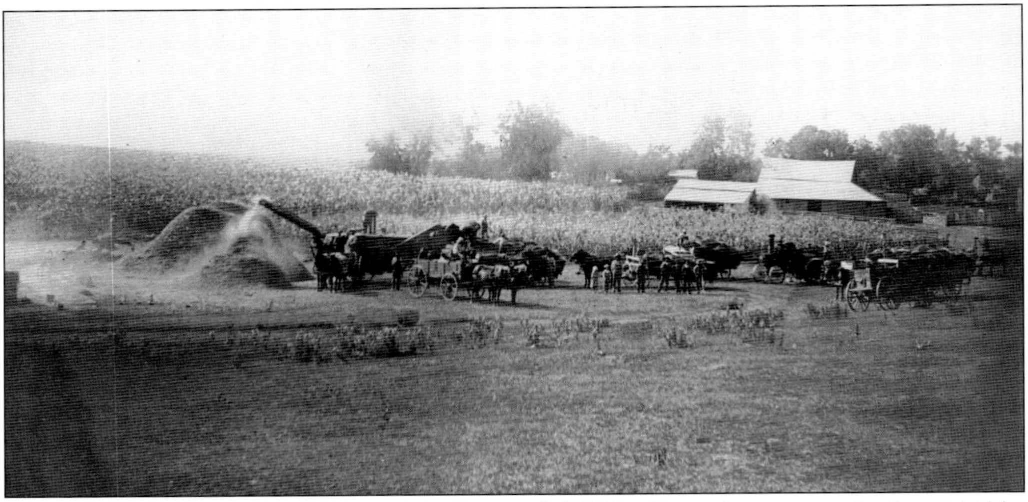

The first threshing machine was invented around 1784 by Scottish engineer Andrew Meikle. Before this tool, grain was separated from the husk and stalk by horsepower and was hand-fed into the machine, which was very time consuming and laborious. The modern combines of today operate with the same components and principles as the machines from the 1800s. This photograph was taken on the farm of Harry and Anna Belle Johnson east of Westboro. (Courtesy of Anna Belle Johnson.)

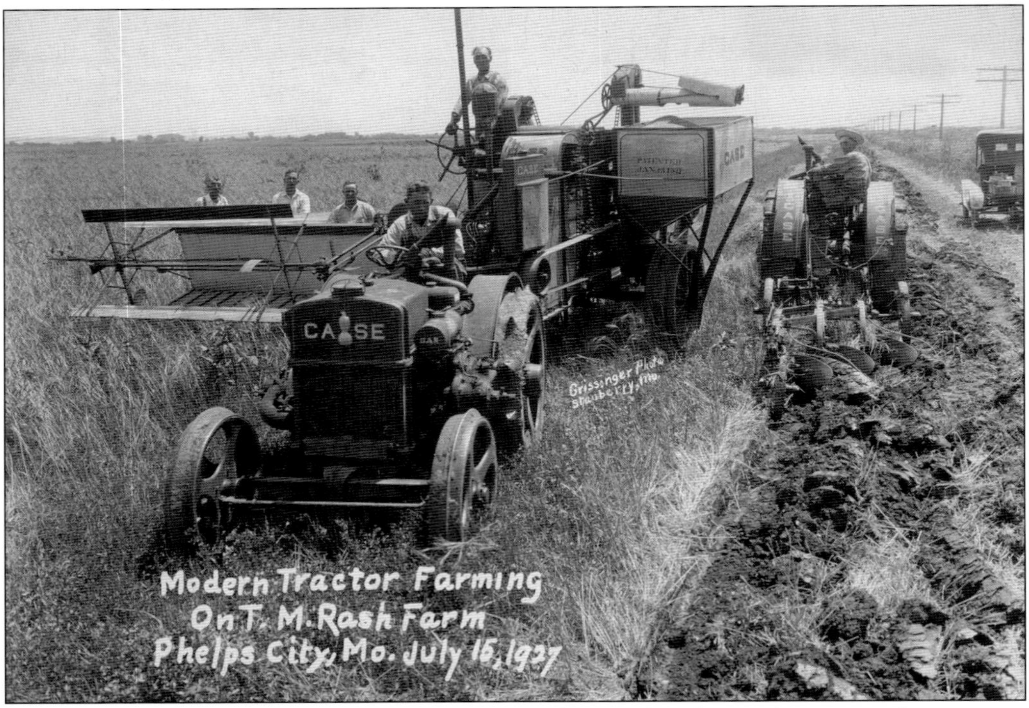

This 1927 farm scene shows a tractor pulling a combine. After the combine ran, other tractors would plow under the stubble and prepare the ground for the next spring. The town of Phelps City sits three miles from the Missouri River on level bottomland. Because of its location, the town floods quite often and few call it home today. The community was formally laid out in August 1868 and sat on the Kansas City, St. Joseph & Council Bluffs Railroad. In 1880, there were 301 residents living in the area. (Courtesy of the *Atchison County Mail.*)

Three
EDUCATION

The earliest schoolhouses in Atchison County were log cabins, and most of the earliest records have been lost to time; however, substantial records remain beginning in 1876. In that year, there were 4,198 white persons between the ages of 6 and 20 in Atchison County, with 11 "Negroes," six male and five female. The average number of school days in a year was 76, and there were 130 teachers. By 1881, records show that there were a total of 5,018 students, 78 schoolhouses, and 121 teachers—69 men and 52 women—in the county.

In 1872, a "List of Rules for Teachers" was issued. The rules, reprinted here from *The Country Schools of Atchison County*, are quite revealing of the times:

1. Teachers each day will fill lamps, clean chimneys.
2. Each teacher will bring a bucket of water and a scuttle of coal for the day's session.
3. Make your pens carefully. You may whittle nibs to the individual taste of the pupils.
4. Men teachers may take one evening each week for courting purposes, or two evenings a week if they go to church regularly.
5. After ten hours in school the teachers may spend the remaining time reading the Bible or other good works.
6. Women teachers who marry or engage in unseemly conduct will be dismissed.
7. Every teacher should lay aside from each pay a goodly sum of his earnings for his benefit during his declining years so that he will not become a burden on society.
8. Any teacher who smokes, uses liquor in any form, frequents public halls, or gets shaved in a barber shop will give good reason to suspect his worth, intention, integrity and honesty.
9. The teacher who performs his labor faithfully and without fault for five years will be given an increase of twenty-five cents per week in his pay, providing the Board of Education approves.

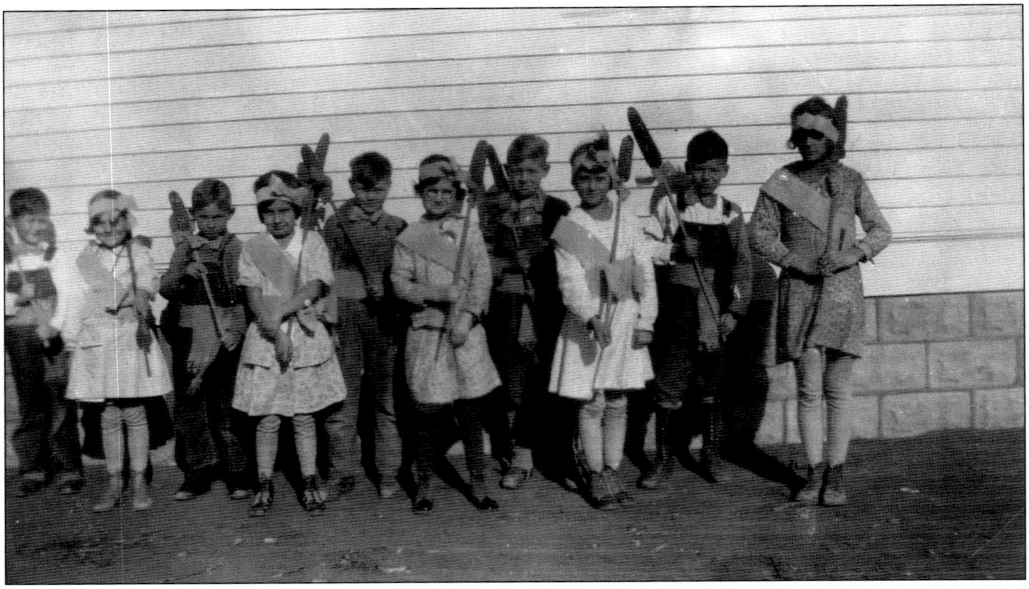

In the days before hybrid corn, farmers picked the seed for the coming year by keeping the best ears of corn. An ear with a small cob and deep kernels was kept safe from mice and hung up to dry, usually in the corncrib. When the Corn Show was held in Westboro, farmers displayed their best ears and compared them with neighbors in the area. Judges came from as far away as Columbia. (Courtesy of Phil and Meta Hull.)

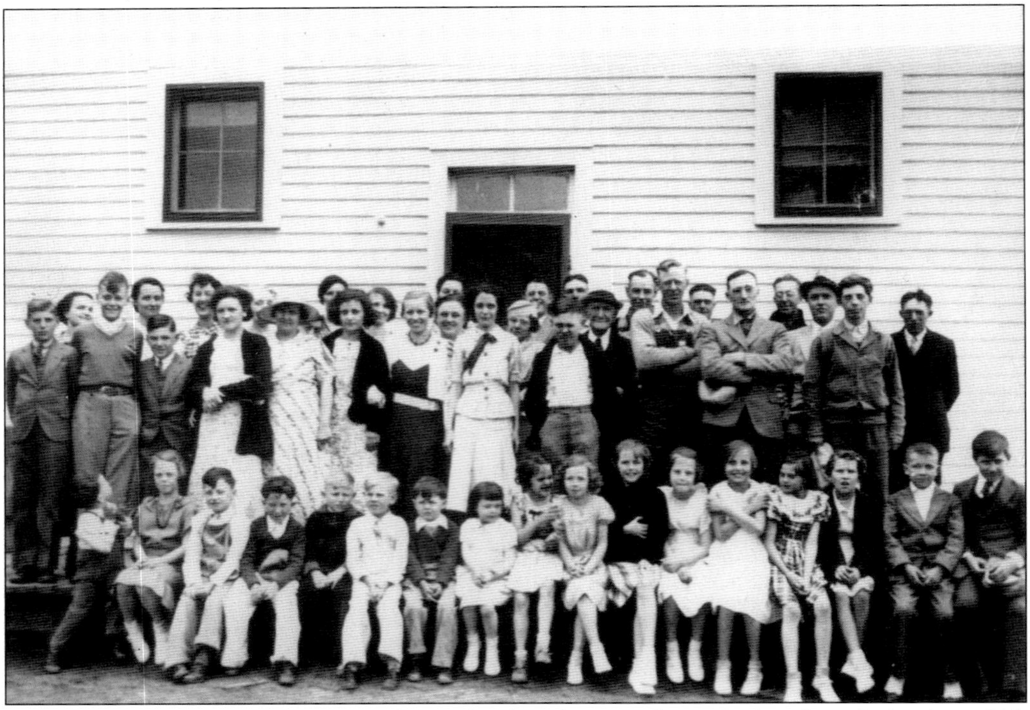

Students at the Morning Sun School pose for this photograph on the last day of school in 1935. The school, built in 1880 two miles west of Westboro, is still standing. During the 1905–1906 school year, the total enrollment was 18 but the average daily attendance was only nine. The teacher's salary was $45 per month. (Courtesy of George and Patty Laur.)

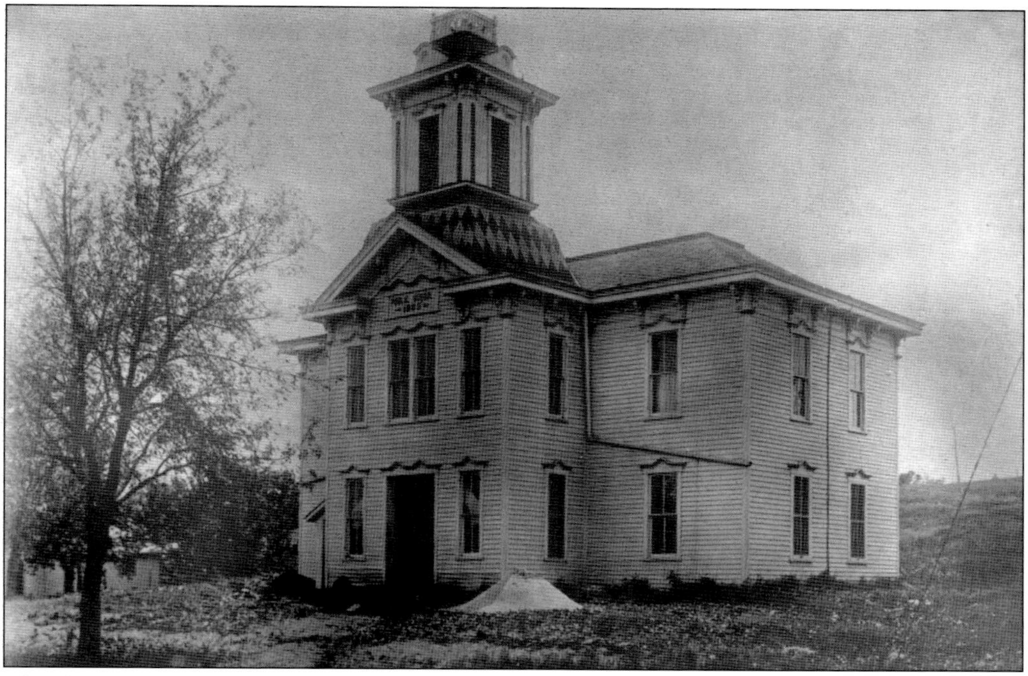

The old Westboro School was built in 1883 for $1,500 by two men, a Mr. William J. Raynolds and a Mr. James Grainger. Located three miles south of the current town of Westboro, the school was destroyed by a cyclone on July 13, 1883, with nothing but splinters left to save. In 1917, the last school in Westboro was built of brick at a cost of $15,000. (Courtesy of George and Patty Laur.)

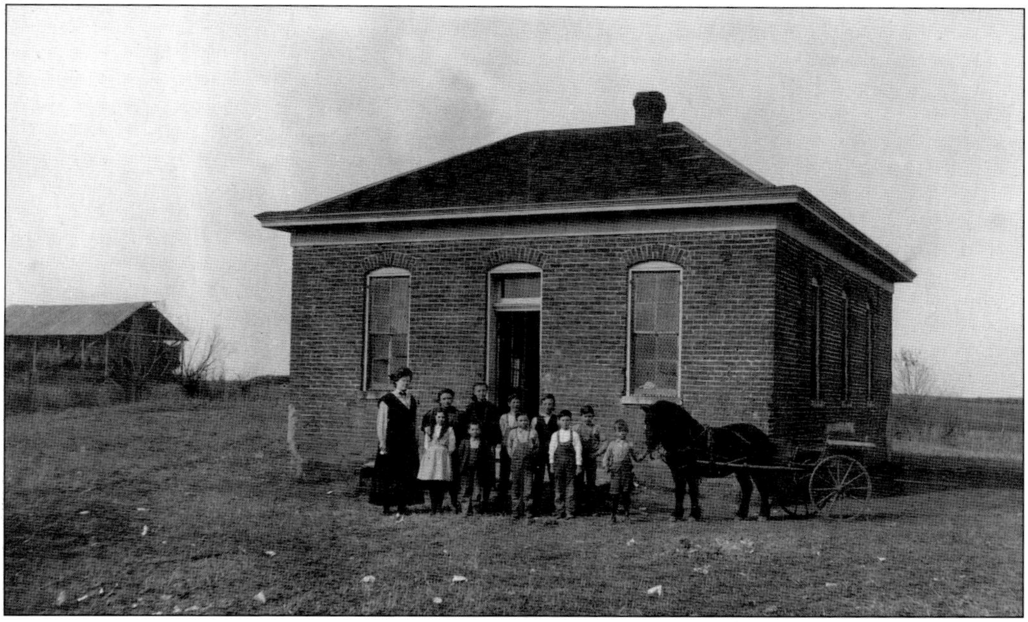

Happy Hill School is seen here around 1908 with teacher Nona Carothers and her students, from left to right, (first row) Vesta Andrews, Norah Hurst, Callie Sears, Harley Miller, and Galen Andrews; (second row) Burgie Lash, Owen VanMeter, Wesley Andrews, Freddie Daugherty, and Everette Miller. This school was eight miles east and four miles north of Tarkio. (Courtesy of the Atchison County Historical Society.)

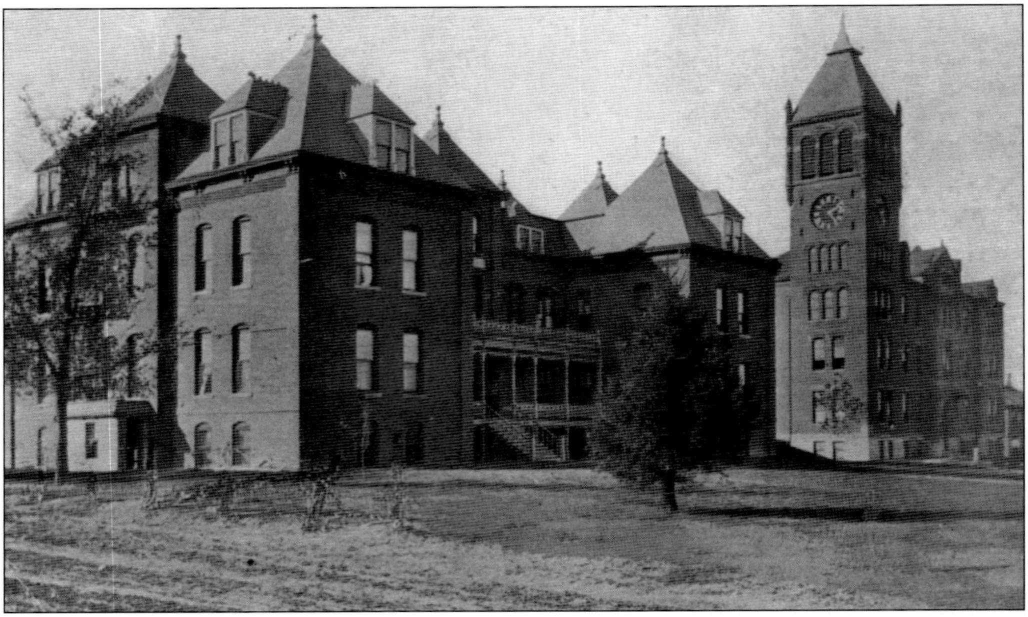

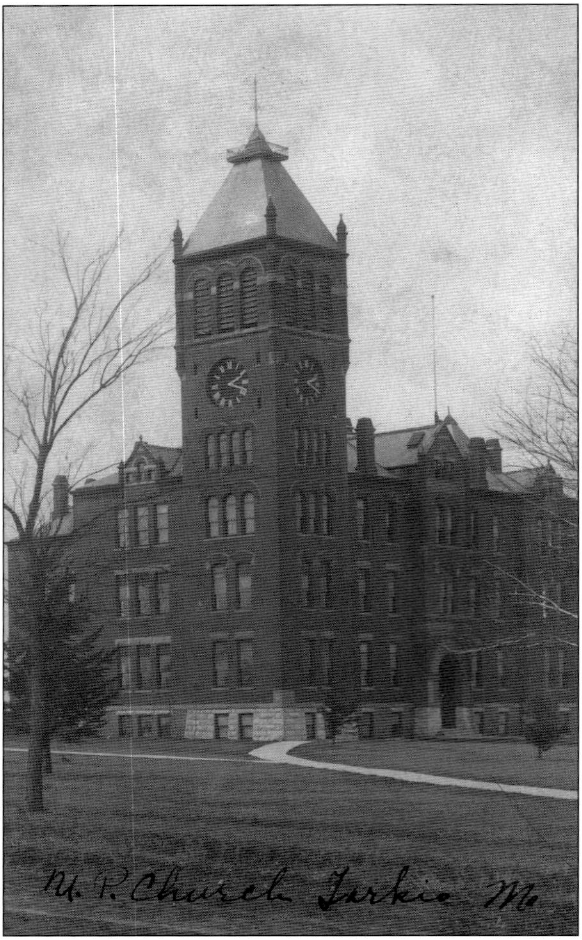

David Rankin wanted the Atchison County Courthouse to be built in Tarkio, so he went ahead preparing for it. When this did not happen, Rankin built Tarkio College instead. Marshall Hall is seen here on the left, and the first Old Main, which later burned to the ground, is on the right. (Courtesy of Hon. Corey Herron.)

Tarkio College was first known as Tarkio Valley College and Normal Institute and opened in August 1883 with 11 students. One of its major benefactors was local farmer and statesman David Rankin, who was a big proponent of improving oneself through education. This building was destroyed by fire in January 1892 and again in January 1930. Tarkio was ahead of its time, as what is now Northwest Missouri State University, a short distance away in Maryville, did not officially open until 1905 and still thrives today. (Courtesy of Hon. Corey Herron.)

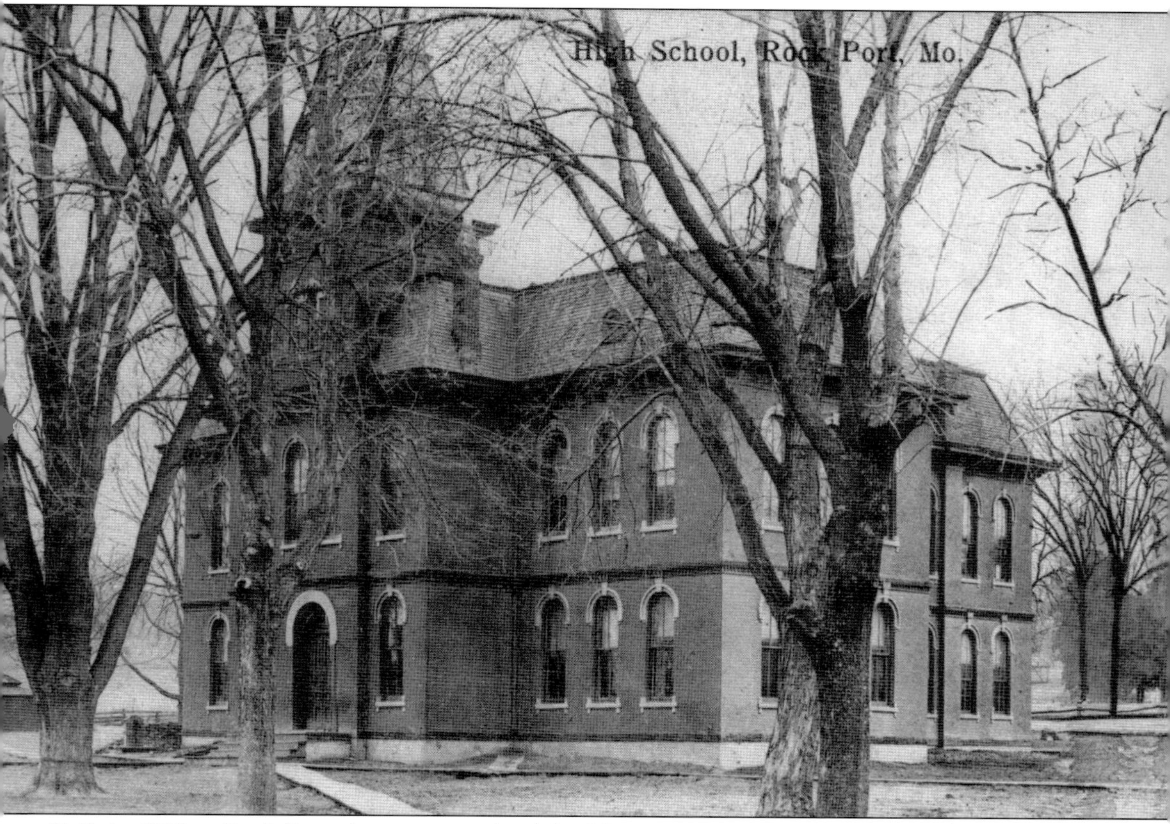

Built in 1892 in Rock Port, this two-story brick building was constructed at a cost of $17,500 and had seven rooms. The seven departments provided three years of high school study. Before it was built, school had been held in a building constructed by the Masons and the South Methodist Church. This postcard is dated March 7, 1911. (Courtesy of Hon. Corey Herron.)

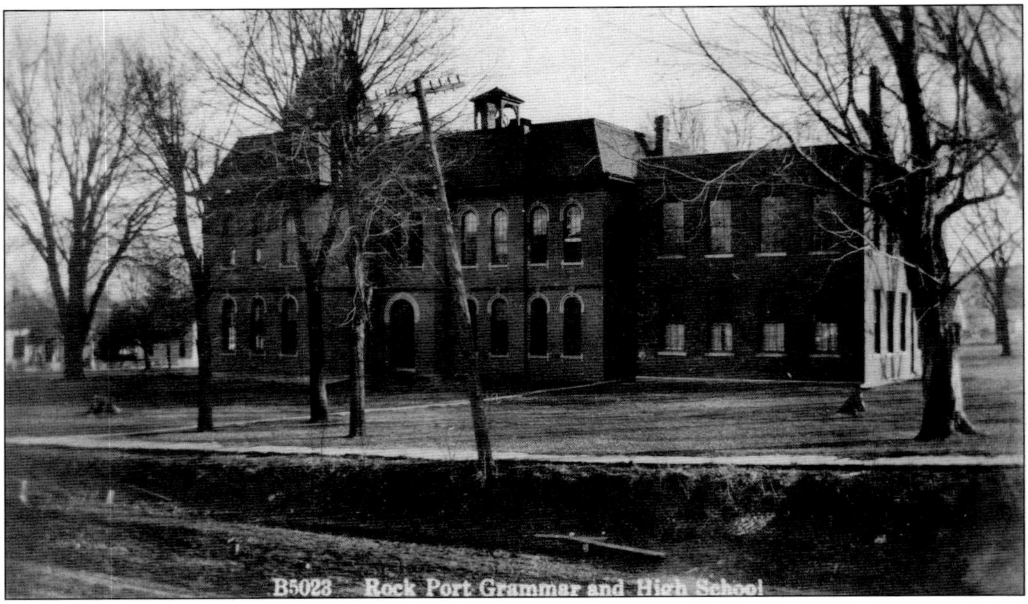

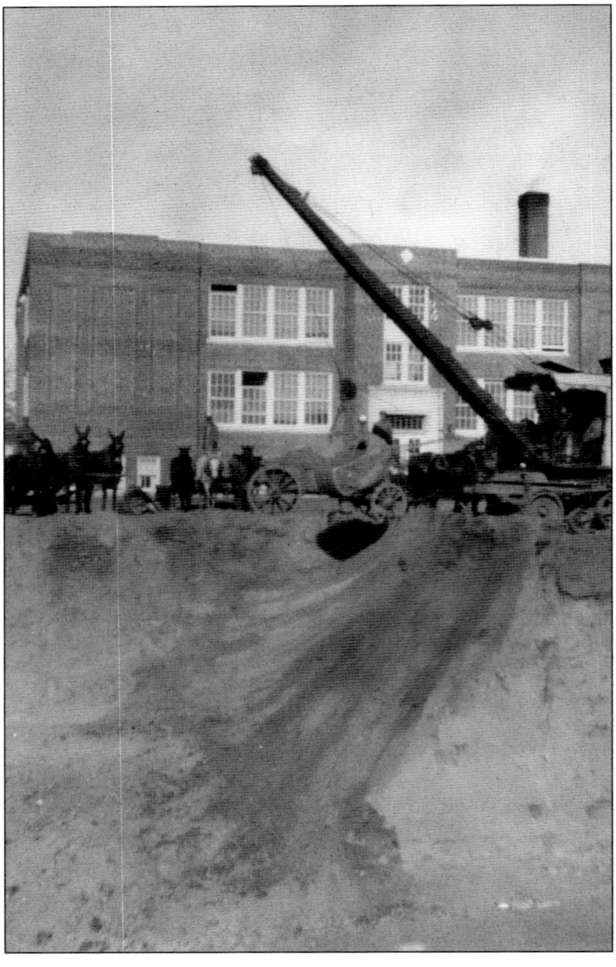

Around the time Rock Port was being settled, the Civil War erupted and caused all school records from that era to be lost. During that time, school was held in private homes and on a farm north of Tarkio; there was a young ladies seminary as well. The first organization of the Rock Port school system was recorded on April 8, 1965, and called District No. 2, with W.G. Bartholomew, P.A. Thompson, and J.D. Dopf as elected directors. (Courtesy of Hon. Corey Herron.)

A dragline with teams of horses and mules moves dirt in front of Fairfax High School in 1933 or 1934. In a story still told around Fairfax today, the assistant foreman hung himself in the school gym in December 1925 because he felt so badly about not completing the school construction on time. The school was eventually finished, and the first students were taught there in 1926. (Courtesy of Betty Wennihan.)

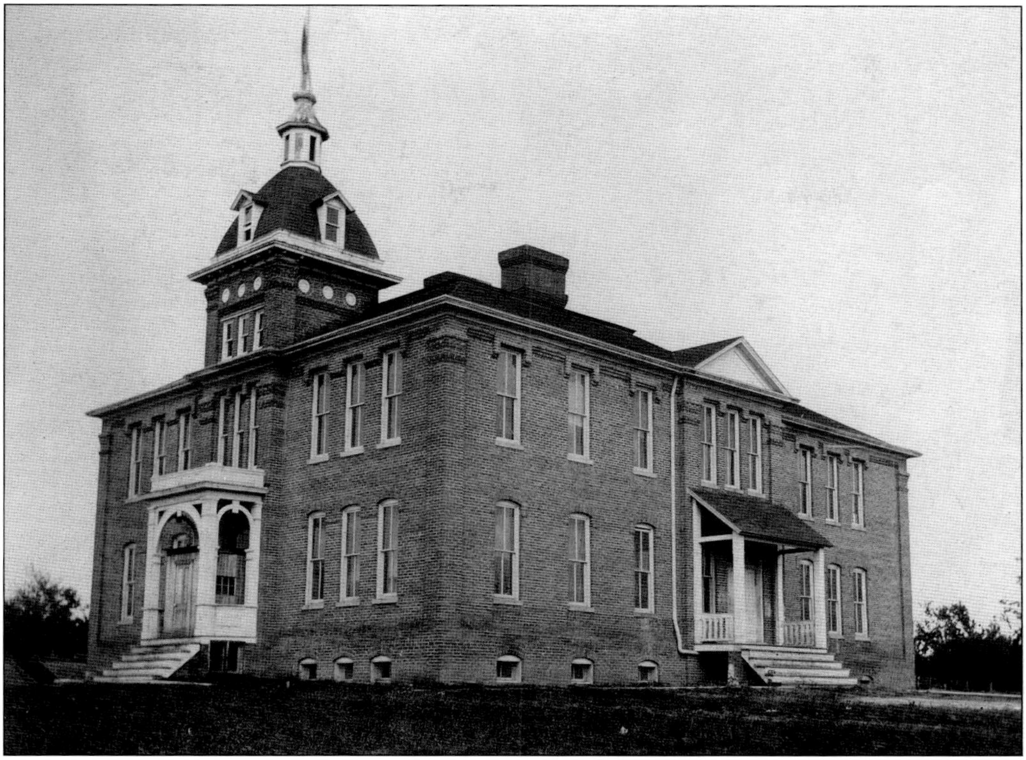

Fairfax High School was built on a high hill in 1896 after a $10,000 bond was issued for its construction. The two entrances faced east and south, and the building served as both an elementary school and a high school. This building was torn down in 1925, and the present Fairfax High School was built the following year. (Courtesy of Betty Wennihan.)

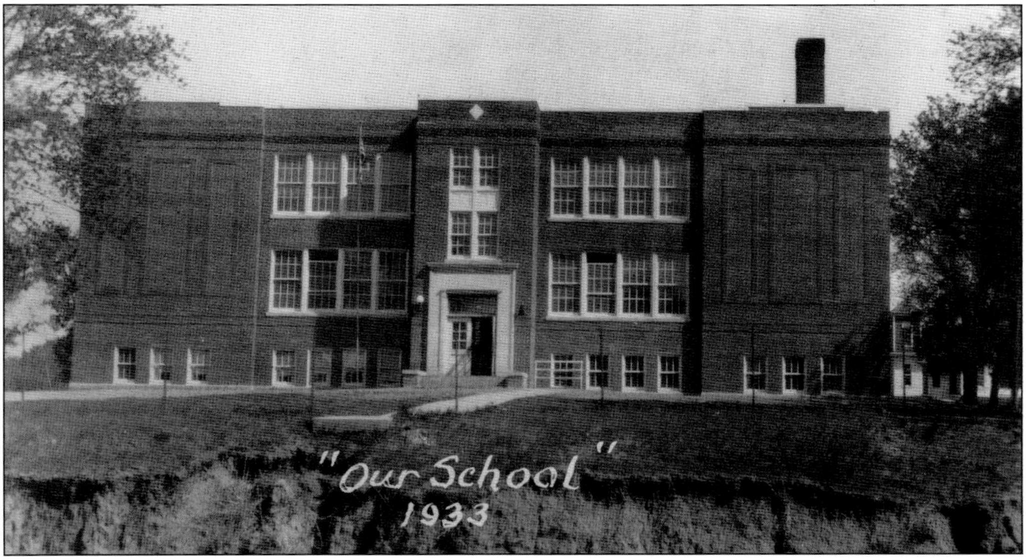

The new Fairfax High School first opened in 1926 and is still in use today. In 1925, ballot bonds in the amount of $51,000 were voted in on the third ballot. On March 19, 1926, the new building was dedicated, and the modern, three-story building was put into use. (Courtesy of Betty Wennihan.)

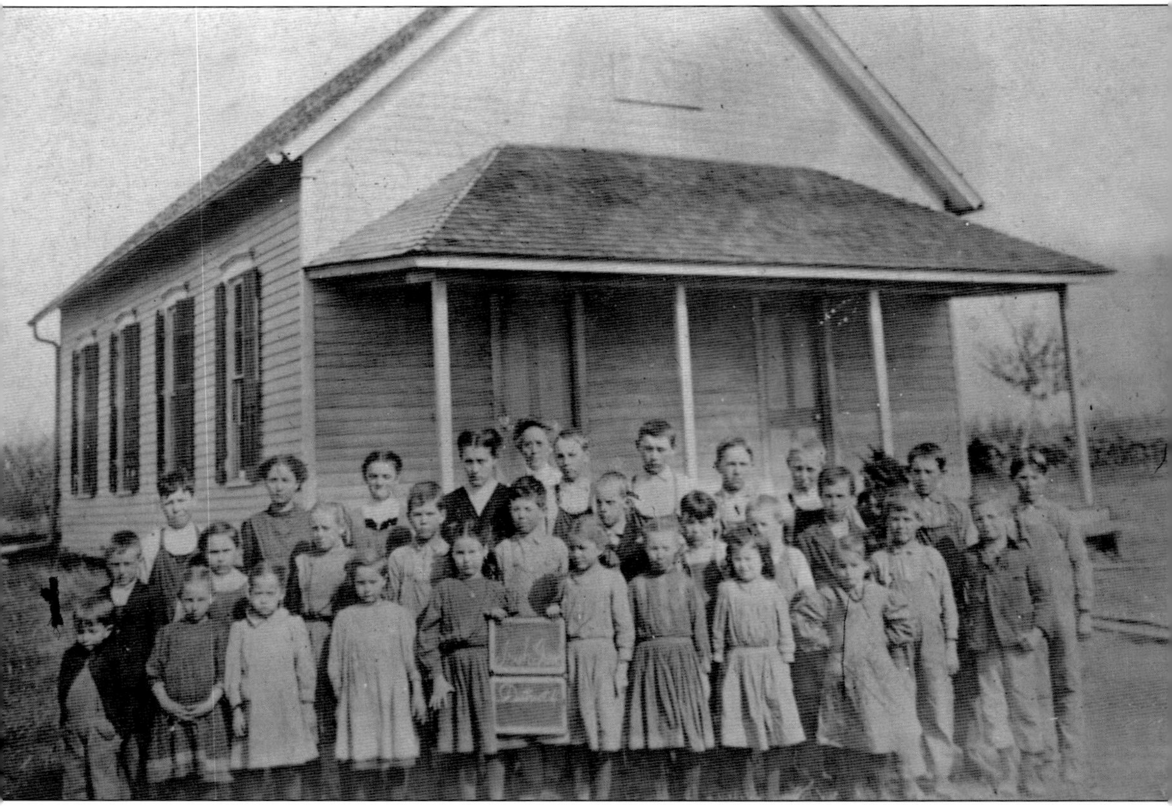

The first school at Irish Grove was a log cabin that was built in 1838 and located three miles west and a half-mile south of Fairfax. The name Irish Grove was derived from two Irish brothers who settled near here by the name of Murphey. Teacher Anna Laird is seen here in the back center with her students in 1908. The last class attended school at Irish Grove in 1943. (Courtesy of Betty Wennihan.)

This church, originally English Grove United Presbyterian Church, was built for $1,500 in 1872 and demolished in 1981. The church had organized in 1858. English Grove was a trading post located on a trail established by Mormons that ran from Liberty, Missouri, to Kanesville, Iowa (now Council Bluffs.) (Courtesy of Betty Wennihan.)

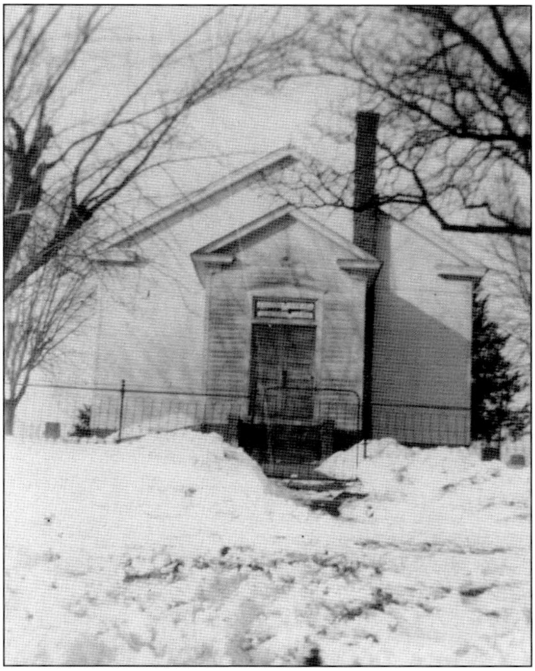

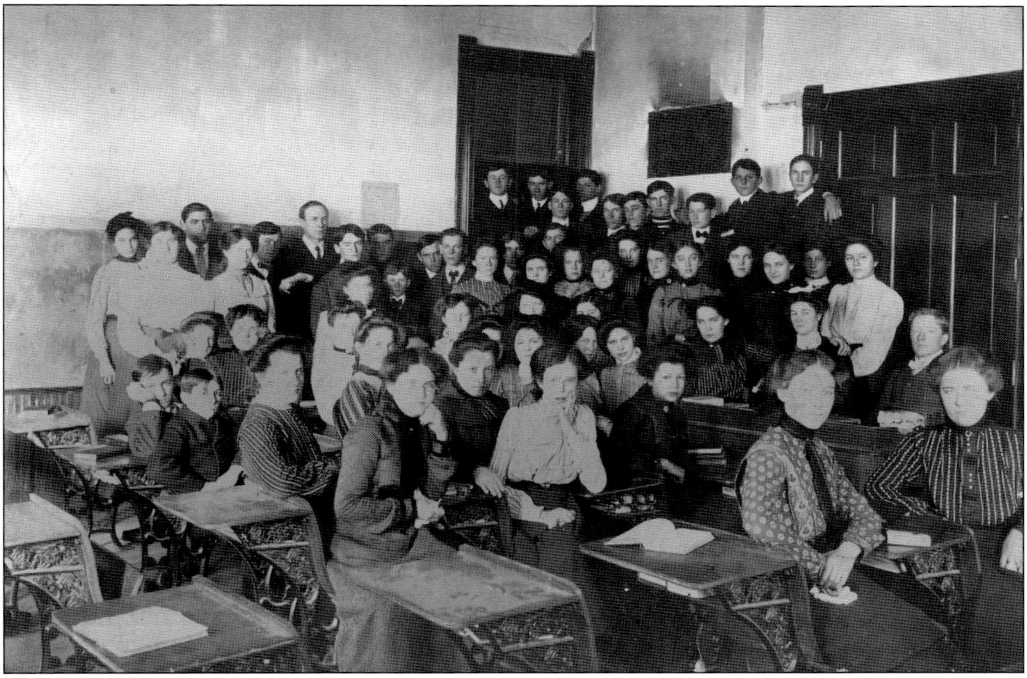

In center of the back row with his hair parted down the middle is Basil P. Hunter, who lived most of his life in Fairfax. He graduated from Fairfax High School in 1905. Along with his father, Dr. James A. Hunter, Basil believed in being active in the community and in city affairs. Both men belonged to the Presbyterian Church, the Masonic Lodge, and other civic organizations. Basil was on a committee that assisted in raising funds to establish Fairfax Community Hospital, and Dr. Hunter was a petitioner who helped incorporate the town of Fairfax. Basil owned his own successful general merchandise business in Fairfax and retired in 1965. (Courtesy of Betty Wennihan.)

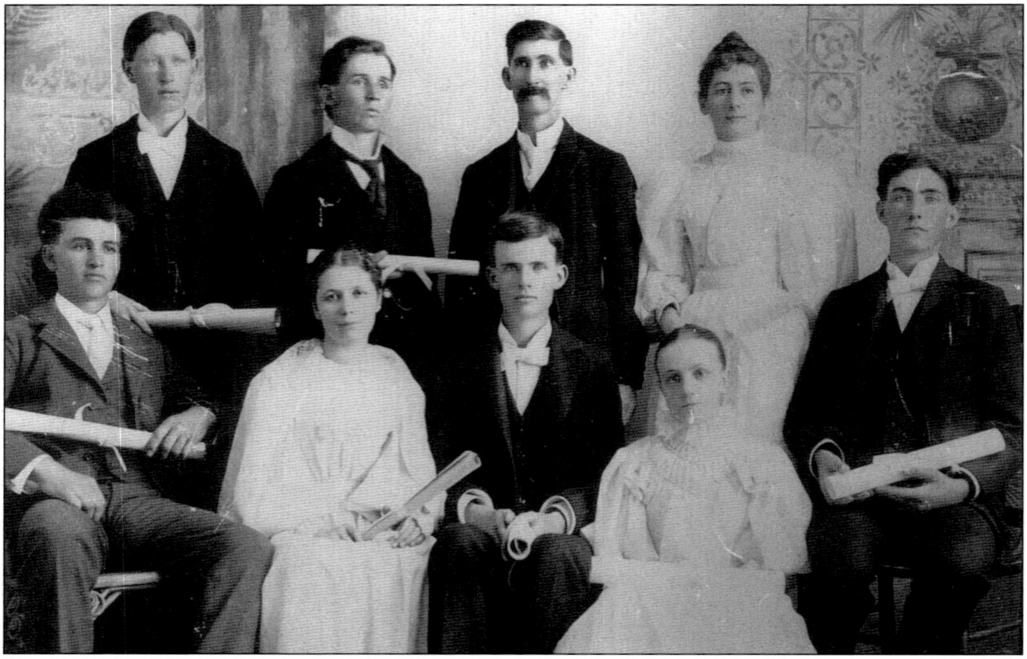

Fairfax's beginnings were due to the Burlington Railroad, which came through in 1881. The president of the railroad, Charles Perkins, put up a large tract of land for sale in the area. Perkins also donated the land for a city park and stated in the deed that "the community was to keep the park in good shape with a neat fence" that was properly painted. If the town did not keep up these requirements, the city park grounds would revert to its original owner. The Fairfax Independent School District was formed in April 1883 and had its first graduating class, seen here, in 1896. (Courtesy of Betty Wennihan.)

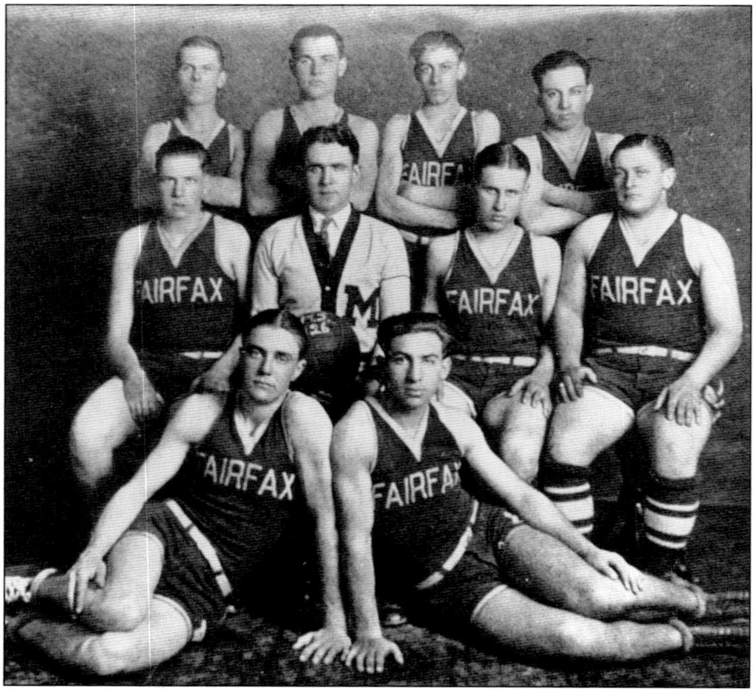

The 1926 Fairfax High School basketball team included, from left to right, (first row) W.P. Green and Lee Wrinkle; (second row) Clair Whitford, coach Lloyd Waller, Charles Ruddle, and Edward Catron; (third row) Russell Walker, Leo Donadlson, Dick Catron, and Guy Wrinkle. (Courtesy of Betty Wennihan.)

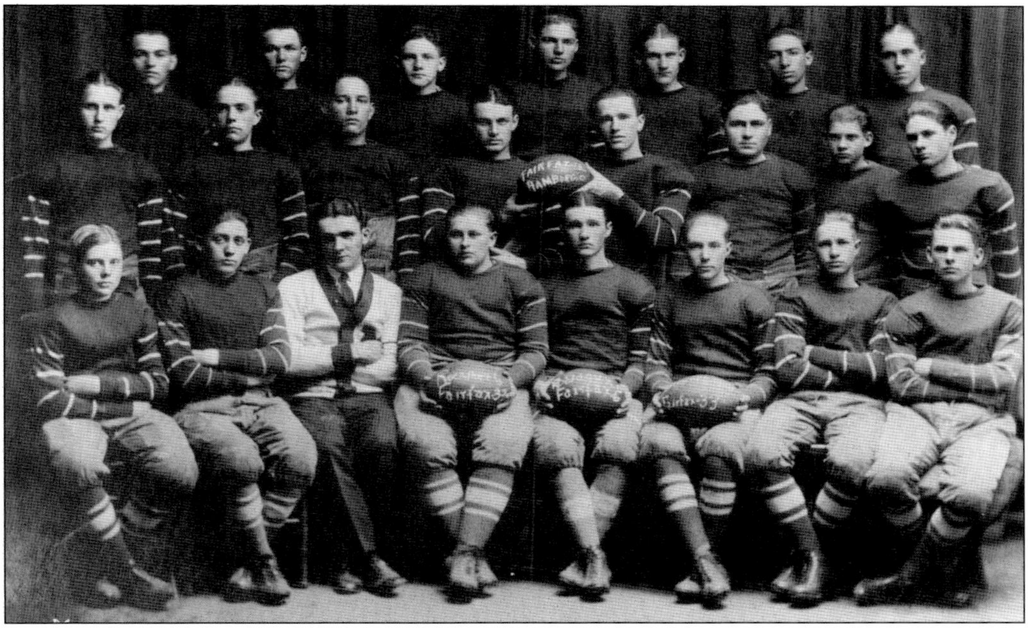

The 1923 Fairfax High School football team went undefeated and proudly display the final scores of their games on footballs in their team photograph. They beat Rock Port, Robidoux, Hamburg, and Mound City by a combined score of 84-12. (Courtesy of Betty Wennihan.)

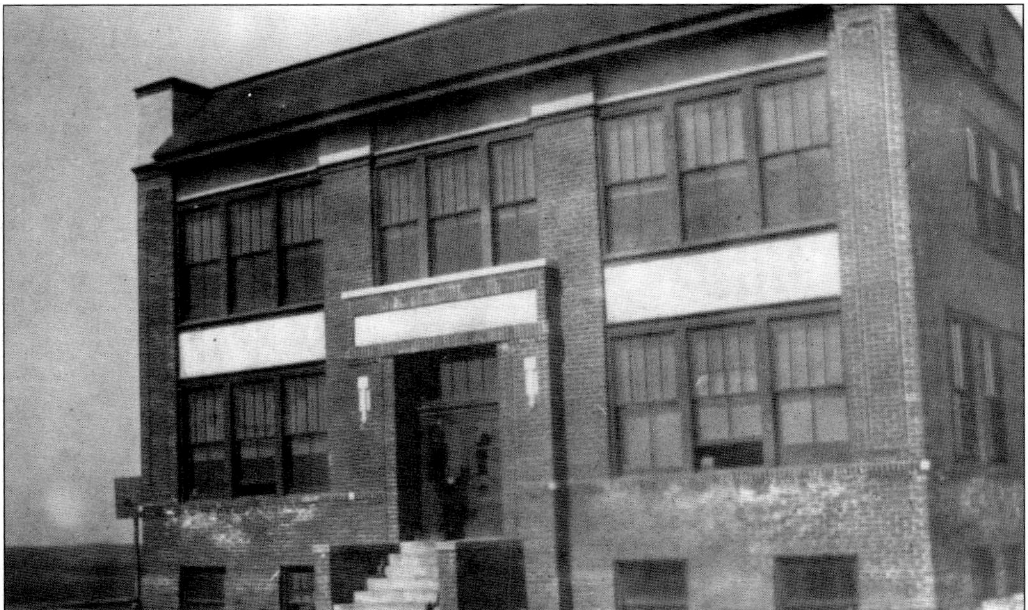

As more people moved west and to the cities, where the jobs were, there was less need for rural schools. Daleview School cost $18,000 to build in 1918 and had a full basement, four classrooms, and an auditorium on the top floor. The Daleview School District was a consolidation of the schools in West Point, Walkups Grove, South Center (commonly known as Littell), Mount Salem, and Spring Valley. Daleview School had its last graduating class in 1944. (Courtesy of Betty Wennihan.)

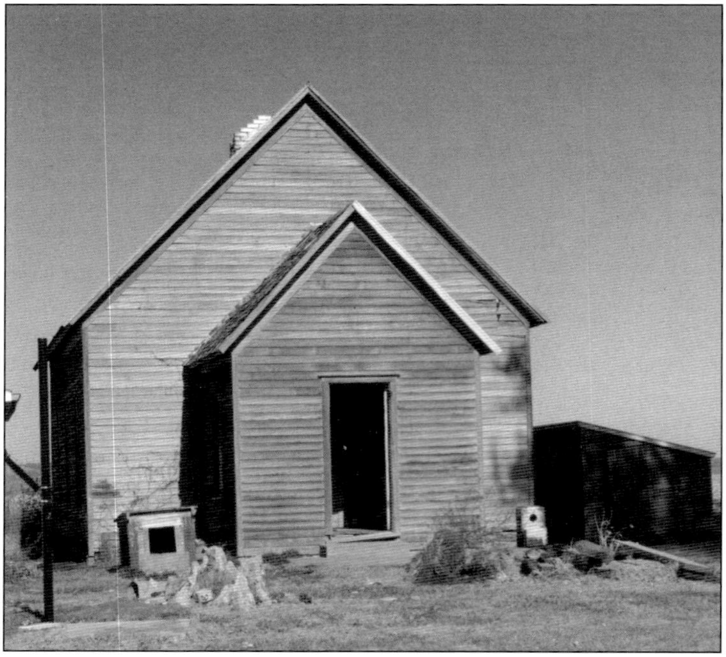

Bethany School, also called Ellison, was four or five miles north of Watson and was the last one-room schoolhouse in Nishnabotna Township. The school had an average daily attendance of 19 and a full enrollment of 29 in 1905–1906. The school had an organ and a water bucket in the hall, and students each had a "folding drink cup" to fill with water. (Courtesy of Kay Gibson.)

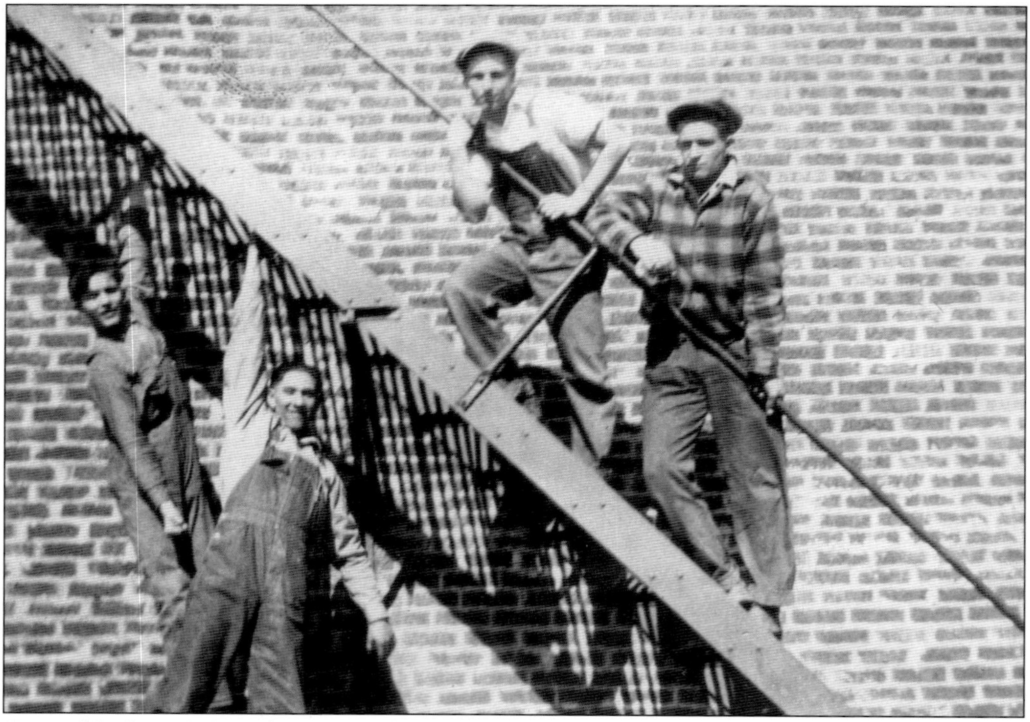

Opened before 1872, Irish Grove School was located a half mile south and three miles west of Fairfax. According to early settlers of the area, Irish Grove was the first school in Clark Township. By 1919, Irish Grove had consolidated with the Hillsdale and Waits schools, and the high school was located in the Pleasant Valley Church. Seen here horsing around outside the church are, from left to right, Wayne Jones, Jim Thompson, Ralph Bennington, and Winston Irvin. (Courtesy of Betty Wennihan.)

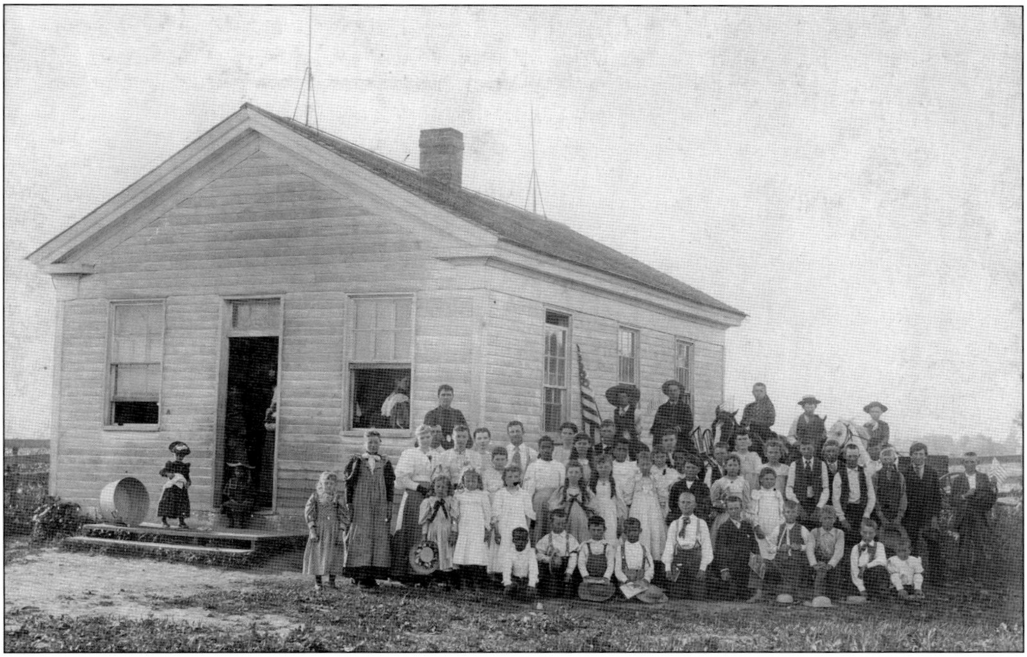

Schoolchildren line up for a photograph on the first day of school at Cooper School, with teacher Hattie Sutton is in the back left in a dark dress. The August 20, 1891, *Atchison County Mail* reported that Sutton had taught three years of school at Cooper School. (Courtesy of Betty Wennihan.)

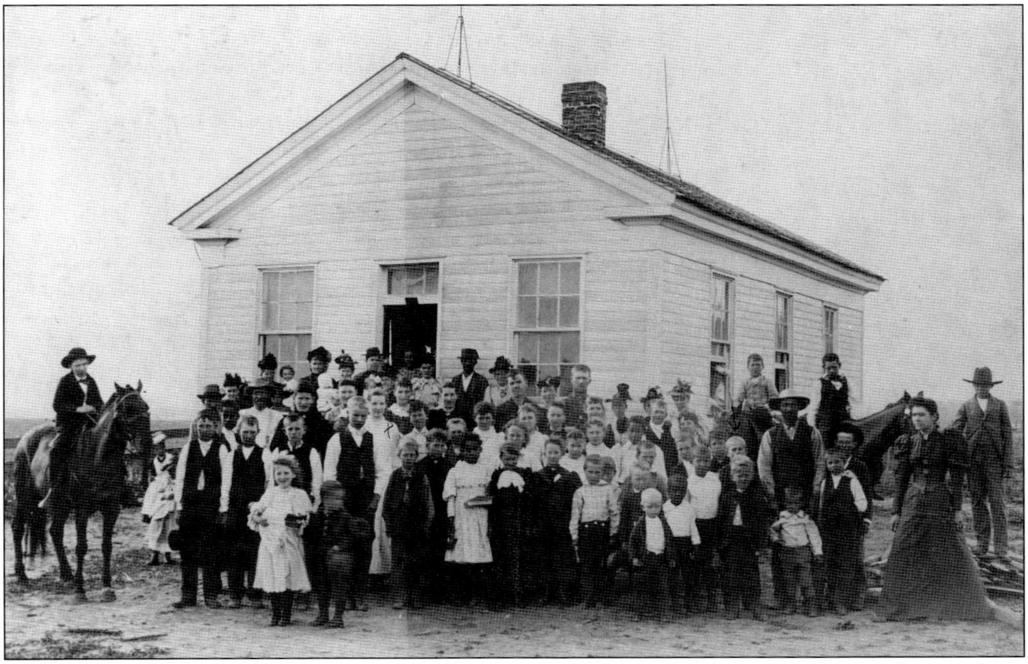

The earliest year Cooper School is reported in county records was 1889, when it received tax money from the district, but it was likely in existence earlier. The school closed in 1950. Some students who attended Cooper School through the years included Harmon Harms; Willie and Hanna Meyerkorth; Mary, Logan, and Josie Goodlow; and George and Fay Clark. Teacher Hattie Sutton is seen here in the front right in a dress. (Courtesy of Betty Wennihan.)

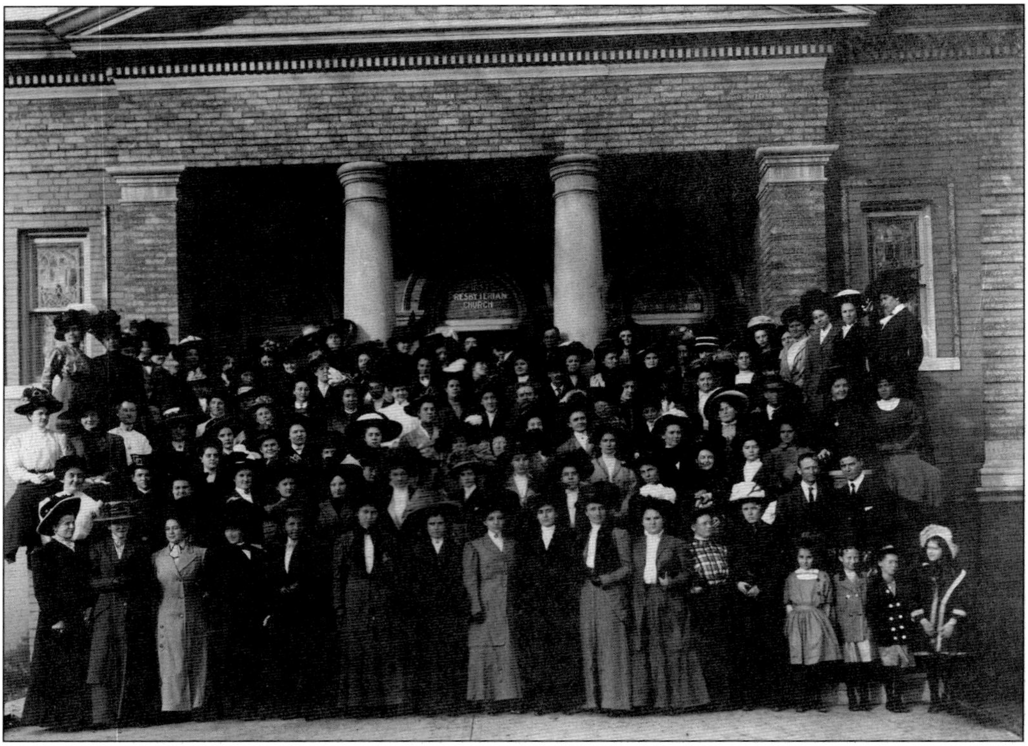

The Teacher's Institute at First United Presbyterian Church is seen here in the late 1920s with county superintendent Sally Grebe second from left in the front row; she retired in 1927. Joseph A. Thompson was at one time the minister of the church and came to Tarkio to lead Tarkio College. (Courtesy of the Atchison County Historical Society.)

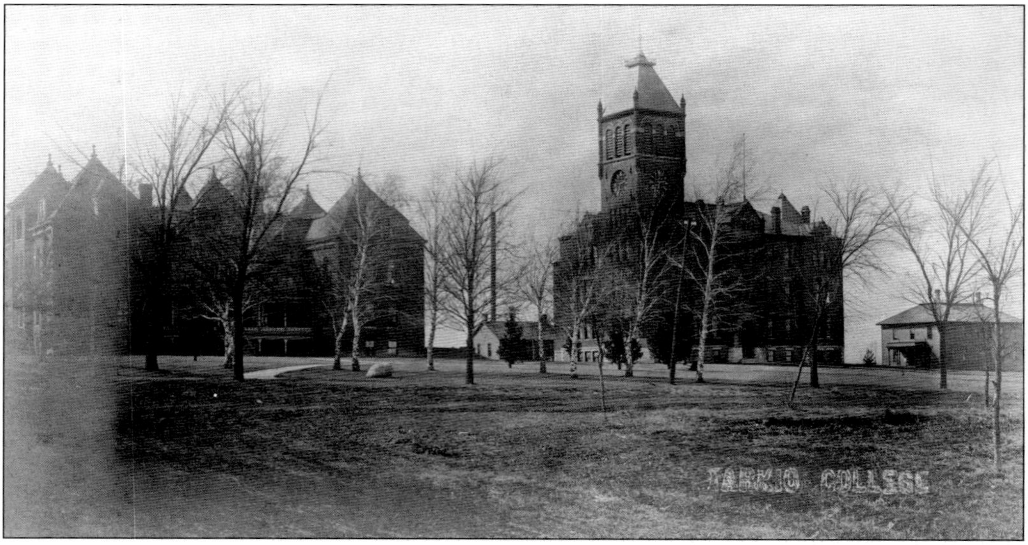

Marshall Hall (left) and the Administration Building (right) are seen here on the campus of Tarkio College. The Administration Building burned on January 19, 1930, and was replaced by a structure that still stands today. David Rankin tried to bring the county seat to Tarkio, building what he hoped would become the county courthouse. After Rock Port was named the county seat, Rankin's building became Tarkio College. (Courtesy of the Atchison County Historical Society.)

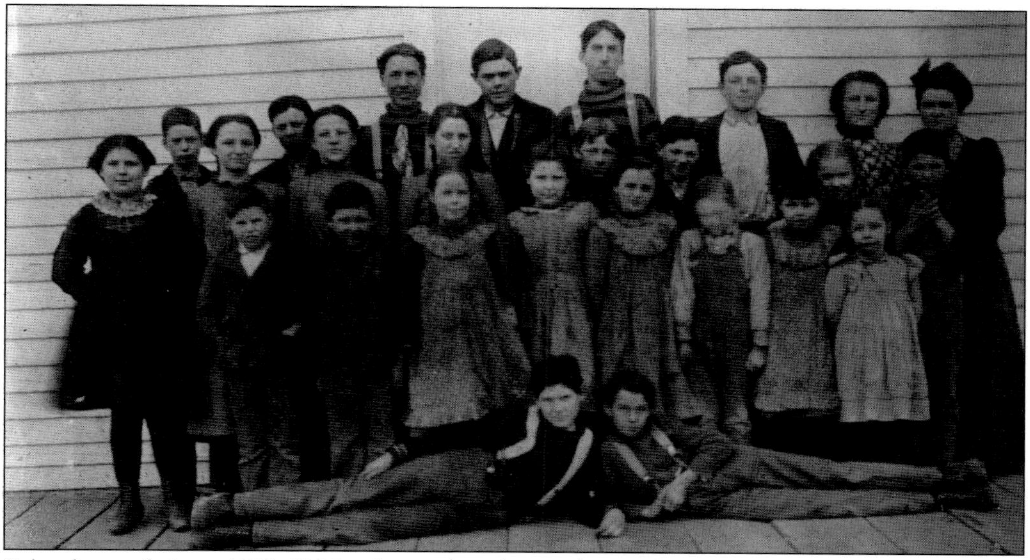

School records from 1905–1906 indicate that the yearly enrollment at Morning Sun School was 18 and the average daily attendance was nine. There are several reasons for the low attendance rate, including illness and the necessity for children to work on the farm. These students stand in front of the school, which still stands two miles west of Westboro, in 1905. (Courtesy of George and Patty Laur.)

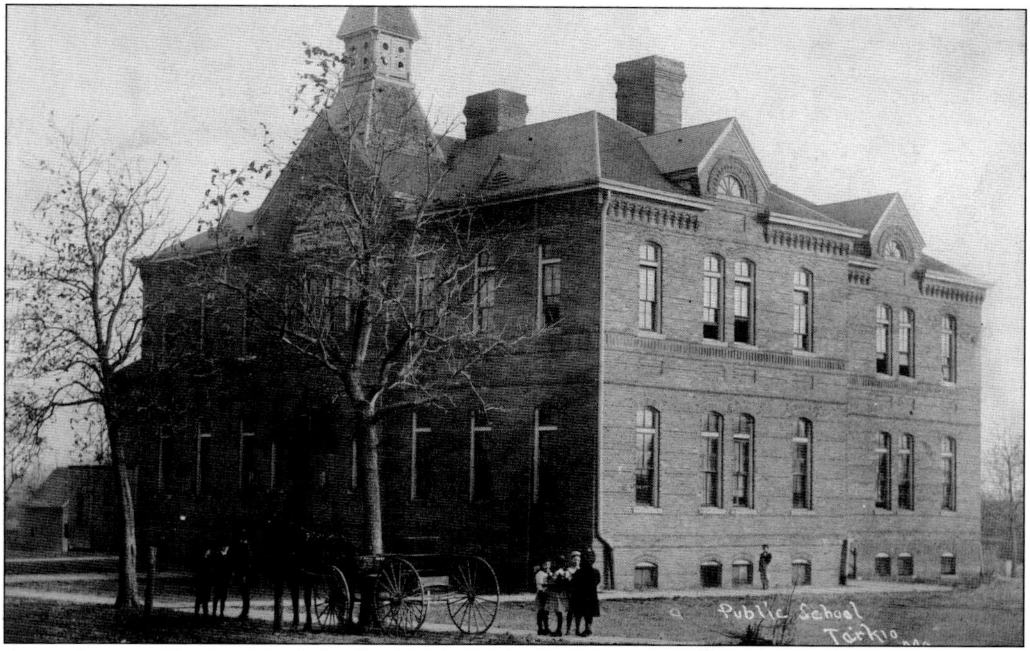

According to *The Country Schools of Atchison County*, "The Tarkio faculty of 1891–92 included W.D. Grove, Principal, Kate Solomon, Sallie McMullen, Sarah Shoenhaire, Ella Rolofson, and Mrs. Maude Grove. There must have been something special in Mrs. Grove's being on the faculty, as is was practically a capital crime for a superintendent at that time to even recommend a married woman as a teacher." This Tarkio public school was built in 1895 and was the third constructed in the area. The first school was on Main Street and the second burned down in 1893. (From *The Country Schools of Atchison County*.)

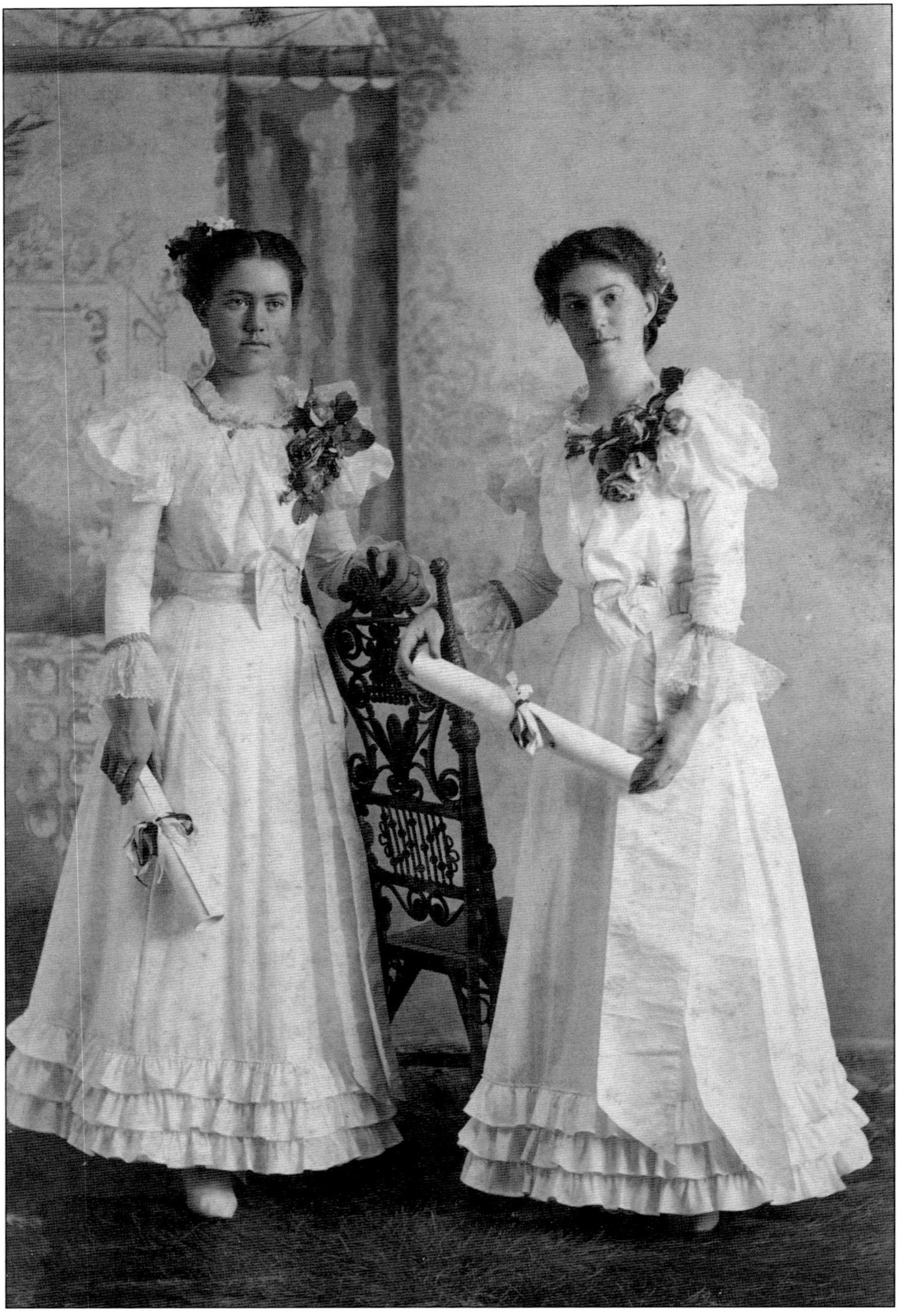

In March 1927, the Phi Kappa chapter of the National Honor Society began at Tarkio High School when it received its charter. The organizing sponsor was Mrs. Edgar Adams. There was a senior chapter for older students and a junior one for younger students in seventh, eighth, and ninth grades. The junior chapter was disbanded a few years later, and the national office advised the senior chapter to drop the Greek name of Phi Kappa and be instead known simply as the National Honor Society. (Courtesy of the Atchison County Historical Society.)

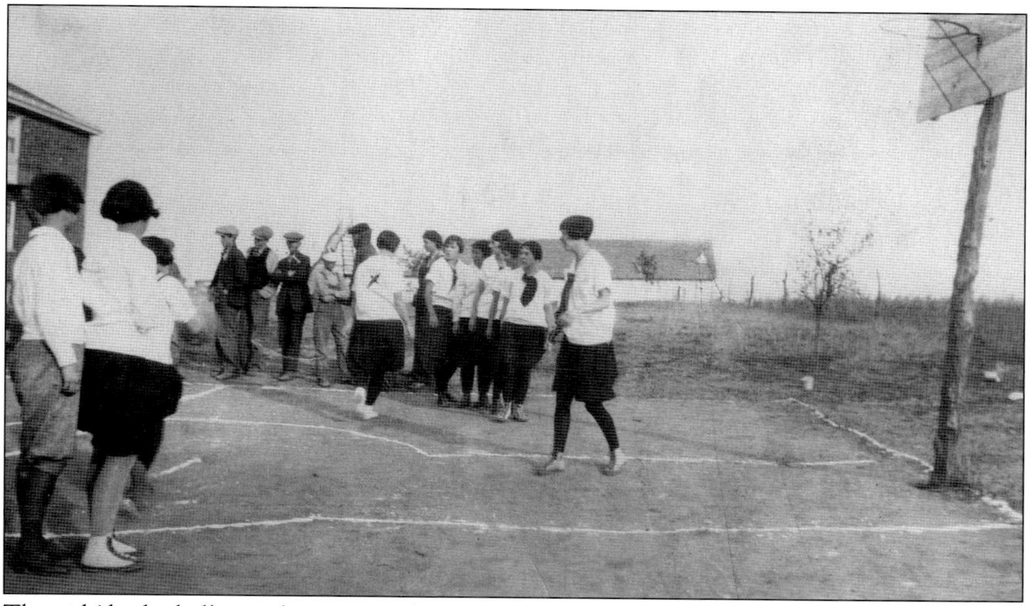

The girls' basketball team began at Tarkio High School around 1915. Instead of traveling to away games by bus as they do today, the girls traveled by train. If the team arrived early enough, they would eat lunch with their opponents and then visit afternoon classes. If they arrived later, they would go right to warm-ups for the game. After the game, there was usually a slumber party at the home of one of the opponents, and the team would leave on the next morning train. (Courtesy of Maxine Staples.)

According to county court records, the common school district officially began in Atchison County on April 13 or 14, 1846. Lone Star School, seen here, was nine miles east and one mile south of Tarkio. The last time there was a one-room schoolhouse in the county was in 1957, when Star School, near Rock Port, closed for good. It had opened its doors for the first time in 1898. (Courtesy of the Atchison County Historical Society.)

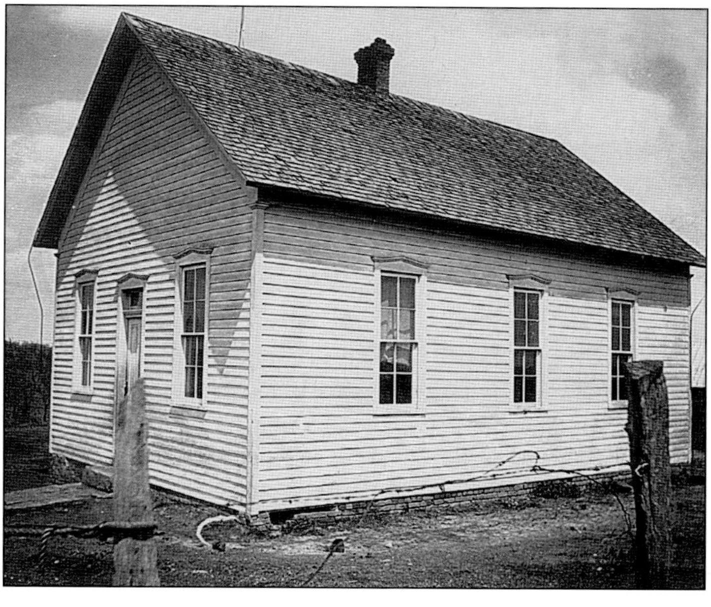

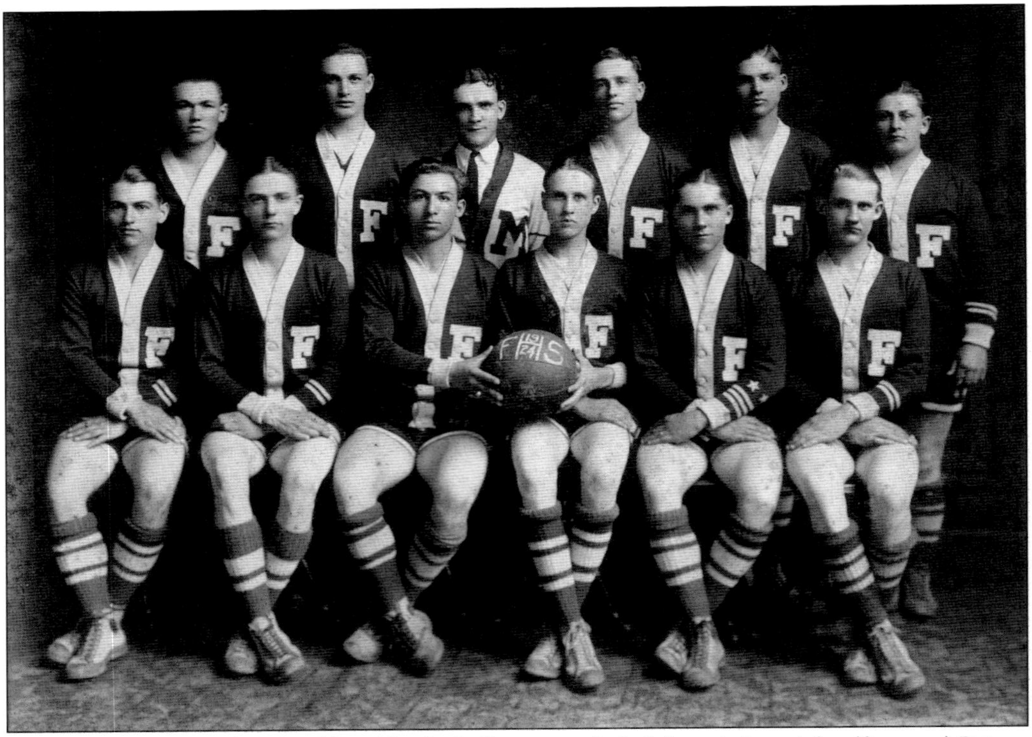

The 1924 Fairfax High School boys' basketball team included, from left to right, (first row) Prime, Green, Wrinkle, Ruddell, Mapes, and Burns; (second row) Donaldson, Cortner, coach Waller, Jones, Martin, and "Pug" Catron. Catron was a druggist in Fairfax for many years. (Courtesy of Betty Wennihan.)

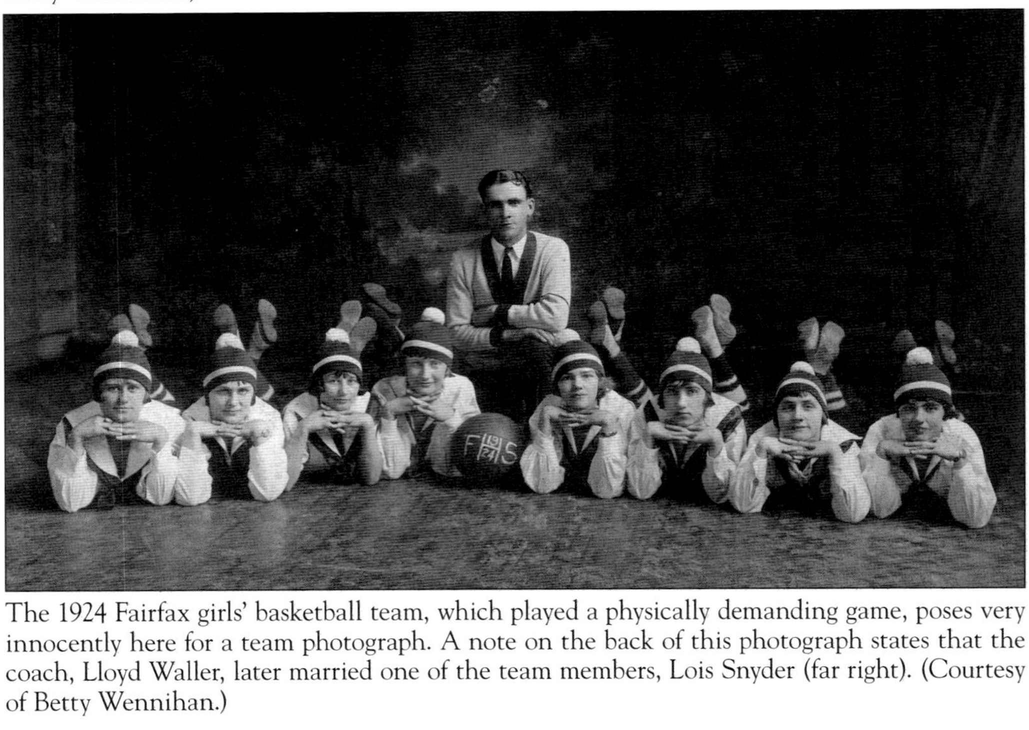

The 1924 Fairfax girls' basketball team, which played a physically demanding game, poses very innocently here for a team photograph. A note on the back of this photograph states that the coach, Lloyd Waller, later married one of the team members, Lois Snyder (far right). (Courtesy of Betty Wennihan.)

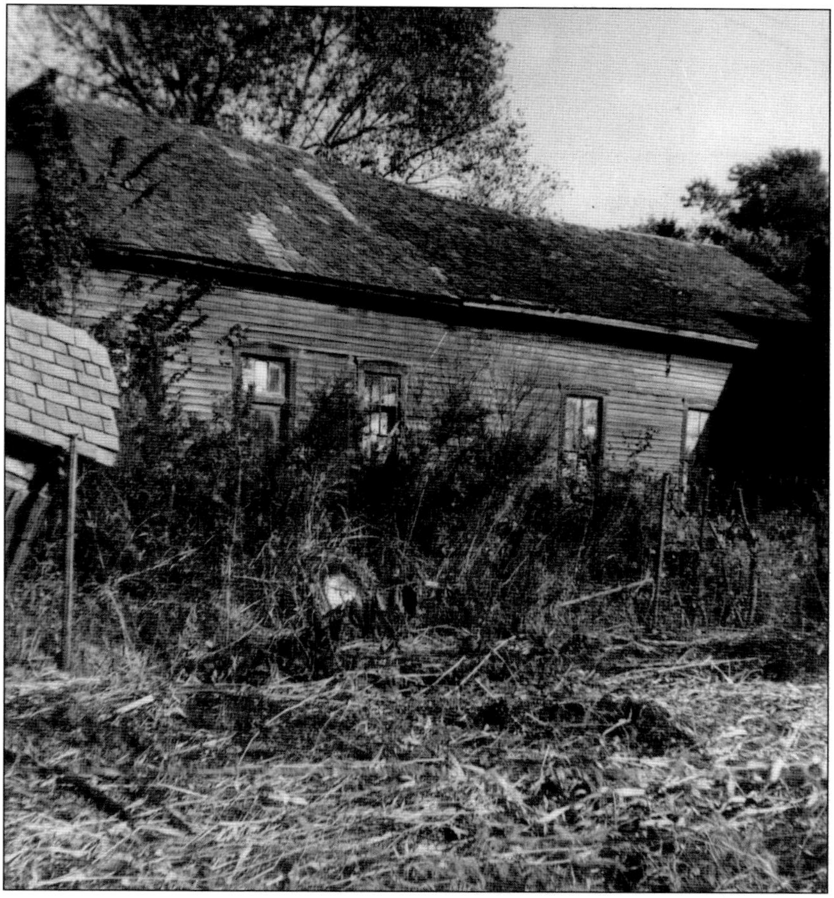

The first public school (at right) was built in Watson for $1,700 in 1870 and later moved across the street. The old building was then used as an opera house for a time. In the early days, there were 70 students enrolled at Watson, and they enjoyed the large shade trees on the campus (below). (Both, courtesy of Kay Gibson.)

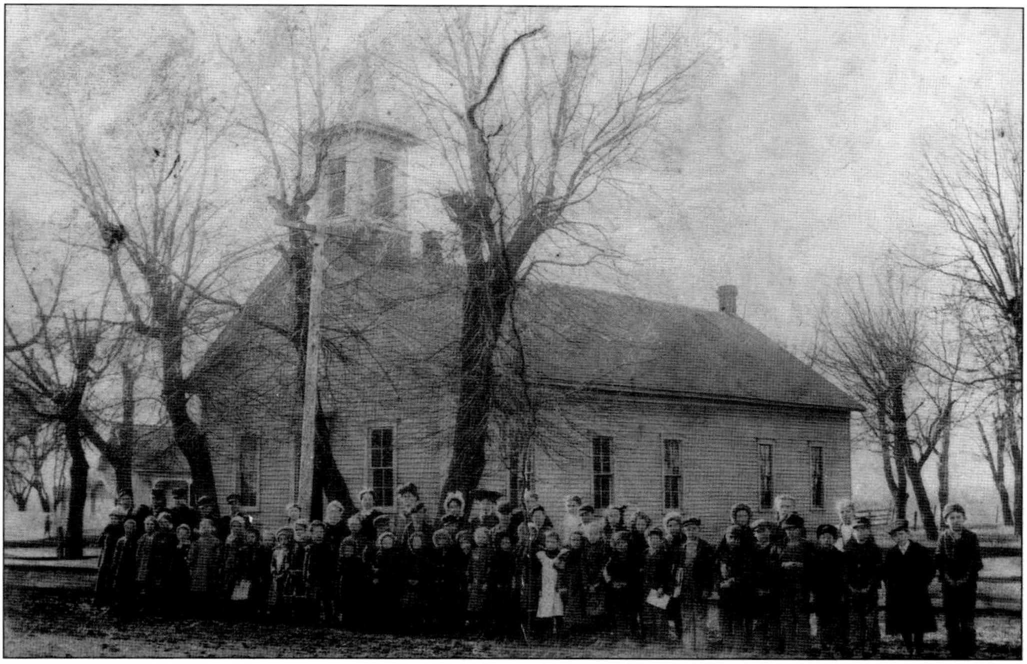

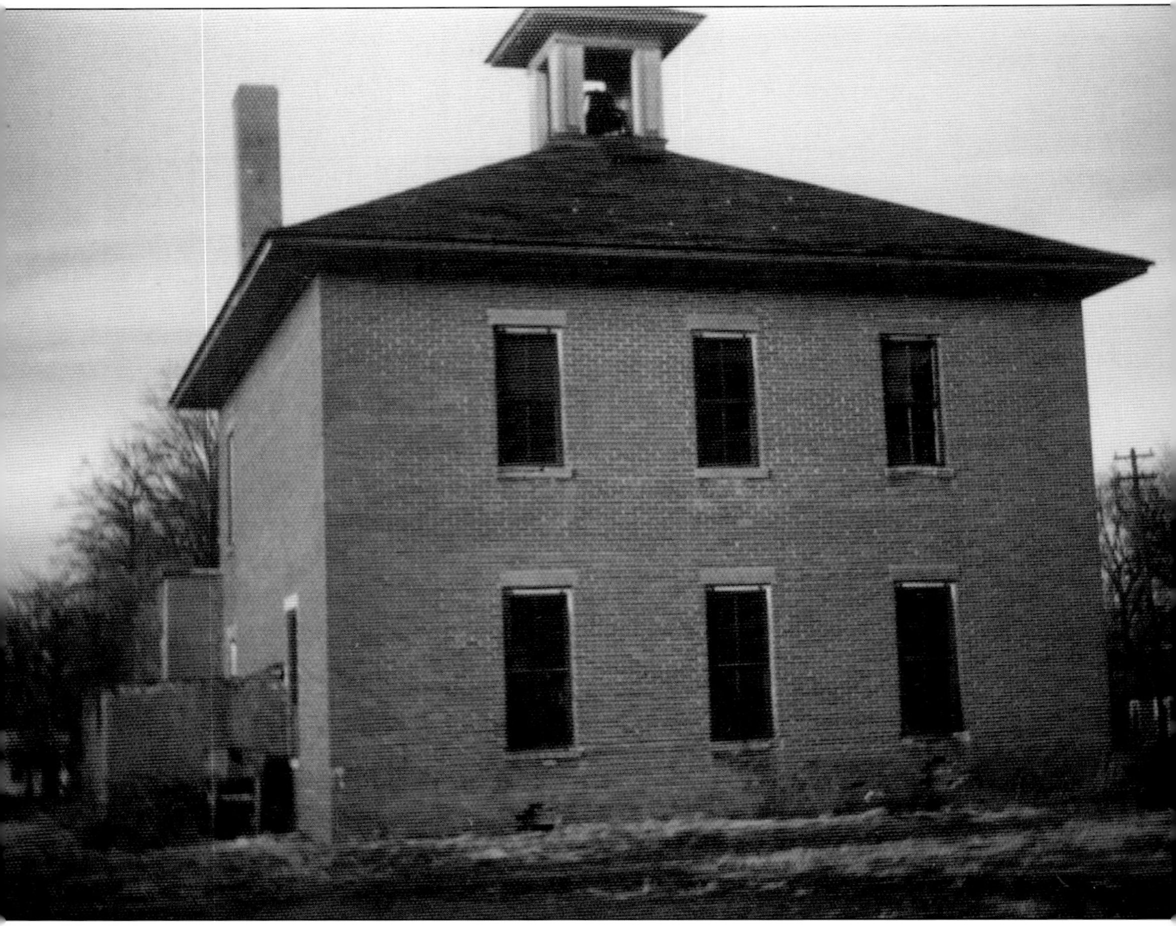

Its location in the rich Missouri River bottomland on the main line of the railroad made Watson a busy town. In 1892, Watson was ranked the second-busiest shipping point in the county. The public schoolhouse seen here was built in 1914 in Watson. (Courtesy of Kay Gibson.)

This c. 1905 image of Tarkio College football players shows that they had padding on their legs but little elsewhere. Dick Low (left) and "Skete" Graham proudly pose for the shot. In these days before a bridge was built to connect Atchison County to Brownsville, Nebraska, the Tarkio team had to row across the river in boats in order to play the rival team at Peru College in Peru, Nebraska. (Courtesy of George and Patty Laur.)

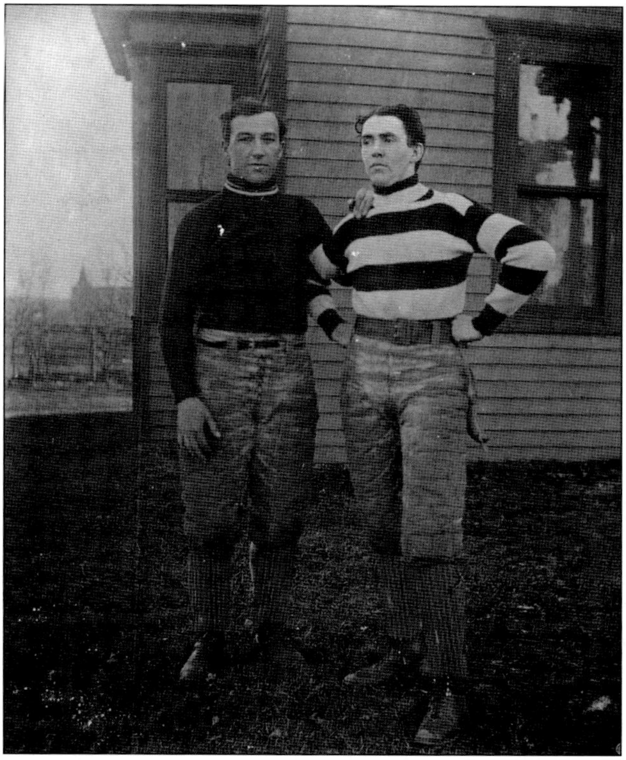

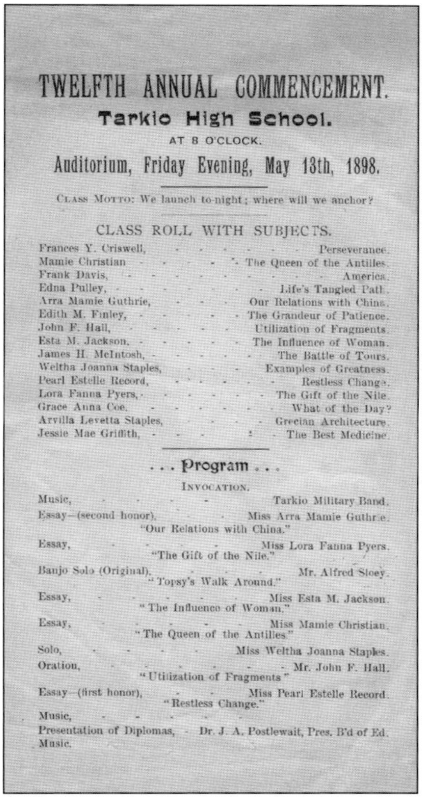

TWELFTH ANNUAL COMMENCEMENT.

Tarkio High School.

AT 8 O'CLOCK.

Auditorium, Friday Evening, May 13th, 1898.

CLASS MOTTO: We launch to-night; where will we anchor?

CLASS ROLL WITH SUBJECTS.

Frances Y. Criswell,	Perseverance.
Mamie Christian	The Queen of the Antilles.
Frank Davis,	America.
Edna Pulley,	Life's Tangled Path.
Arra Mamie Guthrie,	Our Relations with China.
Edith M. Finley,	The Grandeur of Patience.
John F. Hall,	Utilization of Fragments.
Esta M. Jackson,	The Influence of Woman.
James H. McIntosh,	The Battle of Tours.
Weltha Joanna Staples,	Examples of Greatness.
Pearl Estelle Record,	Restless Change.
Lora Fanna Pyers,	The Gift of the Nile.
Grace Anna Coe,	What of the Day?
Arvilla Levetta Staples,	Grecian Architecture.
Jessie Mae Griffith,	The Best Medicine.

... Program ...

INVOCATION.

Music, - - - - - Tarkio Military Band.

Essay—(second honor), - - - Miss Arra Mamie Guthrie.
"Our Relations with China."

Essay, - - - - - Miss Lora Fanna Pyers.
"The Gift of the Nile."

Banjo Solo (Original), - - - - Mr. Alfred Sloey.
"Topsy's Walk Around."

Essay, - - - - - - Miss Esta M. Jackson.
"The Influence of Woman."

Essay, - - - - - - Miss Mamie Christian.
"The Queen of the Antilles."

Solo, - - - - - Miss Weltha Joanna Staples.

Oration, - - - - - - - Mr. John F. Hall.
"Utilization of Fragments"

Essay—(first honor), - - - Miss Pearl Estelle Record.
"Restless Change."

Music, - - - - - -

Presentation of Diplomas, - Dr. J. A. Postlewait, Pres. B'd of Ed.

Music.

The program for Tarkio High School's 1898 commencement includes the title of the lectures for that day. Interestingly, some of them covered issues that are still in the forefront of the US culture today, including "Our Relations with China" and "The Influence of Woman." (Courtesy of the Atchison County Historical Society.)

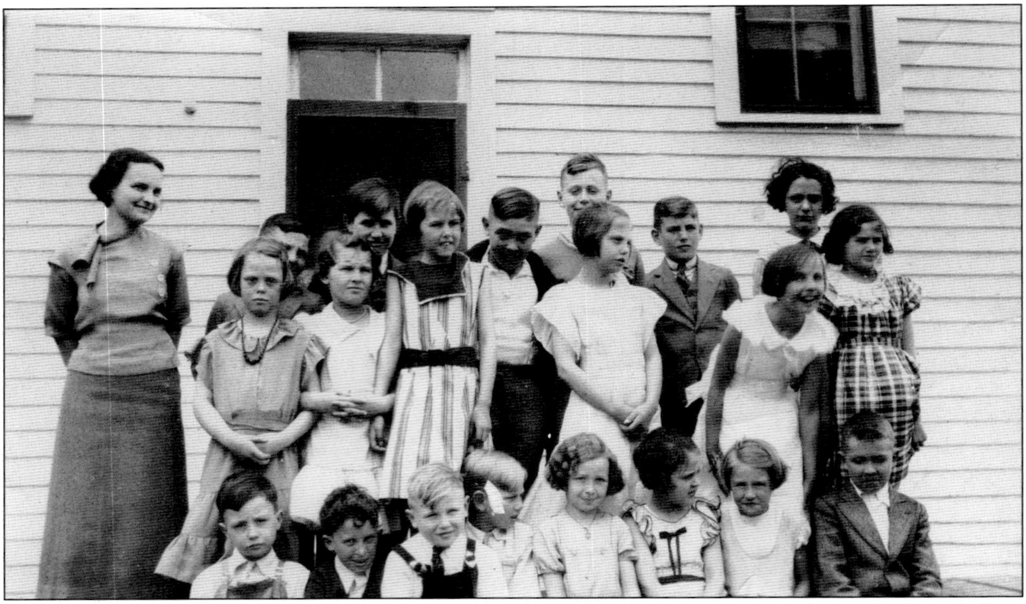

The students at Morning Sun School pose for this photograph in 1935. They are, from left to right, (first row) Waldron, Smith, Hurst, Schoneman, Vette, Miller, Rolf, and Walter; (second row) Waldron, Jones, Rolf, Waldron, Walter, and Hurst; (third row) teacher Mary Rankin, Hurst, Winstead, Jones, Geo. Laur, Hurst, and Miller. (Courtesy of George and Patty Laur.)

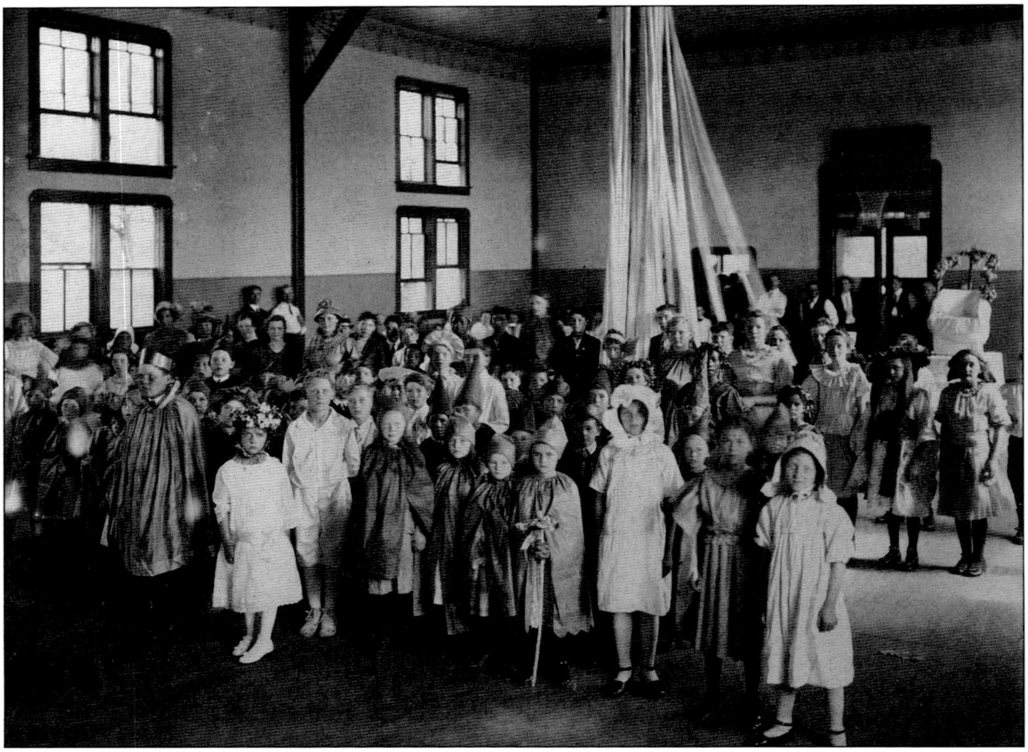

This May Day pageant was held in an Atchison County school in the early 1900s and included costumes, hats of different types, and a king and a queen. Note the chair, or "throne," at the back right with a ring of flowers for a lucky occupant. (Courtesy of the *Atchison County Mail.*)

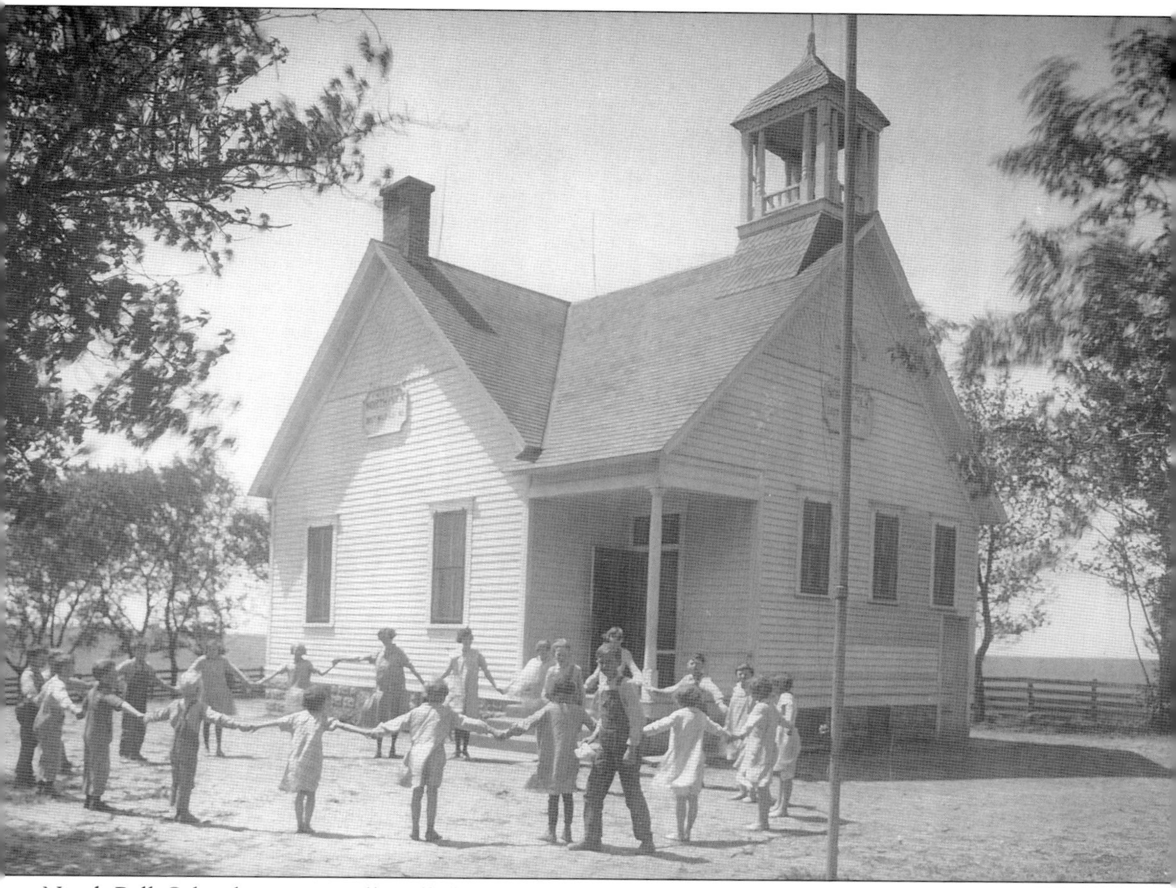

North Polk School was originally called Baker School and was named for two brothers who served on the school board in the late 1800s. When North Polk was built in 1899, it cost $937, with $35 set aside for the stove and $62 for furniture. Jane Salmond was the teacher of this group of North Polk School students and taught at the school from 1916 to approximately 1930. (Courtesy of the Atchison County Historical Society.)

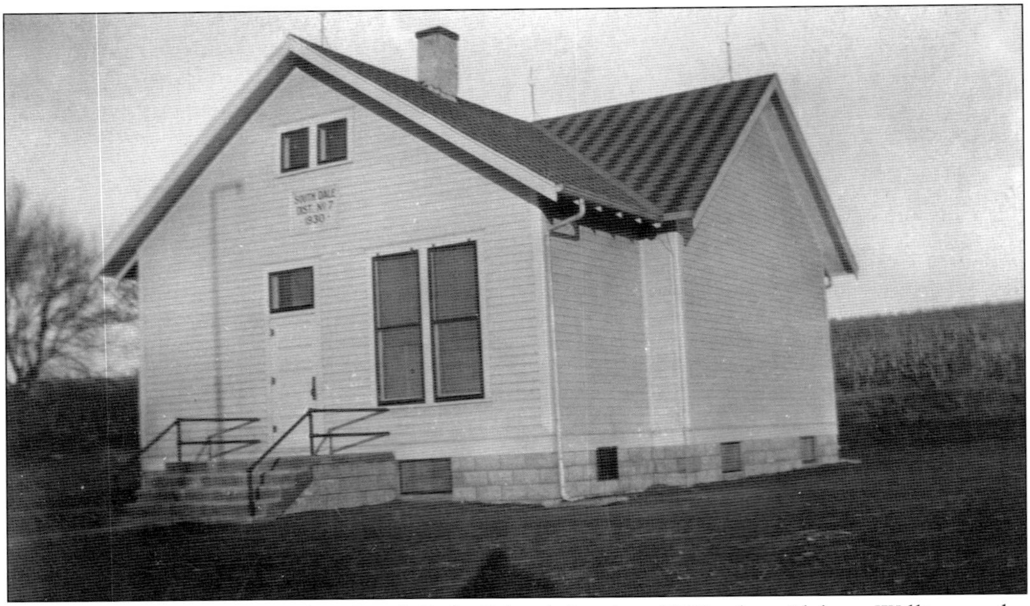

Early county records show that South Dale School dated to 1880, when Idelette Willis was the teacher. According to records from 1904, the house was on land belonging to F.F. Fosket and was one mile east of the old Farmer's City Store. The school's yearly enrollment in 1905–1906 was 42, with an average attendance of 30. Seen here is the second South Dale School, District 7, built in 1930. (Courtesy of the Atchison County Historical Society.)

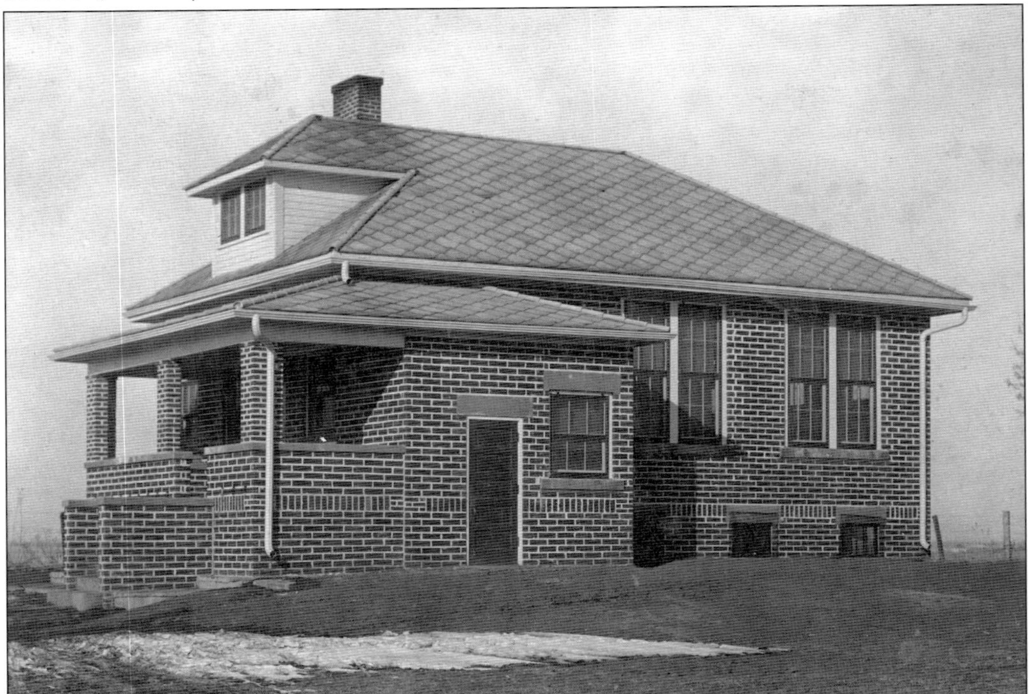

Centerview School, two miles east and one mile north of Tarkio, was built in 1926 after the previous building burned in March 1925. This new school boasted a cyclone cellar and 154 volumes in its library. (Courtesy of the Atchison County Historical Society.)

Four

Getting Down to Business

Many of the businesses that were vital when this county began are no longer relevant in today's world. Brickyards, millers for grain, and leather and harness repairmen are part of industries that are no longer alive; however, the main reason early settlers came here, to find fertile land to farm and raise a family, still applies today. Farmers and ranchers still make a good living raising crops and livestock, even as the number of farmers in the United States declines. The town of Tarkio (population approximately 1,700) still boasts two banks, while Rock Port (population 1,300) also has two, and Fairfax (population 600) has one.

As the horse was overtaken by the automobile, car dealers and auto repairmen were needed in the area. When electricity came to the farms, so too came rural electric co-ops and linemen to install and maintain the lines. Clothing, furniture, and hardware stores were established to help homeowners supply and sustain their homes. Each decade saw the arrival of new businesses where there were none only a few years before.

Today, two of the newest businesses in Atchison County have built almost 100 wind-turbine generators in northwest Missouri: Farmer's City Wind Power and Cow Branch Wind Energy. Studies have shown that the environment in northwest Missouri is a perfect fit for wind turbines. They now dot our horizon, creating a renewable energy source that leaves no greenhouse gases. One of these companies, Iberdrola Renewables, is the second-largest wind operator in the United States and the fourth-largest utility company in the world by market cap. Only 24 of these wind turbines create 50 megawatts of electricity, enough to power approximately 20,000 homes for a year. As citizens of Atchison County look to the future, it is the hope to find and create other jobs and opportunities that were not even thought of just a few years ago.

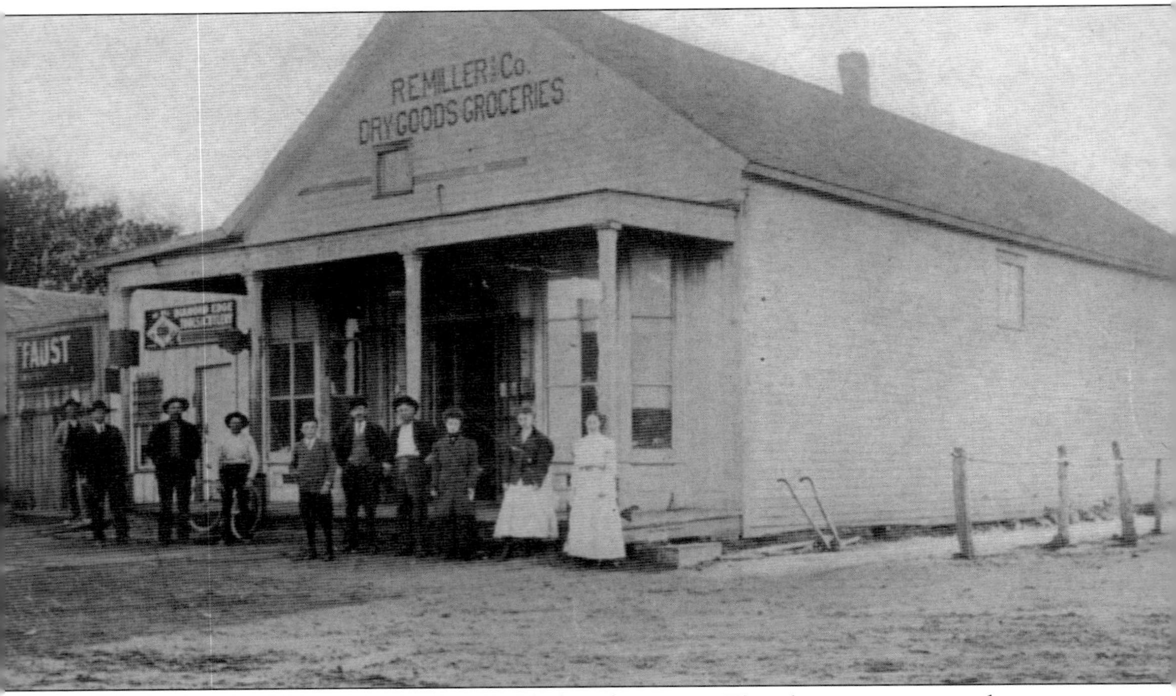

Around 1900, dry goods stores were hubs of activity. They kept many items homeowners needed and offered services to their customers to keep them coming back. Above the front door of the R.E. Miller and Company Dry Goods and Groceries, "post office" is written faintly. The sign in the background advertises Diamond Edge Tools and Cutlery. (Courtesy of Hon. Corey Herron.)

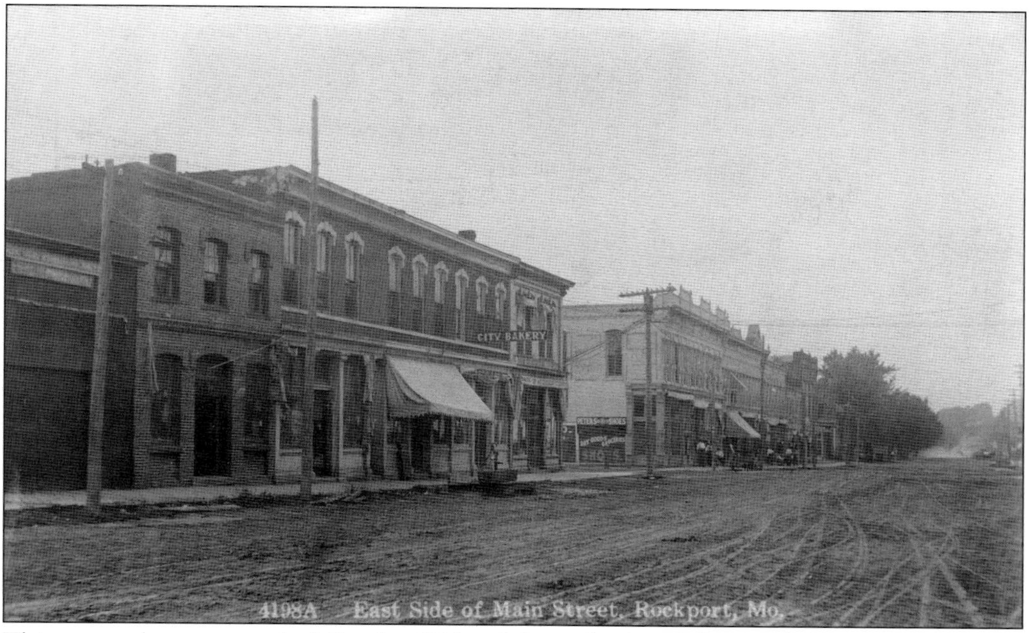

This postcard was postmarked October 1910 and shows the City Bakery and the Bank of Atchison County on Main Street in Rock Port. Across the street is Peter's Shoes, whose sign advertises "Sunflower Shoes, Dry-Goods, Groceries, Shoes." (Courtesy of *Atchison County Mail.*)

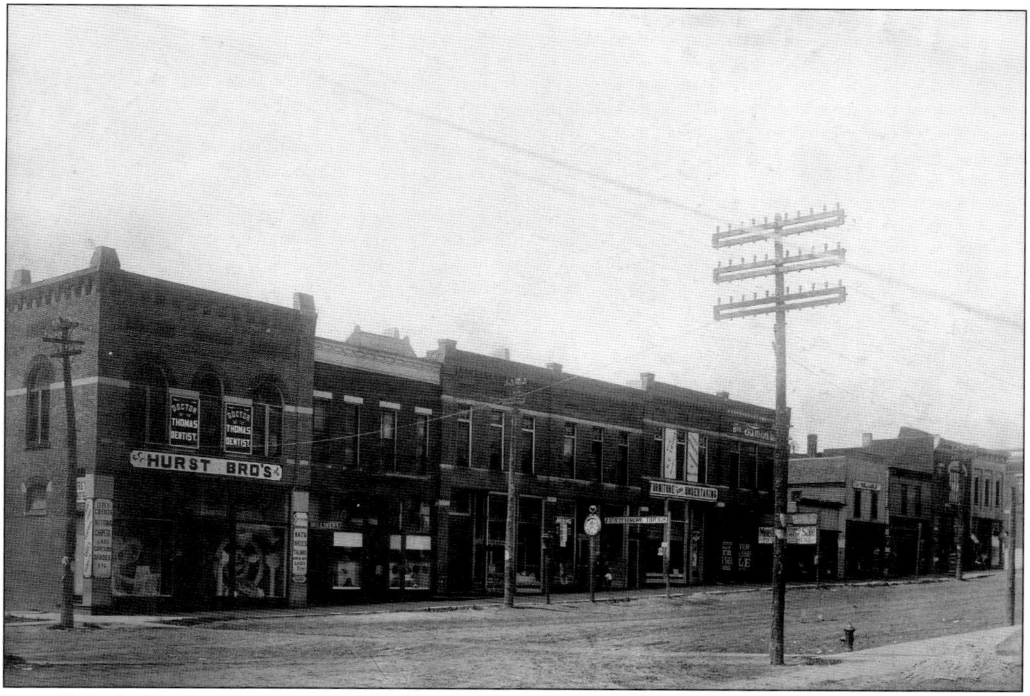

Even though the street was not yet paved, Tarkio had electricity and fire hydrants by this time, showing that it was prospering. Dominating this c. 1902 photograph is Hurst Brothers, which advertised its dry goods on the south side of the street. Next door is a millinery, J.F. Withrow Drugs, and a furniture and undertaking business. (Courtesy of the Atchison County Historical Society.)

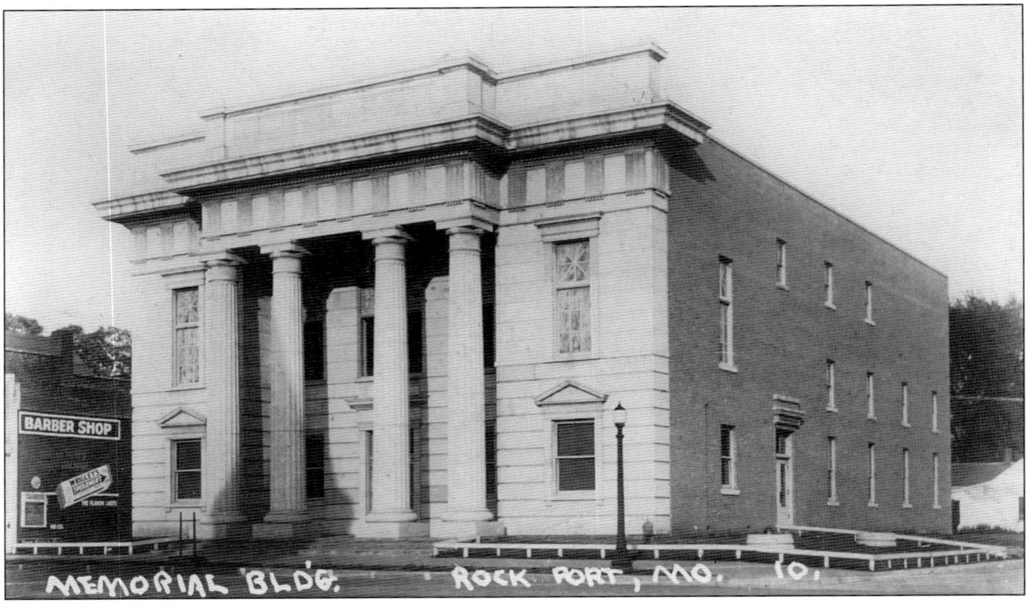

Built in 1920 as a tribute to those who served in World War I, the Memorial Building in Rock Port was paid for entirely with local funding. Approximately $50,000 was pledged by citizens from 1919 to 1921. Movies were shown here in 1922, and many school plays were performed on the stage on the top floor. It was also used for basketball games and a skating rink. Today, the Liberty Theatre is used for productions, while the main floor can be rented for family functions, wedding receptions, and parties. (Courtesy of *Atchison County Mail.*)

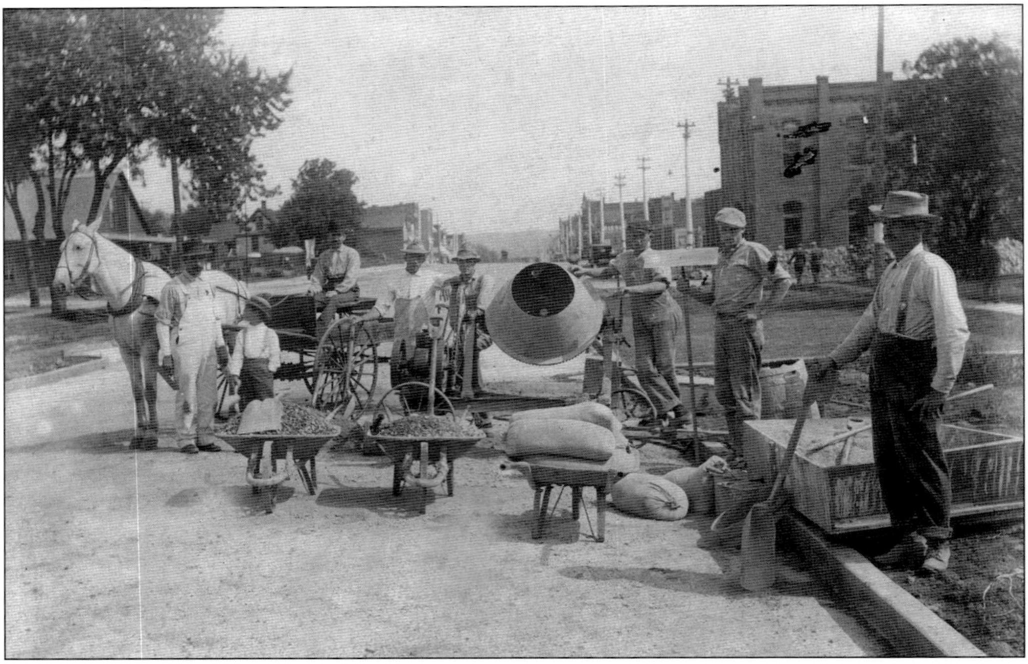

This mixer was responsible for pouring the new curbs for streets in Tarkio. It was labor-intensive work—the concrete came in bags and was mixed by hand—but workers took pride in their craft. Note the horse-drawn buggy in the foreground and the early automobile in the background above the right wheel of the mixer. (Courtesy of the Atchison County Historical Society.)

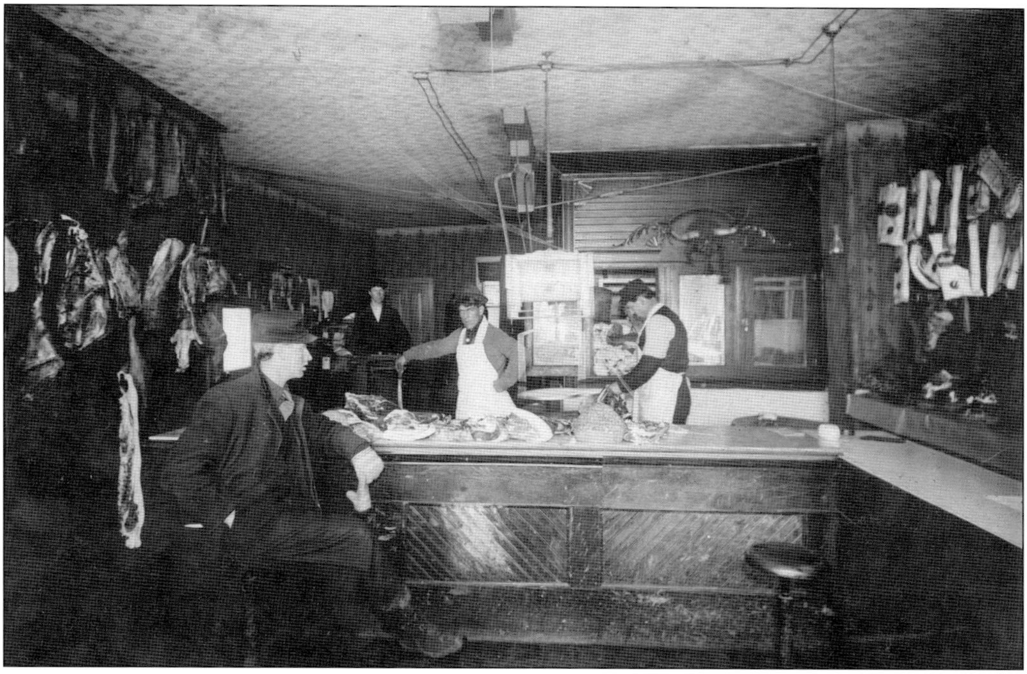

Butcher shops were forerunners to grocery stores and later supermarkets. Fresh meats were prepared and cut to the customer's satisfaction. Today, it would be impossible to pass inspection hanging fresh meats unprotected, as seen here on the left. (Courtesy of the Atchison County Historical Society.)

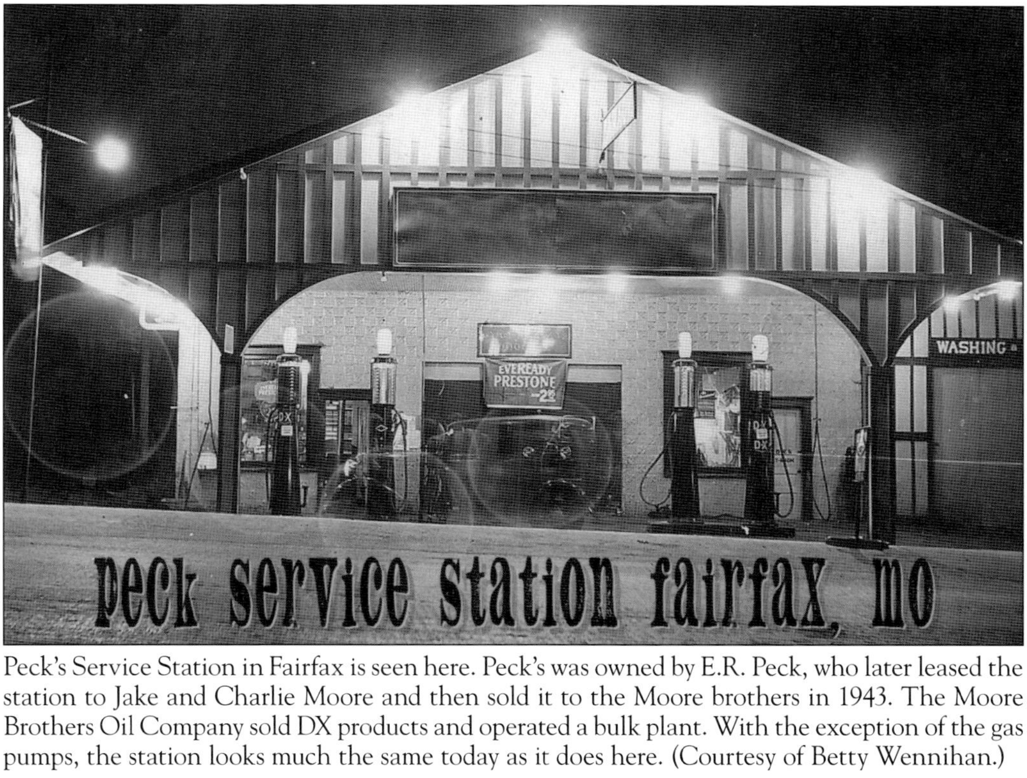

Peck's Service Station in Fairfax is seen here. Peck's was owned by E.R. Peck, who later leased the station to Jake and Charlie Moore and then sold it to the Moore brothers in 1943. The Moore Brothers Oil Company sold DX products and operated a bulk plant. With the exception of the gas pumps, the station looks much the same today as it does here. (Courtesy of Betty Wennihan.)

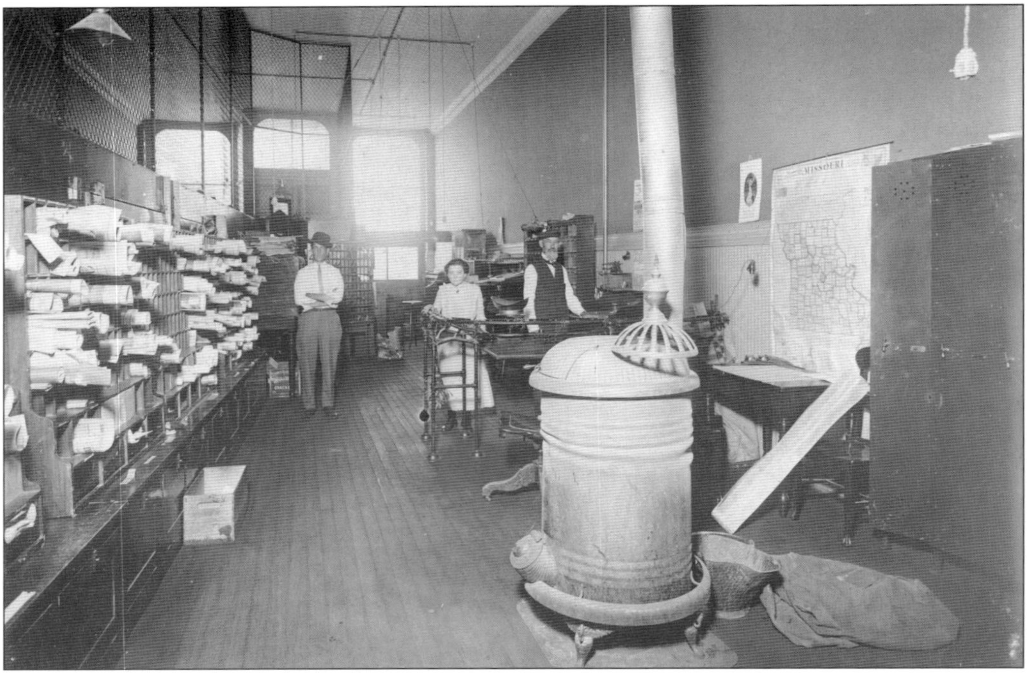

The high ceilings in the buildings of this era were cooler in summer but also harder to heat in winter. The Tarkio Post Office is seen here around 1915, when it was in the old auditorium building. From left to right are Earl Wright, Nellie Dobson, and Frank McKim. Samuel P. Jewell was the earliest postmaster, in 1881, running the post office out of his house, as was common at the time. (Courtesy of the Atchison County Historical Society.)

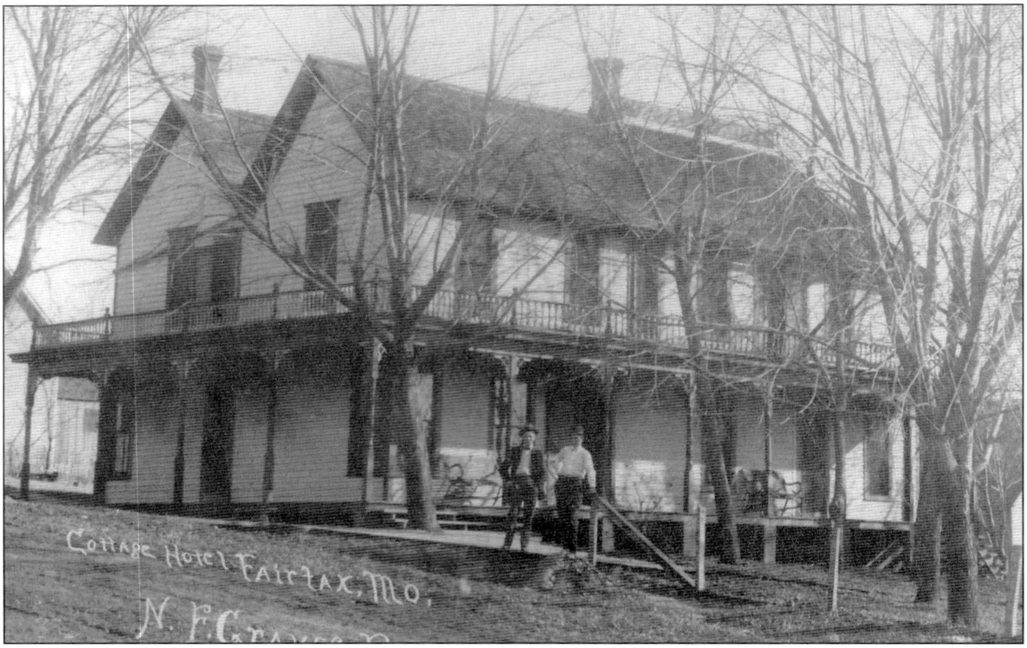

The Cottage Hotel in Fairfax is seen here between 1911 and 1914. Standing in front of the hotel are Archibald Elliot Sharp (left) and owner Ned Forest "N.F." Graves. Sharp was Graves's uncle. The Basil Hunter house was later built on this site. (Courtesy of Betty Wennihan.)

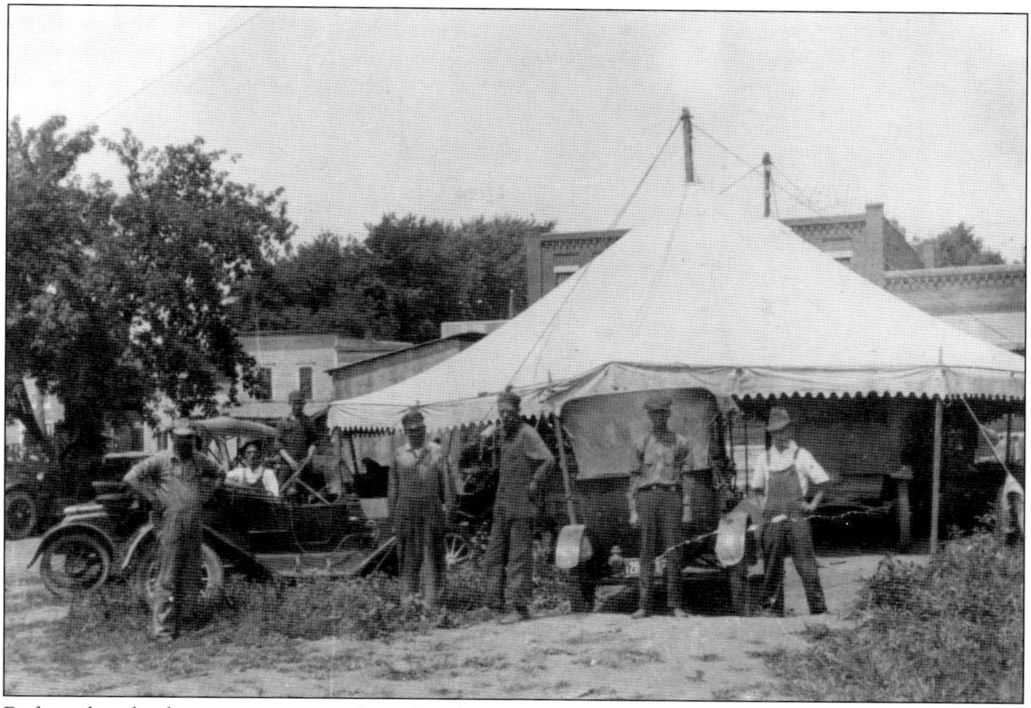

Before they built a garage repair shop, brothers Ed and Bob Harrington operated under a tent in Fairfax. This photograph was taken in 1916 or 1917 and shows workmen along with a few customers (in white). From left to right in dark shirts are Ed Harrington, unknown, Bob Harrington, Joe Harrington, and Earl Harrington. The tent was used throughout the year and in all types of weather. (Courtesy of Betty Wennihan.)

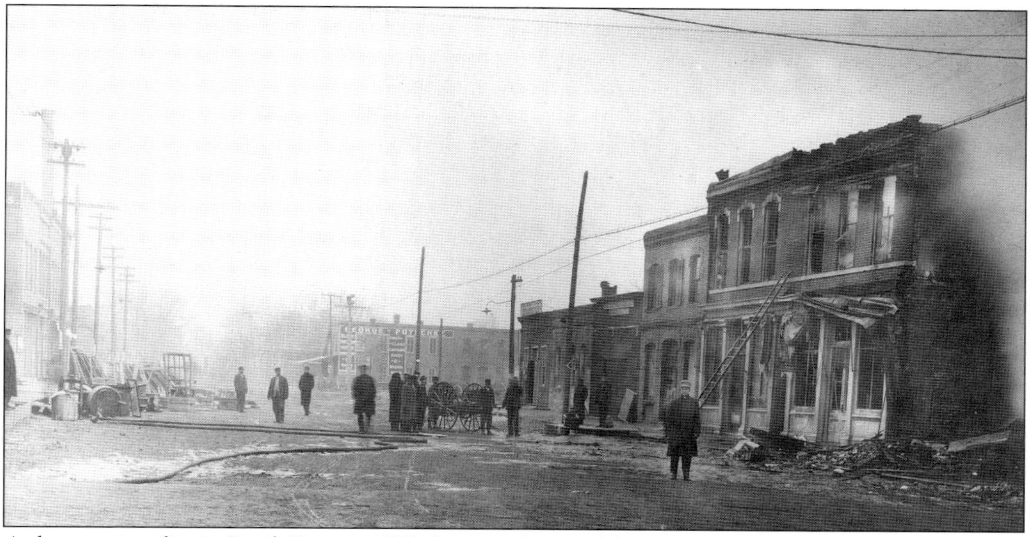

A devastating fire in Rock Port in 1913 destroyed many Main Street businesses, and it is a credit to the firemen that the blaze was stopped at all. Later records show that the fire was stopped at the Chamberlain Building at 315 South Main Street (now Stoner Drug). The following businesses were lost in the fire: Raines Abstract, Holliway Barber Shop, Schoenbeber Clothing, the opera house, the law office of Miles and Mullins, and the law office of Ramsay and Gore. (Courtesy of the *Atchison County Mail.*)

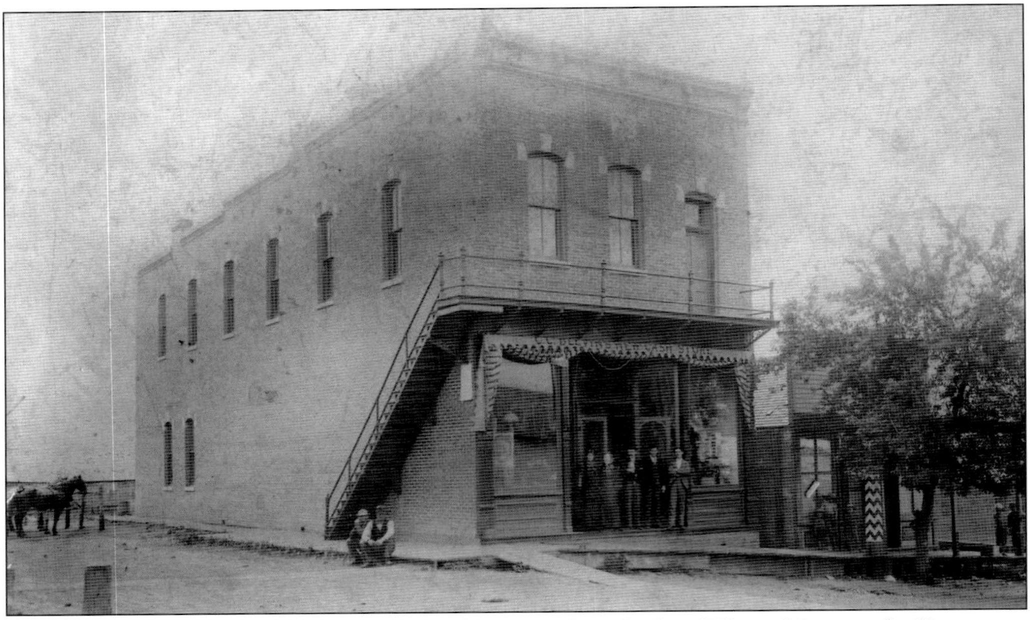

The first brick building in Fairfax, seen here, is identified as White Mercantile Company. The awning reads, "C.C. Blevins New Cash Store." Hackett Furniture, Sims Printing, Pearce Produce, and Pearce Fireworks were all located here at one point in the location's history. This building no longer stands; the Wake Up N Save is presently located on the site. (Courtesy of Betty Wennihan.)

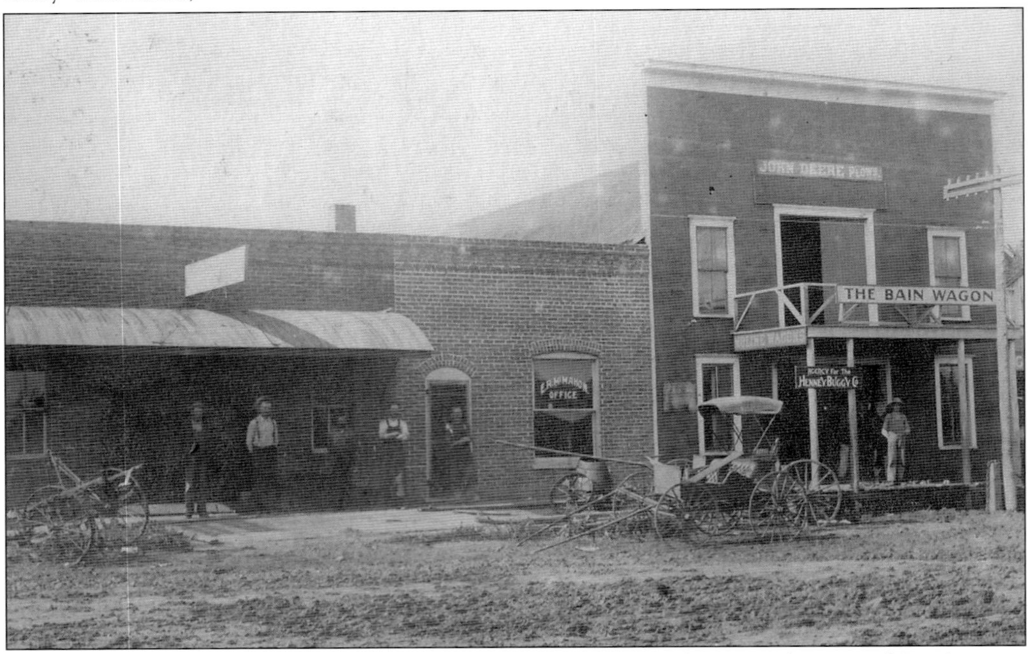

These buildings in Fairfax advertise the office of E.R. McMahon Hardware and Implement, Henney Buggy Co., John Deere Plows, Moline Wagons, and Bain Wagon. Fred McMahon, born in 1899, operated the hardware area of McMahon Hardware and Implement for 31 years until 1945, when the business was sold. He also served three terms as Fairfax's mayor and was in the Missouri General Assembly for 14 years. (Courtesy of Betty Wennihan.)

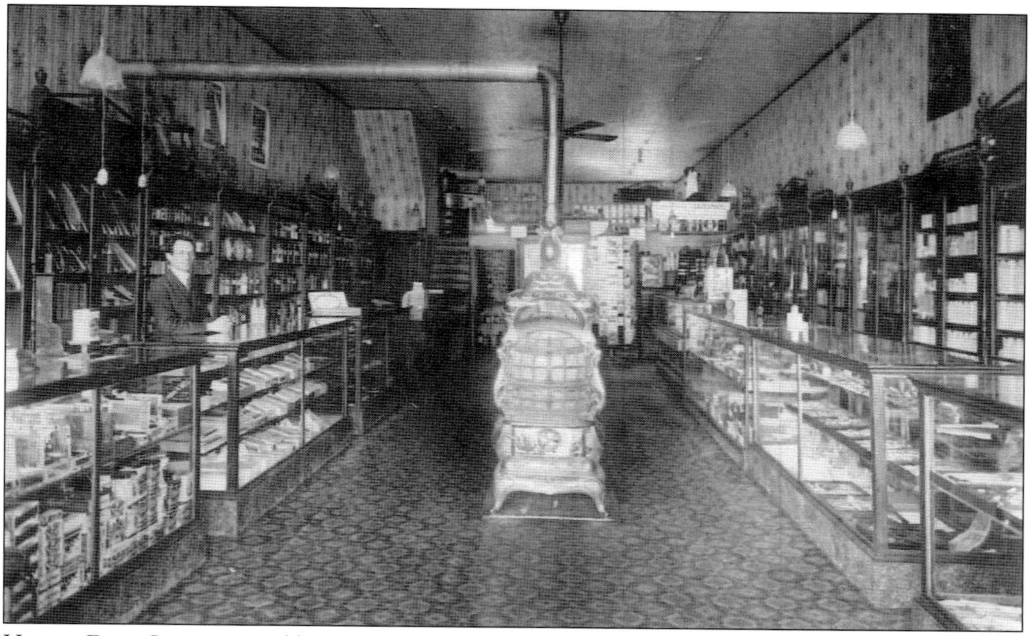

Hunter Drug Store, started by Dr. J.A. Hunter, is seen here when it was run by his son Dr. Owen H. Hunter. As early as 1900, the older Hunter had been in business in Fairfax and also had a store with his sons in Craig. His two sons both joined their father in his practice, and his daughter Beulah also worked faithfully in the store from 1927 until her passing in July 1979—a remarkable legacy. (Courtesy of Betty Wennihan.)

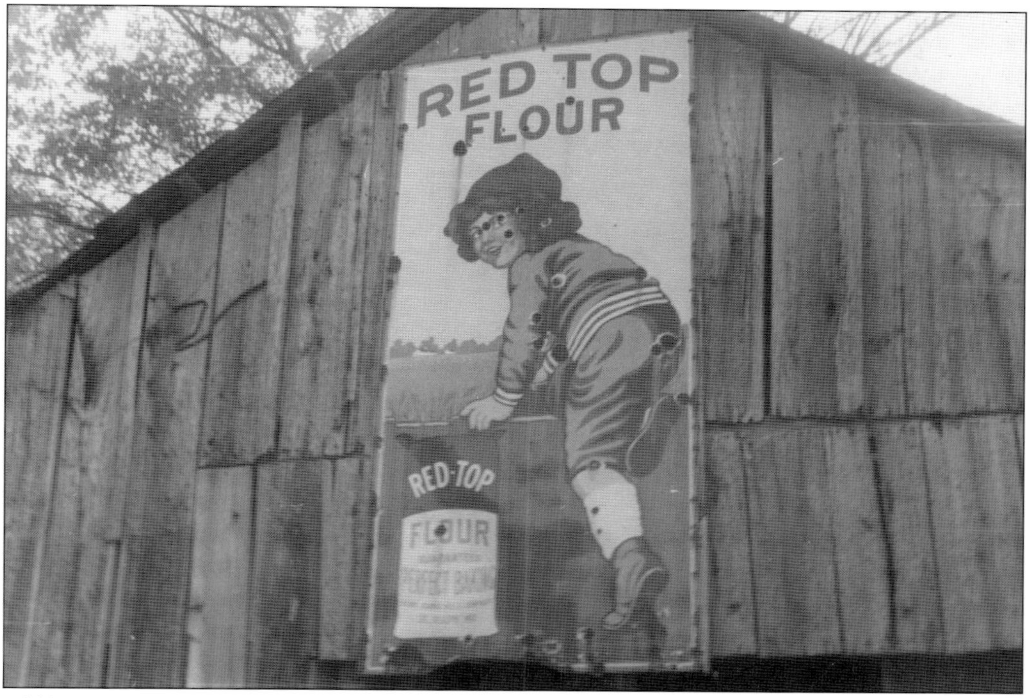

Old barns and buildings close to major roads and highways were chosen for impromptu billboards in the early days. Here, customers are advised to use Red Top Flour. Note the holes in the sign; sportsmen also used these signs for target practice. (Courtesy of Kay Gibson.)

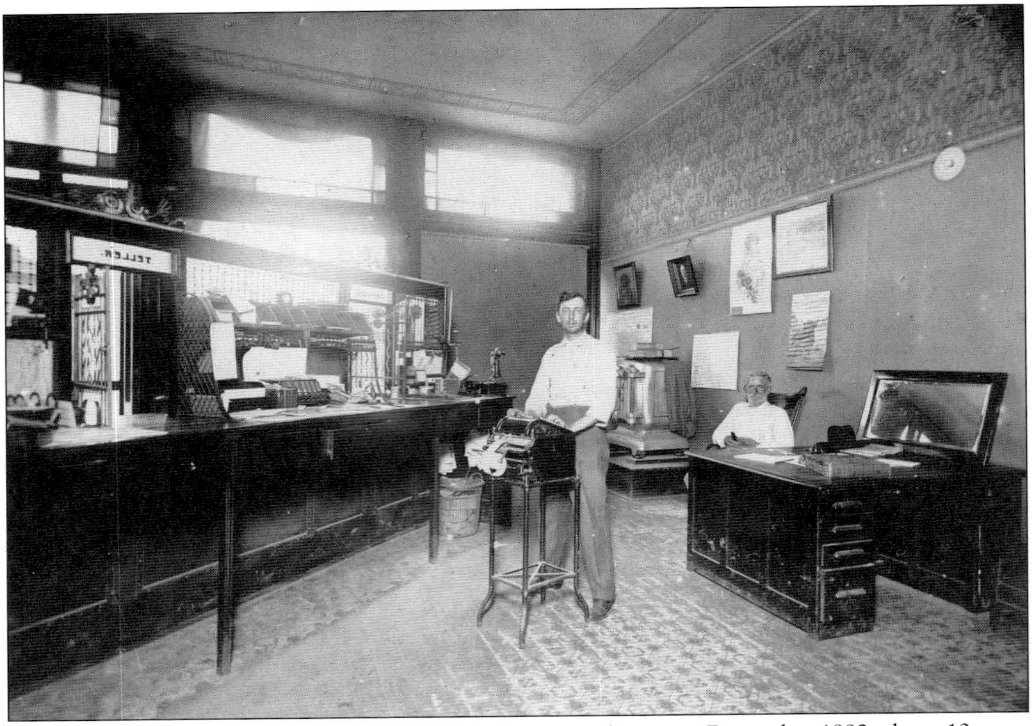

The Exchange Bank of Fairfax (above) received its state charter in December 1892, about 10 years after the railroad came to town. Another bank in the early days in Fairfax was Farmers Bank (below), which opened in 1884. Farmers was not as successful and closed in the 1920s. (Both, courtesy of Bob Alldredge and Exchange Bank.)

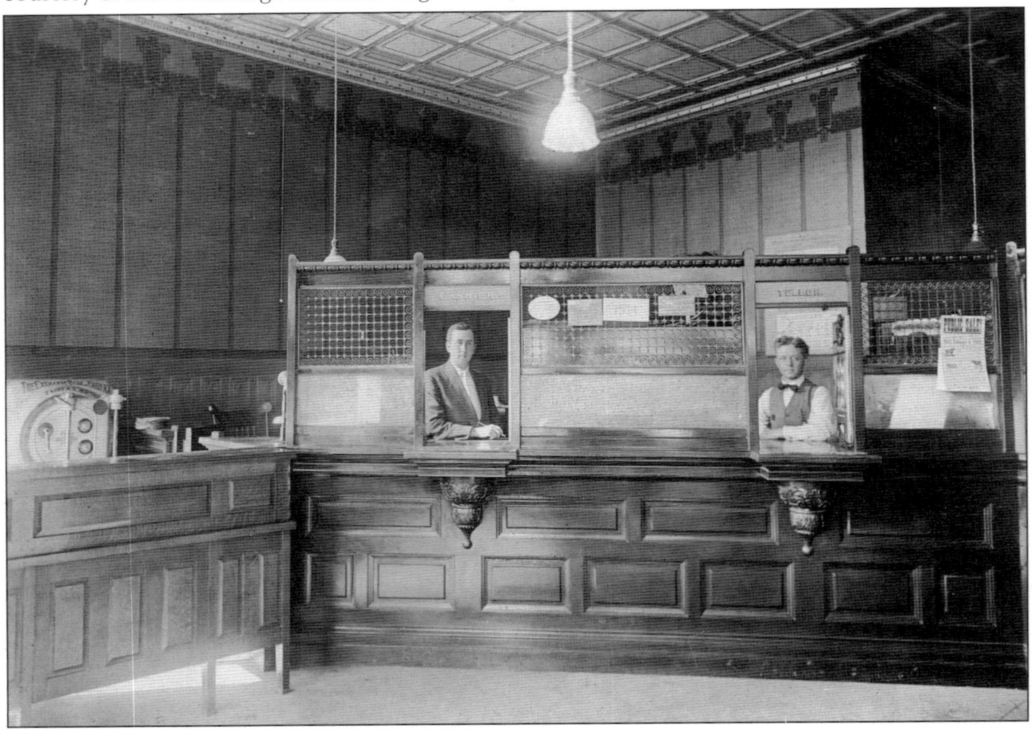

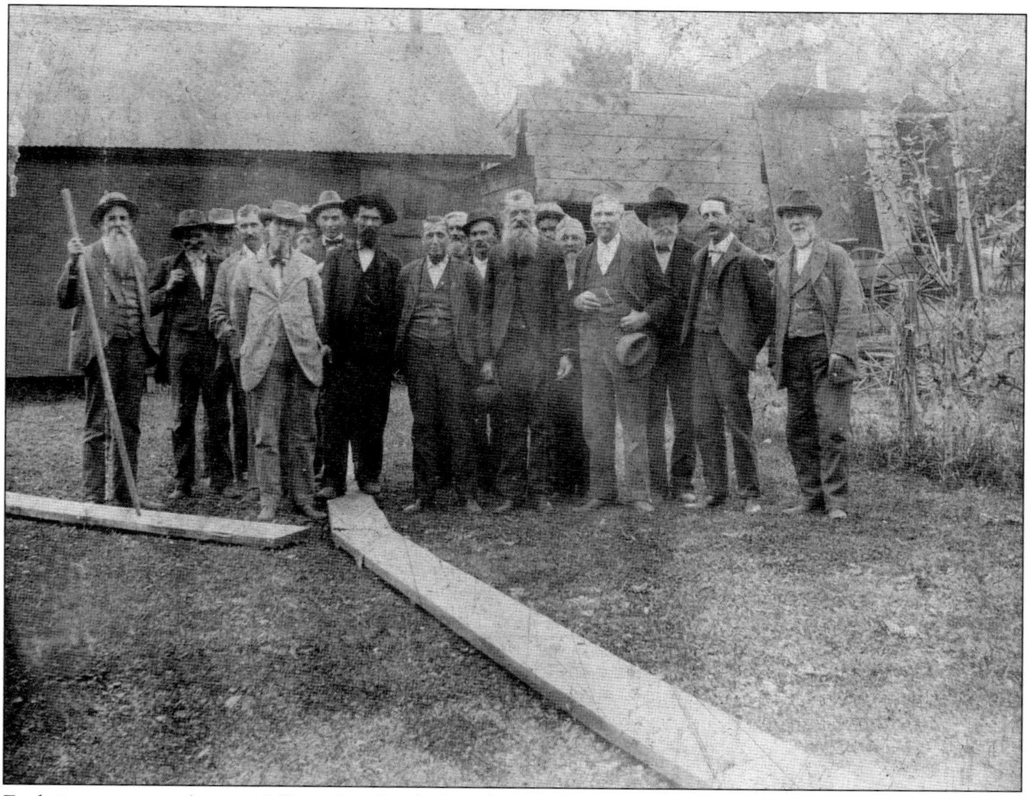

Early investors and townsfolk gather for the breaking of ground on the first Exchange Bank of Fairfax building in 1893. The original stockholders and organizers were S. Ballard, T. Angel, J. Beck, M. Bear, W. Bryan, J. Botkin, W. Christian, A. Carter, R. Curry, G. Creed, F. Holbrook, W. Hedrick, H. Schooler, J. Turner, and many others. (Courtesy of Bob Alldredge and Exchange Bank.)

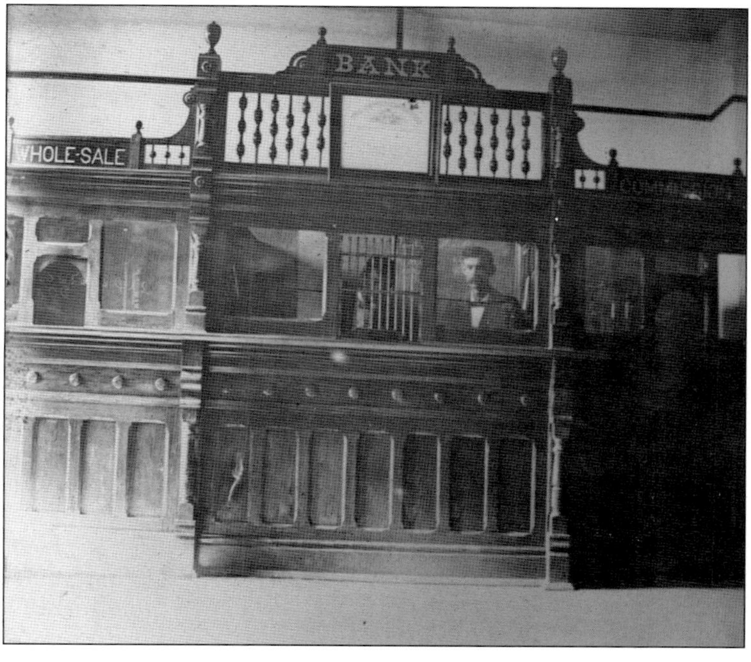

Town records give credit to J.Q. Morris for starting a bank in the second building in Westboro shortly after the Tarkio Valley Railroad came to town. The first building was said to be a grocery store built by Frank Lowe. The bank building and safe are still in use today; the building has been a post office and a café. (Courtesy of George and Patty Laur.)

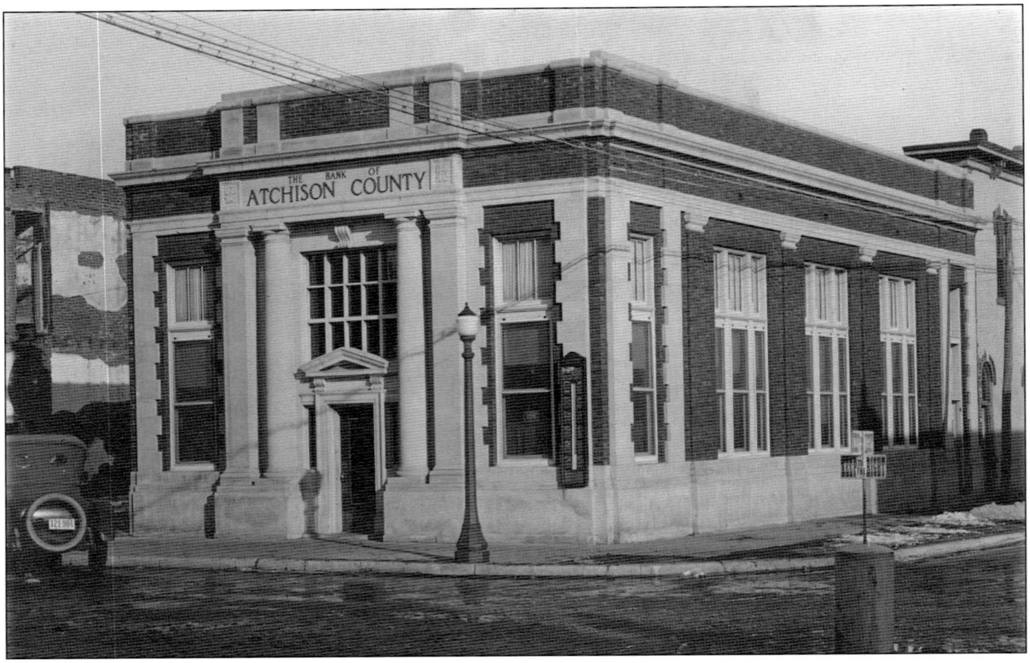

Chartered in 1870, the Bank of Atchison County made this building home beginning in 1920. By 1968, the directors of the bank wanted a new location and moved into the old Citizens Bank temporarily until the new structure was finished. This and the building behind it were torn down to make way for the new bank. (Both, courtesy of the *Atchison County Mail*.)

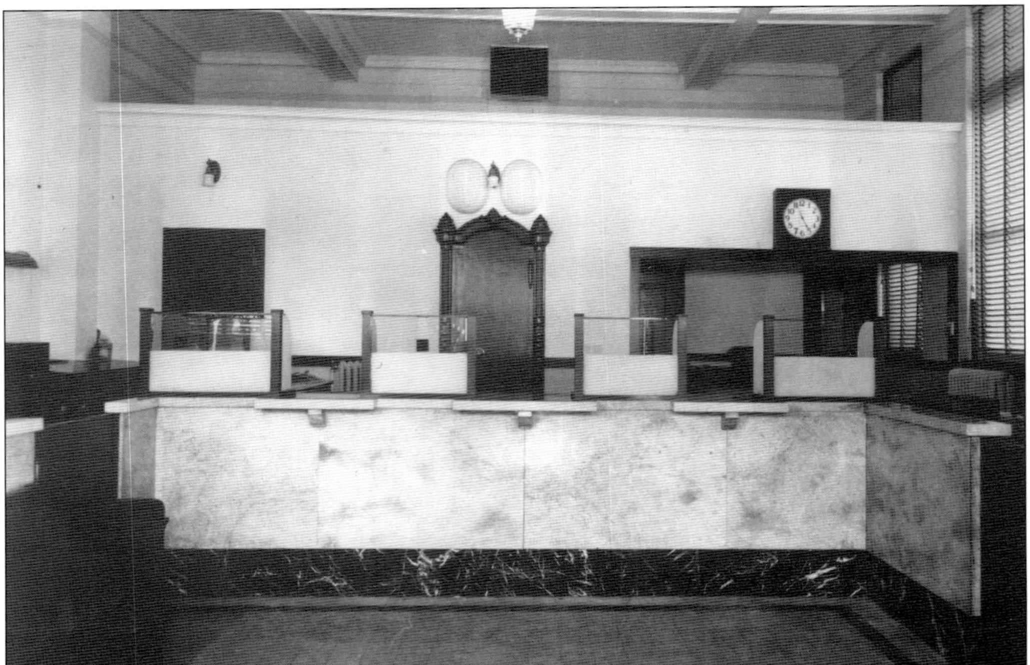

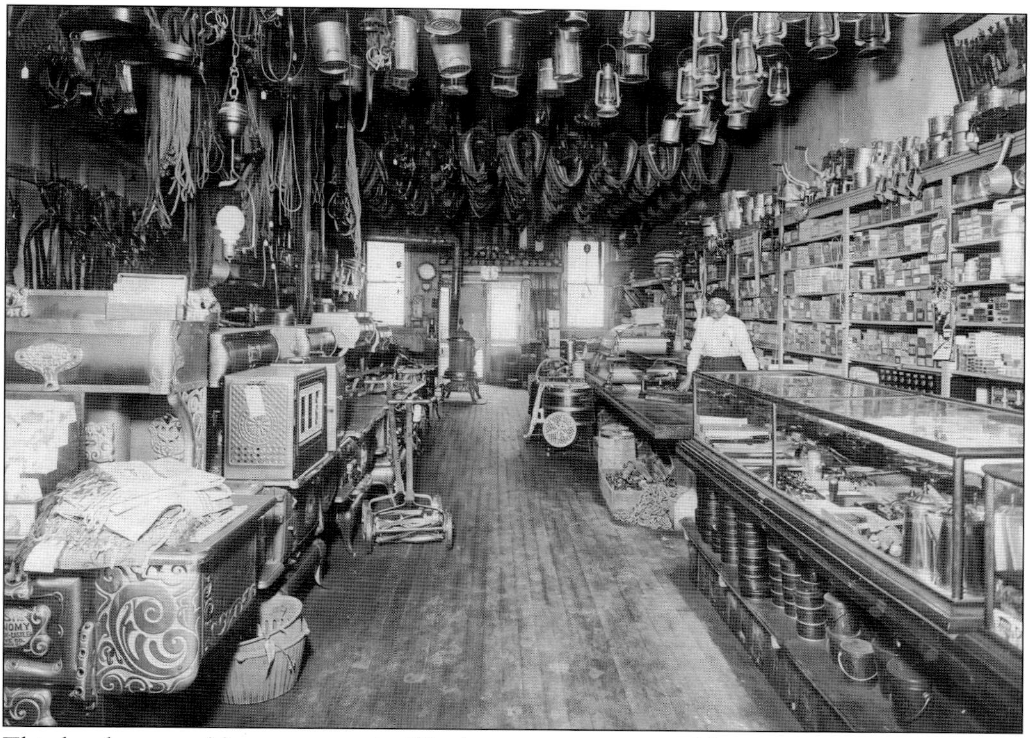

This hardware and harness store in Westboro was once owned by Oscar and Emma Uttvits and Josiah Peck. It was a "do-it all" store, selling many items, including stoves, mowers, sterling silverware, and lanterns, as well as repairing anything made of leather, from harnesses to shoes. Oscar Uttvits (below) came to America from Europe with his parents in 1866 and married Emma Peck in 1888. Oscar and Emma had two daughters: Ethel, who married Fred Bargman, and Laura, who married Ernest Johnson. (Both, courtesy of Marcia L. Frede.)

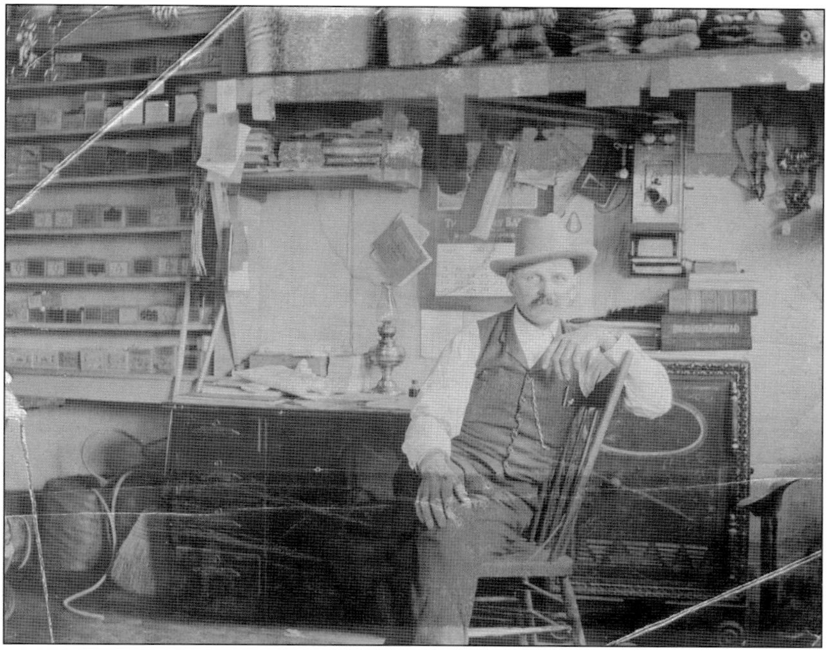

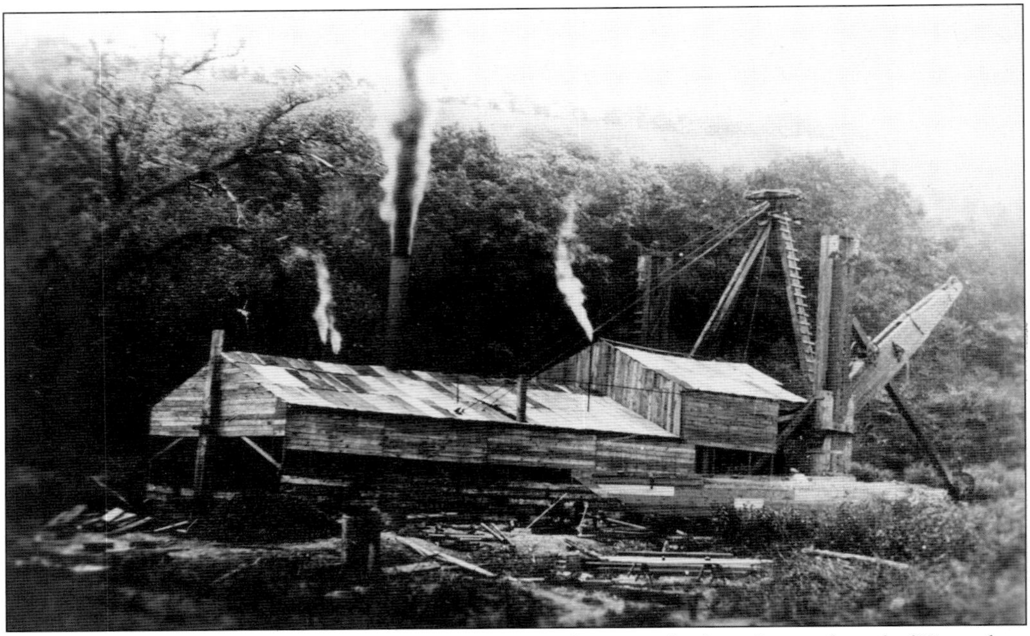

The Pollard and Camel coal-powered dredge boat, seen here, was built at the south end of Horseshoe Lake and was operated by George Marrison and A. Spittler. (Courtesy of Kay Gibson.)

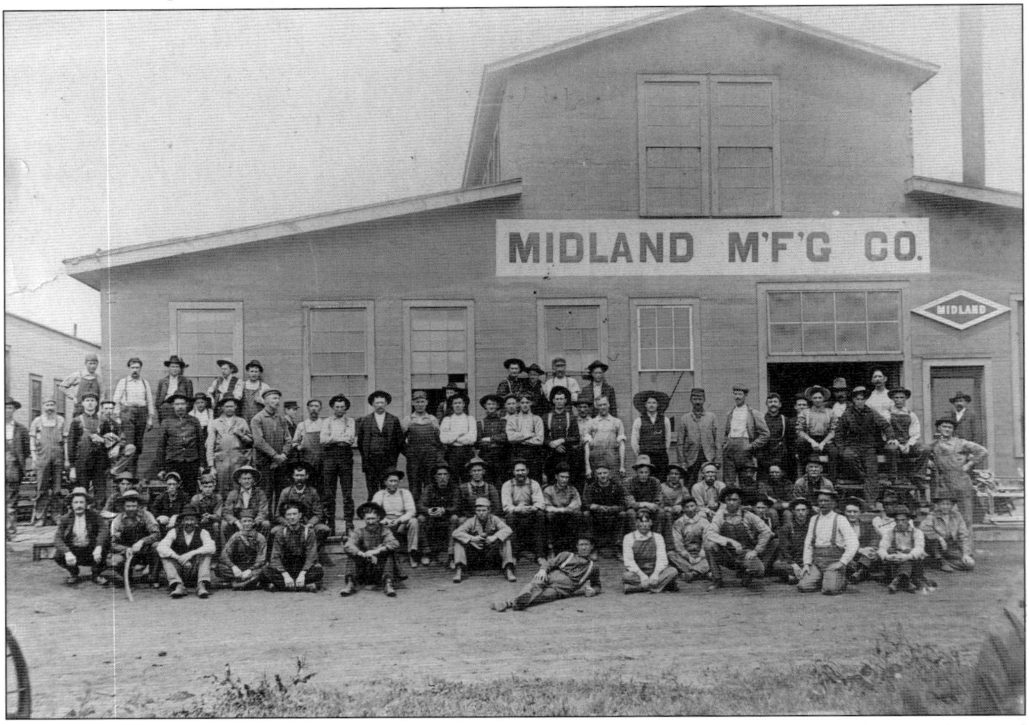

Midland Manufacturing Co. in Tarkio began with David Rankin's backing and manufactured two-bottom steel plows. At one time, Midland employed 140 people. Rankin knew that to be successful, farmers had to cut their production costs, and a two-bottom plow was much more efficient than the single-row plows that many farmers used at the time. (Courtesy of the Atchison County Historical Society.)

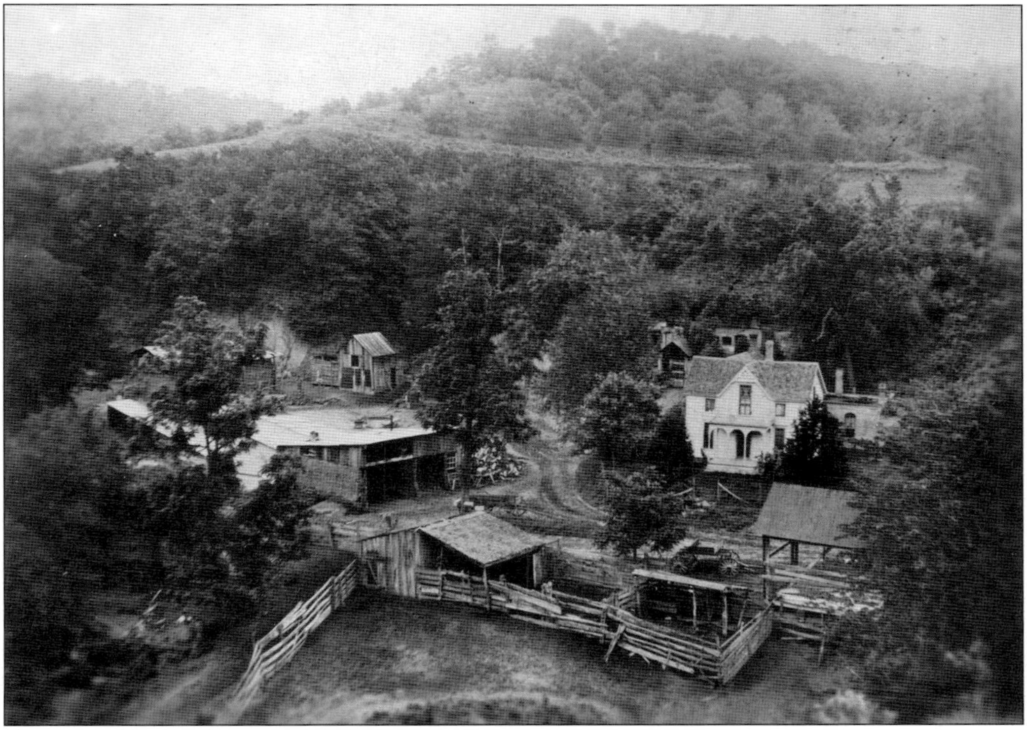

The brickyard in the hills north of Rock Port was very busy because builders wanted to create their new businesses from brick instead of highly flammable wood. The photograph below lists the men as, from left to right, owners Willson Hudson, Bill Clemons, Sammie Hudson, ? Murdock, and Clyde Vonnittie. As a better quality of brick became more available by train, many local brickyards went into the history books. (Both, courtesy of Kay Gibson.)

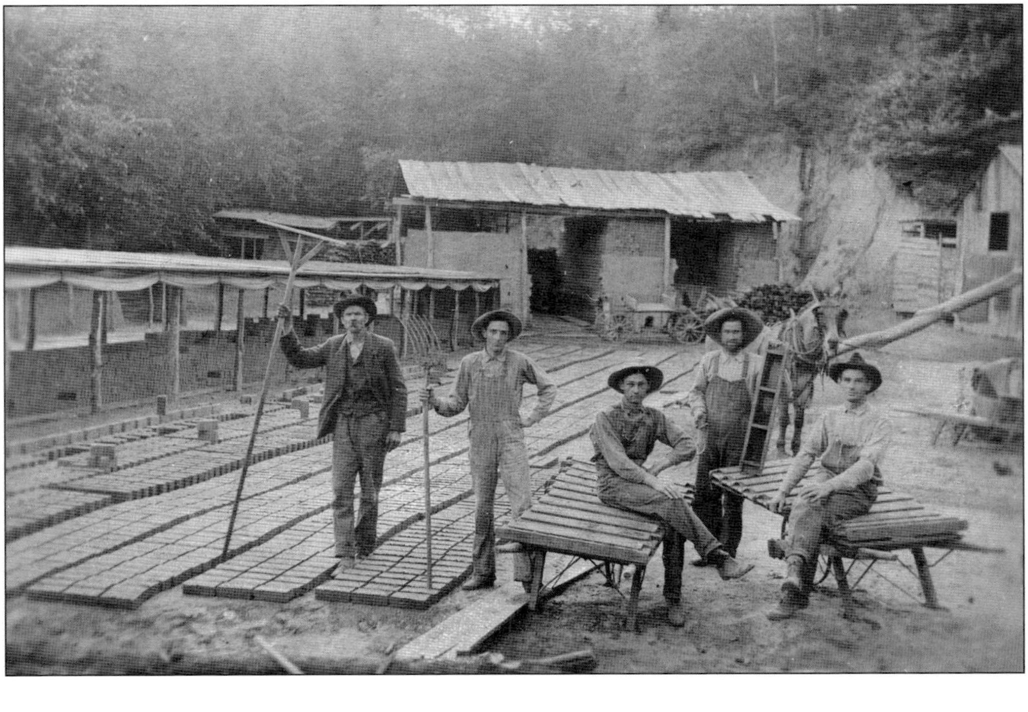

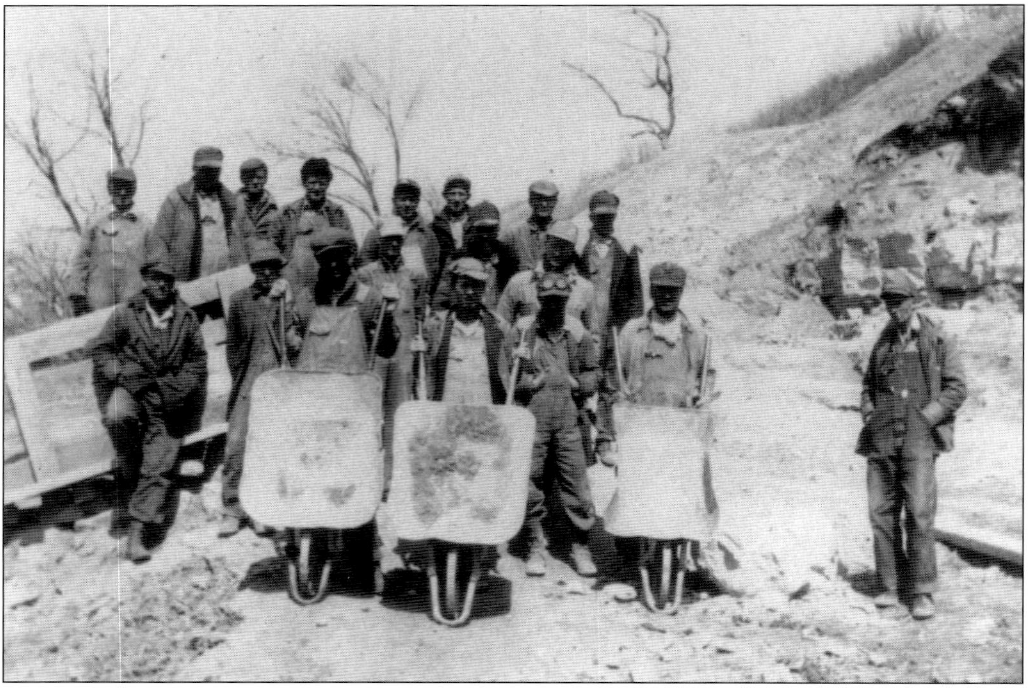

This local Civilian Conservation Corps (CCC) team works on a public project in the Rock Port area in the 1930s. The CCC was part of Pres. Franklin D. Roosevelt's New Deal and was extremely popular with the public. The CCC worked on conservation and natural resource projects from 1933 until World War II, employing single men between the ages of 17 and 23. (Courtesy of Kay Gibson.)

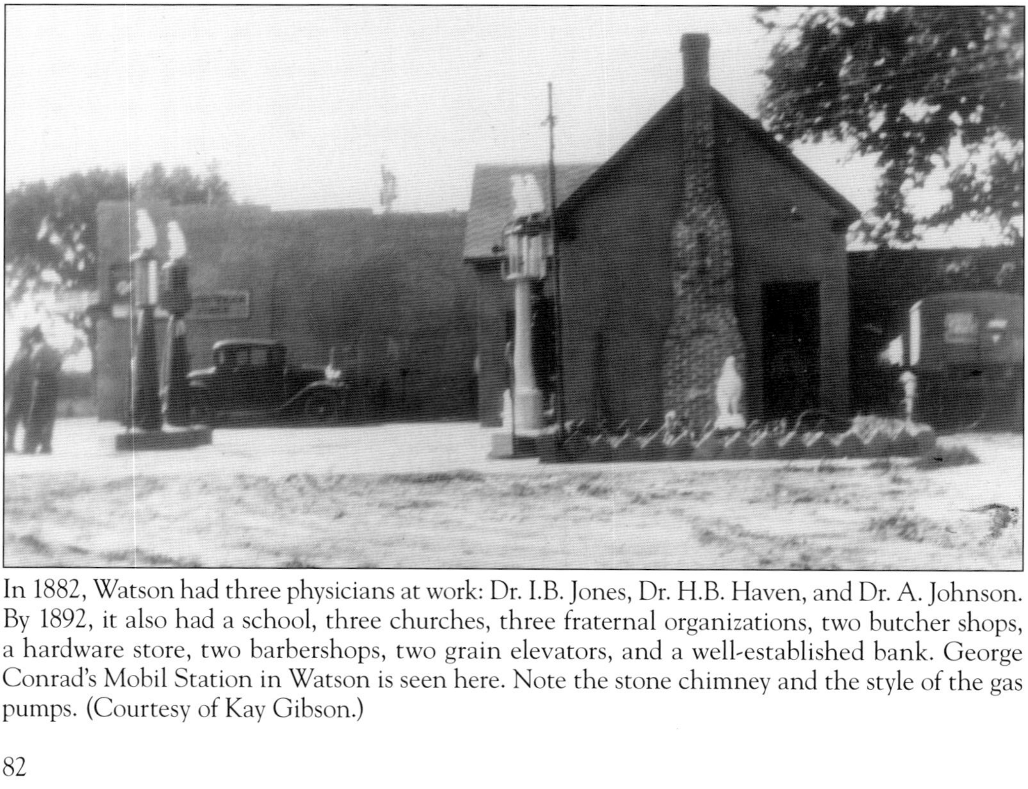

In 1882, Watson had three physicians at work: Dr. I.B. Jones, Dr. H.B. Haven, and Dr. A. Johnson. By 1892, it also had a school, three churches, three fraternal organizations, two butcher shops, a hardware store, two barbershops, two grain elevators, and a well-established bank. George Conrad's Mobil Station in Watson is seen here. Note the stone chimney and the style of the gas pumps. (Courtesy of Kay Gibson.)

These three men hold a banner for Kinzer and Jackson, and the sign in the window advertises 30 percent off warm-weather suits. The earliest shops and stores were made of wood, but later, after fire or decomposition, wooden buildings were gradually replaced with brick buildings, which lasted longer. (Courtesy of Kay Gibson.)

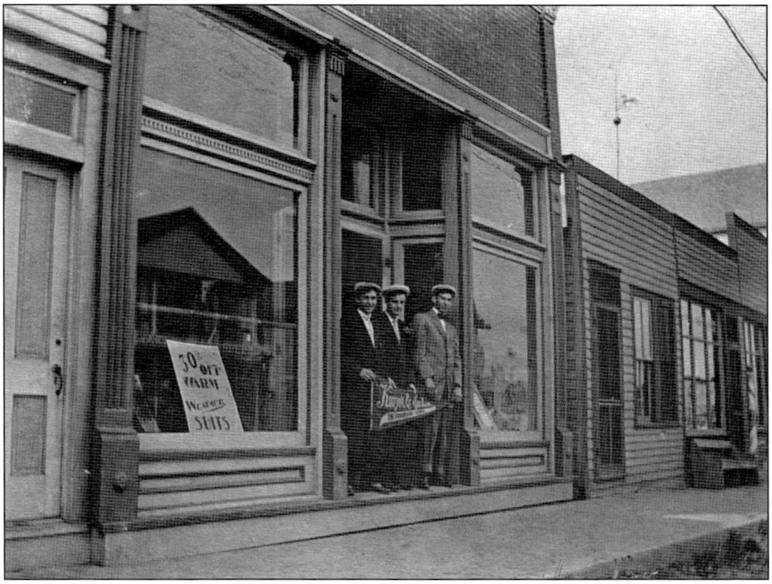

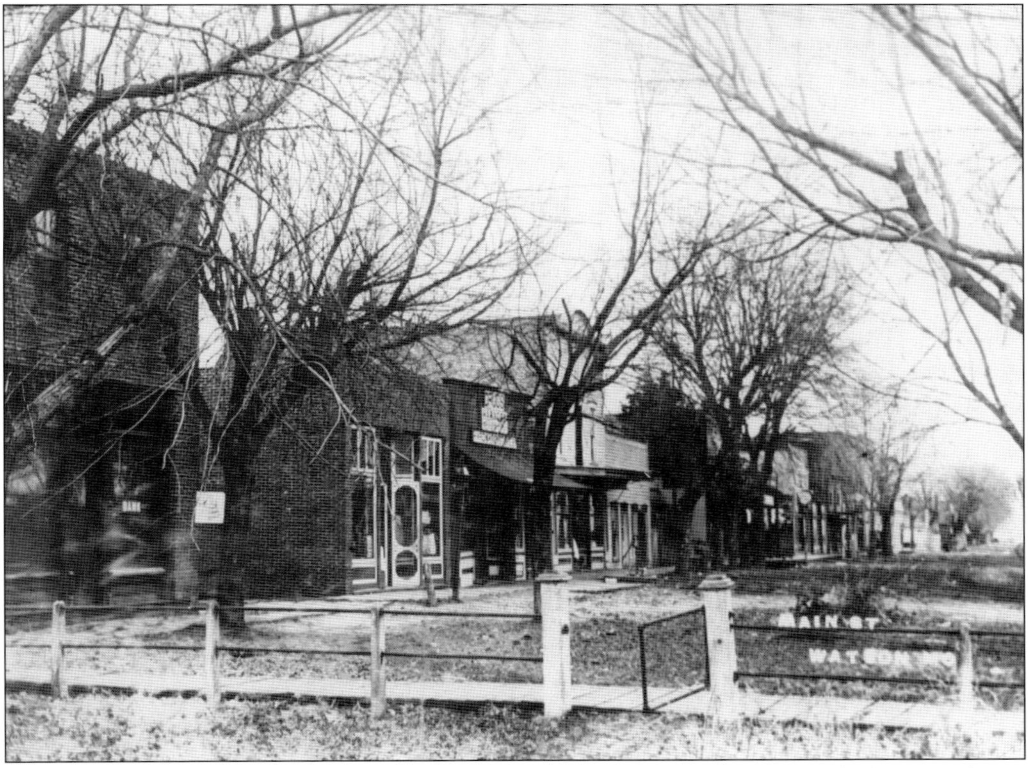

Main Street in Watson is seen here in 1915 when it was a thriving town but before storefronts were built with brick. This is an excellent example of early life in a small town, as the street is not yet paved but city leaders have built a wooden sidewalk to keep residents out of the mud. (Courtesy of Kay Gibson.)

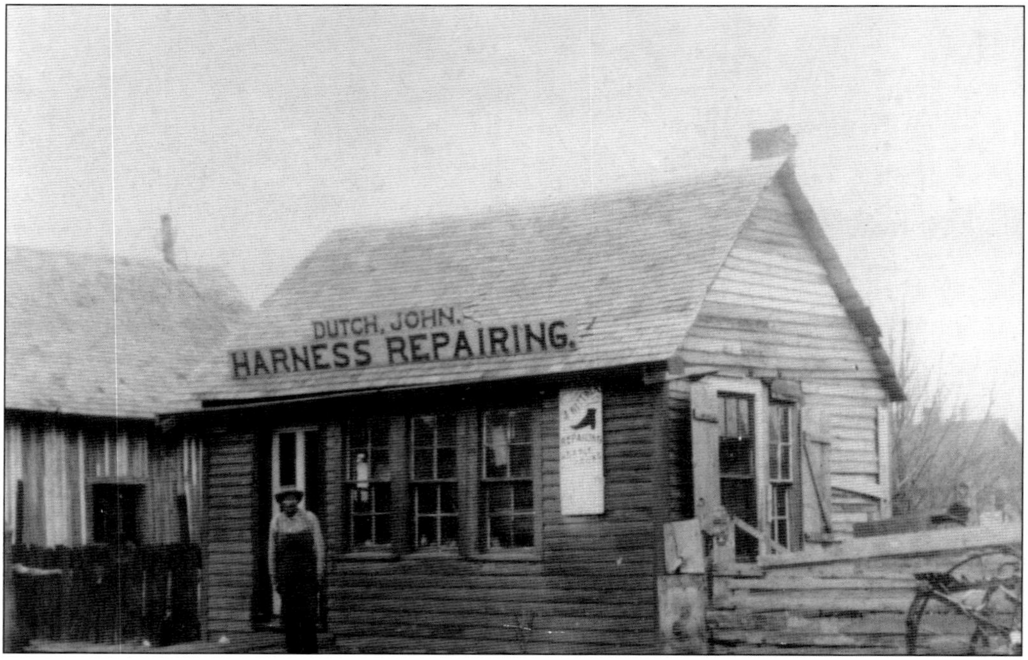

Dutch John Harness Repairing in Watson is seen here in 1907. The sign in front shows a boot, indicating that Dutch John did shoe and boot repair as well. Settled by Marion Good in 1869, he owned the only building at that time, which had been moved from Sonora. G.T. Boston applied for a license for a saloon after he moved a building from Sonora, but it was refused. Undaunted, Boston moved just outside the city limits. (Courtesy of Kay Gibson.)

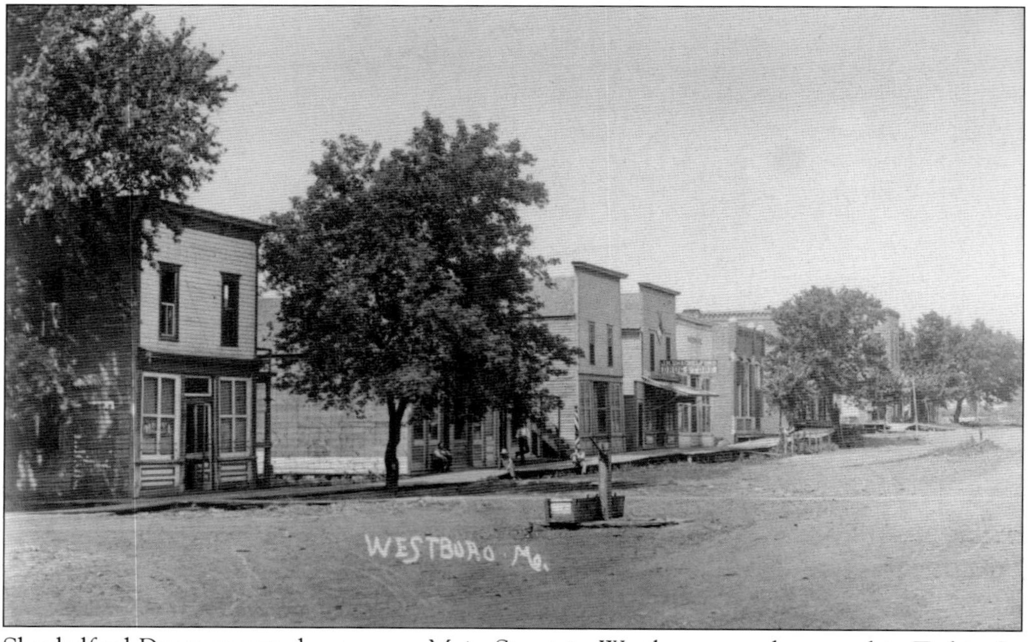

Shackelford Drugs operated a store on Main Street in Westboro, seen here, and in Tarkio. In Westboro's best days, there were three hotels, two general stores, three blacksmith shops, one millinery, two groceries, and a skating rink. Note the water trough in the middle of the street next to the water pump. (Courtesy of the Atchison County Historical Society.)

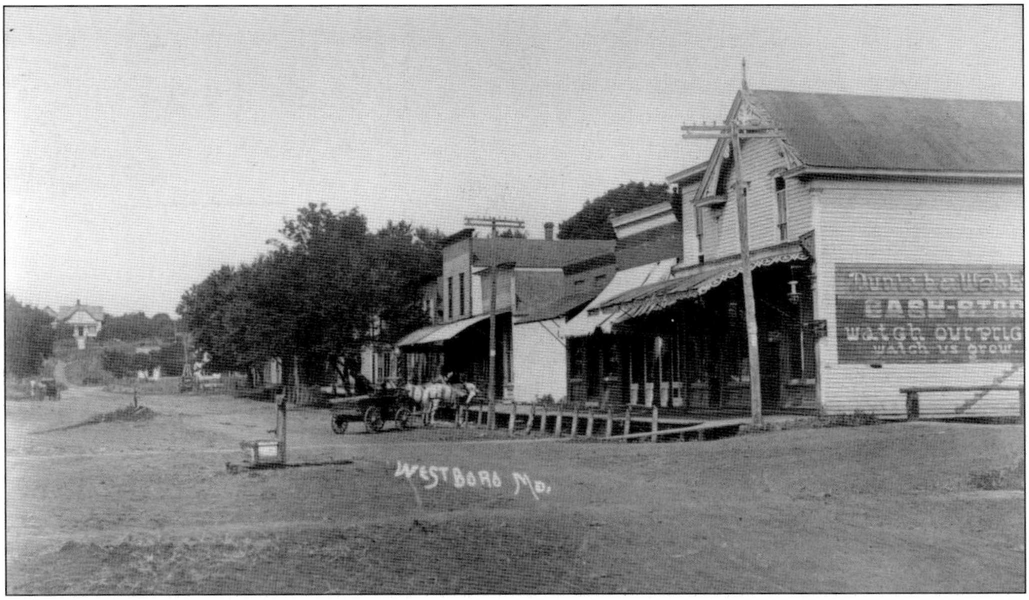

This store was later known as Tucker's Store and Funeral Service and was first run by A.R. Tucker when he bought it in 1914. Tucker's son Scott joined him in the enterprise later that year. The sign on the building on the right states, "Cash Store–watch our prices–watch us grow!" (Courtesy of the Atchison County Historical Society.)

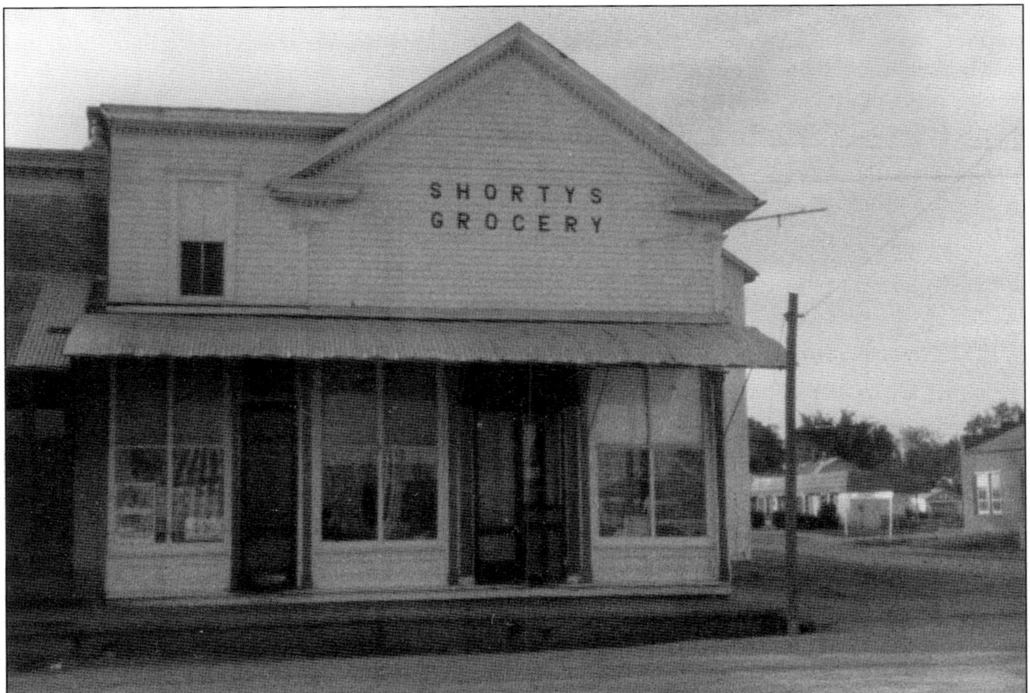

The main part of the building that became Tucker's Store, seen here when it was Shorty's Grocery, was moved to Westboro from Centerview soon after the railroad bypassed Centerview. A.R. retired in the late 1950s, but funeral services, which were first offered in the fall of 1919, were held until the late 1960s when Scott Tucker retired. (Courtesy of Harry and Mary Combs.)

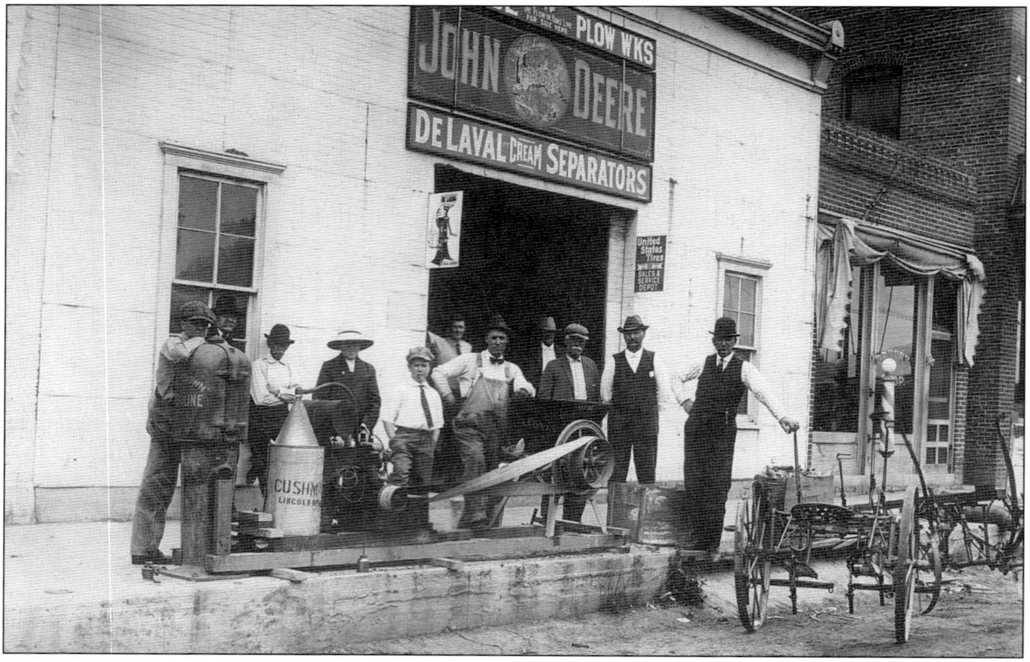

This is Bischof Hardware on Main Street in Rock Port. An early-1900s advertisement reported, "Wm. A. Bischof for Superior Stoves and ranges, Great Western Oak Heaters, Woodmanse Woodmills, Myers Pumps, DeLaval Separators, John Deere Implements, Winona Wagons, Keen Kutter and Sure Edge Tools." William's father, George L. Bischof, came to America from Germany in 1850, and his mother, Phillipine Helmer, from Prussia in 1859. The two raised 12 children, with William born as the fourth child. (Courtesy of the *Atchison County Mail.*)

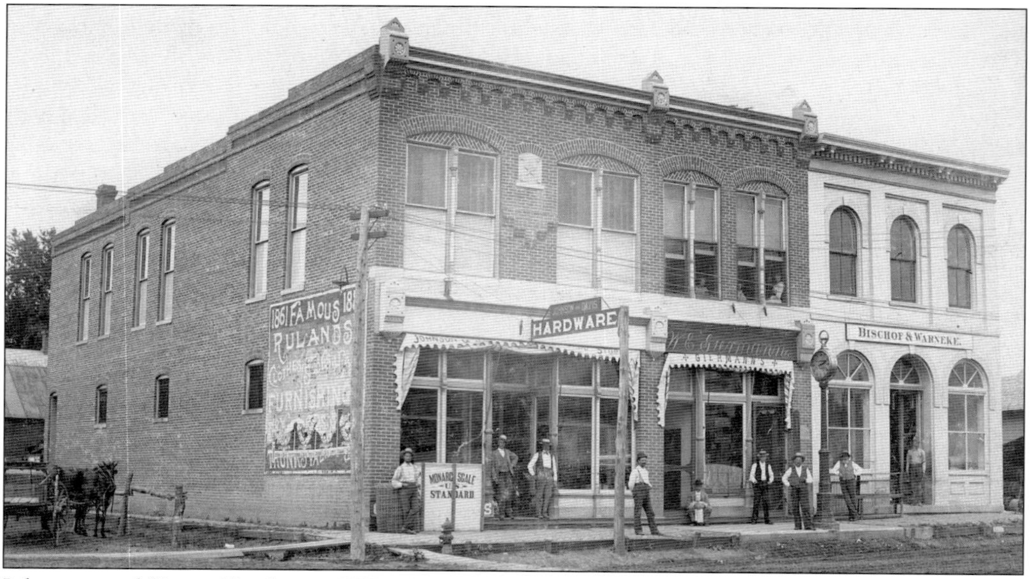

Johnson and Davis Hardware, W.E. Giermann's, and Bischof and Warneke were all on Main Street in Rock Port. Giermann's advertised his services as a jeweler and optician, stating, "The best watch that was ever constructed needs occasional attention." Another advertisement read, "Entrust this important service to us and rest assured that only competent workmen will work on your watch." (Courtesy of the *Atchison County Mail.*)

Five
DAY-TO-DAY LIVING

Whether it is going to church on Sunday or going to work throughout the week, people fall into patterns in life. This chapter shows how Atchison Countians lived and how they reacted to the unexpected events of the last century.

In the early 1900s, men and women throughout the country struggled to make a living and raise their children, especially on the family farm. But the fun times with family were what folks looked forward to the most. Parades, family dinners, vacations, and one-day outings helped people through the toughest of times. These were the pleasures that picked residents up and left an impression on the community.

In the early 1900s, standards of living were quite different. For one, there was no air-conditioning, and the heat of the day abated little at night. There were many nights slept on the floor with the rest of the family, which led to wonderful conversations. Work on the farm in the day was varied, from feeding chickens, cows, horsed and hogs and keeping them healthy to putting up hay in the summer and cutting wood for the cold winter to come. The work was non-stop, and no one was exempt unless they were sick.

For store clerks, the hours were also long. Many general store owners opened their shops at 6:00 a.m. and did not close until 9:00 p.m. To further entice customers to come into their store, services were offered, such as harness and leather repair and boot and shoe repair, because many could not afford new goods as often as they would have liked. Day-to-day life was never dull, and people from Atchison County did the best with what they had and kept a lookout for better days ahead.

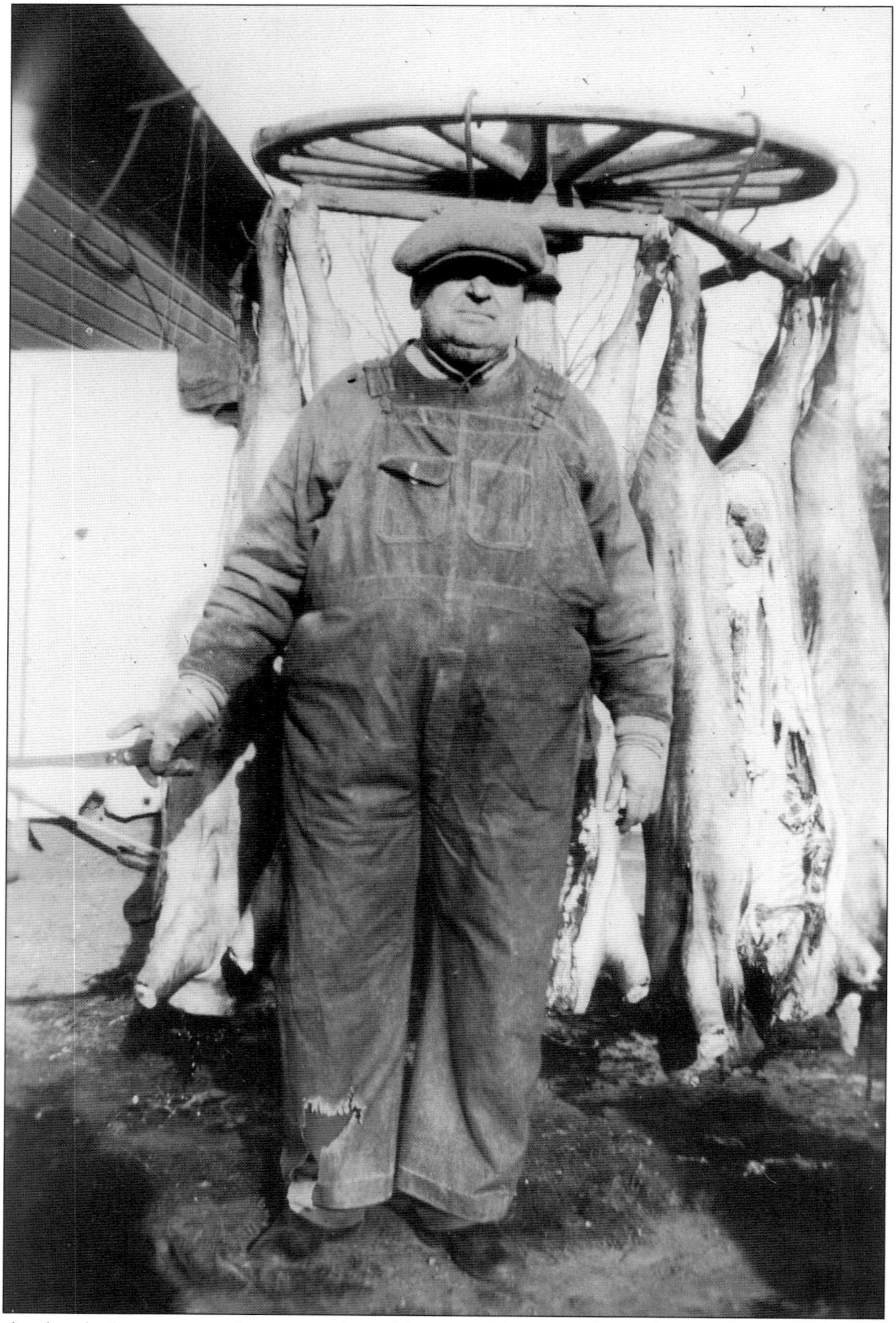

In the days before supermarkets, several neighbors would get together at butchering time or anytime there was work to be done to help one another and share in what was a difficult job. Harmon H. Harmes is seen here on a butchering day near Milton, seven miles south of Rock Port. Note the wagon wheel and single post used to hang the meat. (Courtesy of Betty Wennihan.)

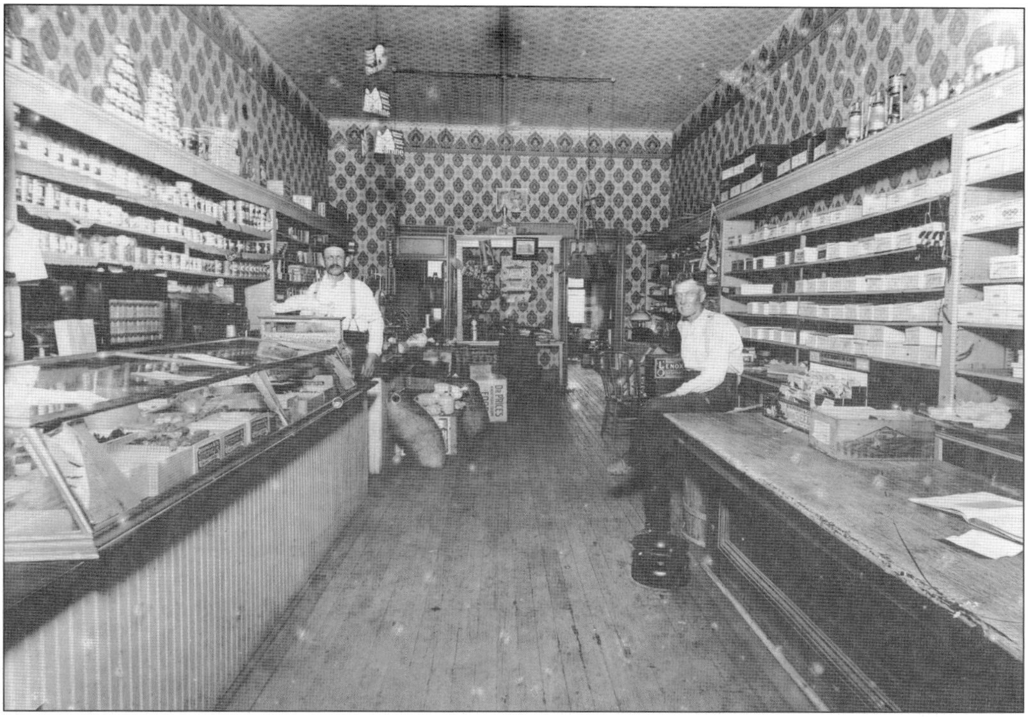

General stores in every town endeavored to provide quality products at the lowest price with friendly customer service. An early advertisement for the Klump Brothers store in Tarkio proclaimed that they offered "prompt delivery to all parts of the city. Highest prices paid for produce, butter and eggs." (Courtesy of the Atchison County Historical Society.)

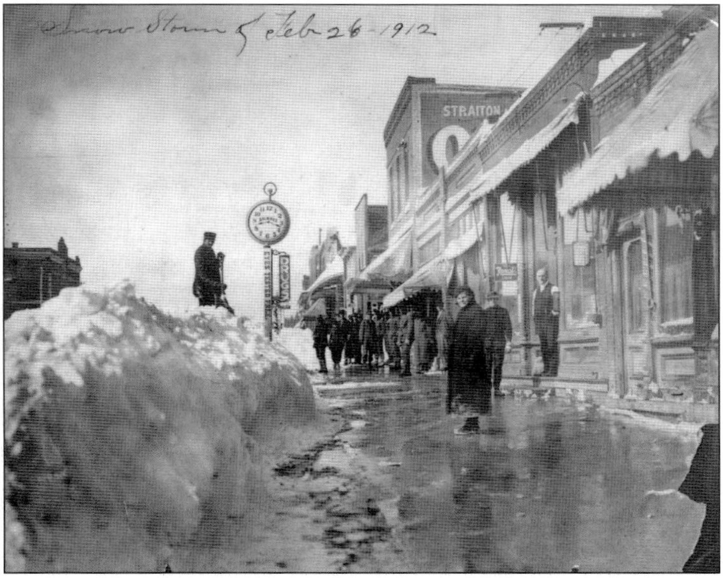

Life in small towns hit by large snowfall could be inconvenient, but on remote farms it could be deadly. In some instances, the storms hit so rapidly that children would be caught going to or coming home from school. Even adults, particularly teachers walking home from school or cattlemen tending their livestock, could be caught out in the low temperatures and blinding snow. (Courtesy of the Atchison County Historical Society.)

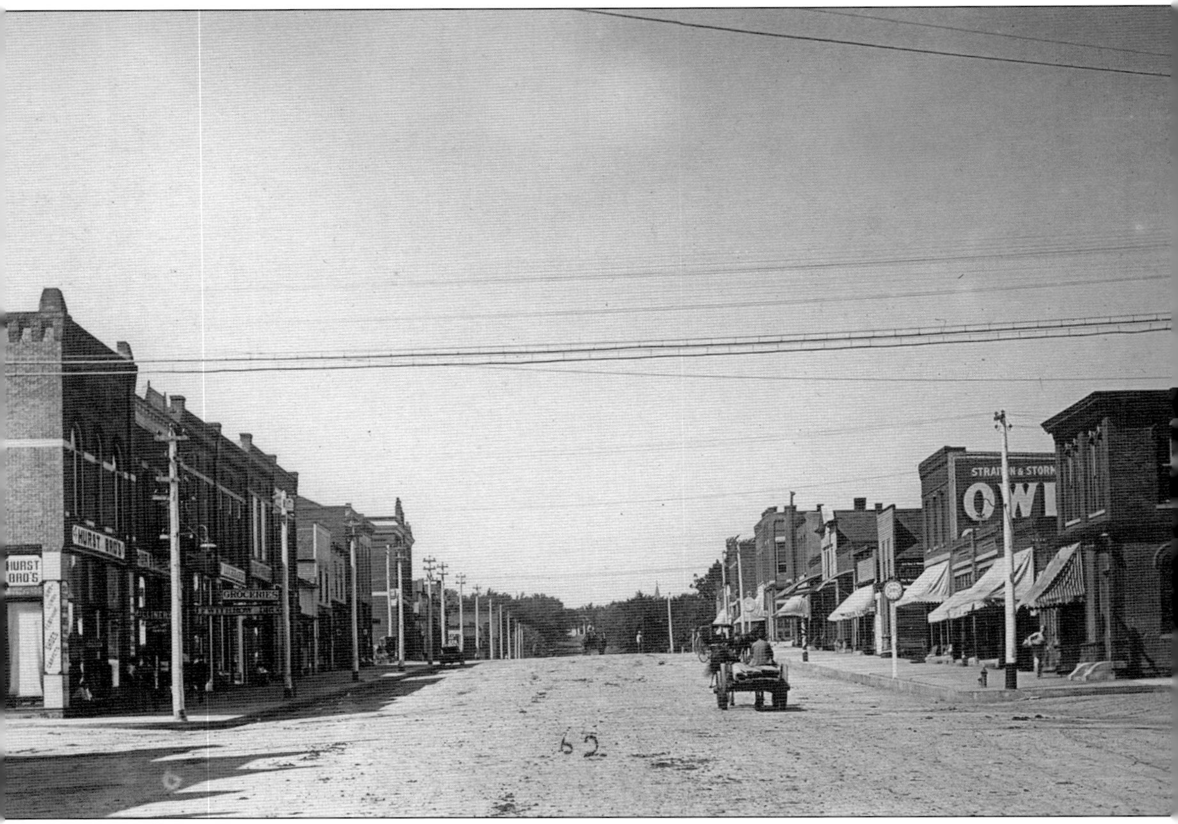

Before Main Street in Tarkio was paved, this was a typical afternoon scene, with Hurst Brothers on the south side (left) advertising dry goods, clothing, shoes, and carpets. The store was run by Henry and James Hurst. Henry was also the president of Farmers Bank. On the same side of the street, there was a millinery, J.F. Withrow Drugs, and Luckhardt Groceries. Notice the two clocks on the north (right) side. (Courtesy of Hon. Corey Herron.)

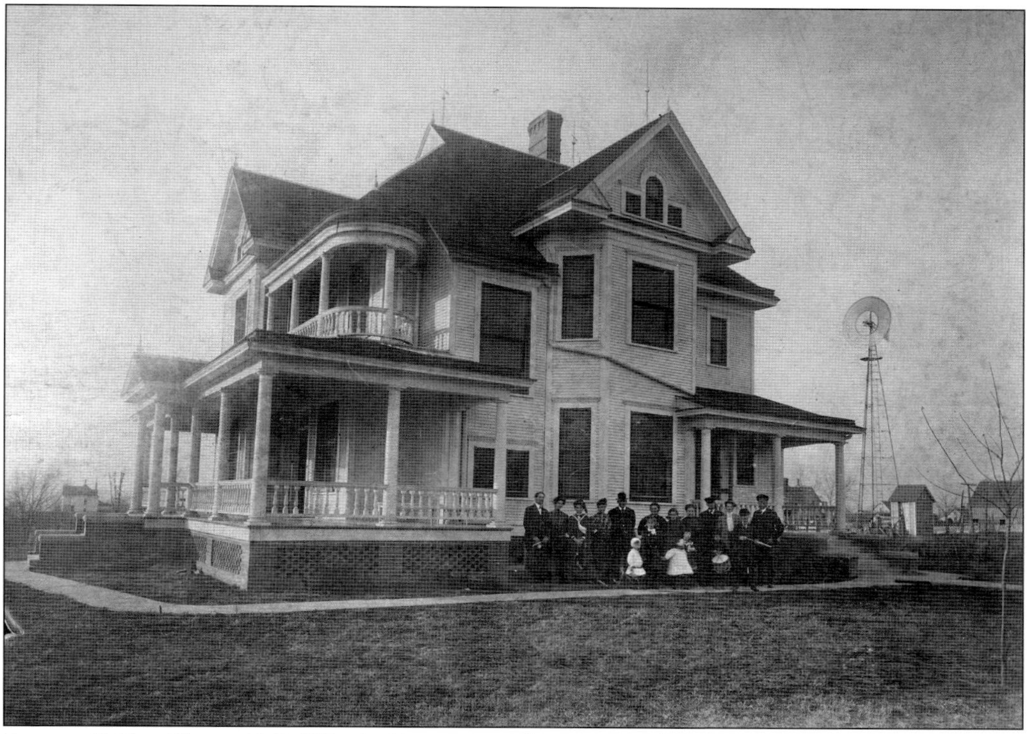

Born in 1848 in Illinois, E.C. Whitford later married Emma Strickler in 1871 and moved to Fairfax in 1873, where they raised five children. Whitford had a loan business and later purchased stock in the Fairfax Exchange Bank, becoming the majority stockholder and president of the bank. This home is lovingly cared for today by Harry and Mary Combs. (Courtesy of Harry and Mary Combs.)

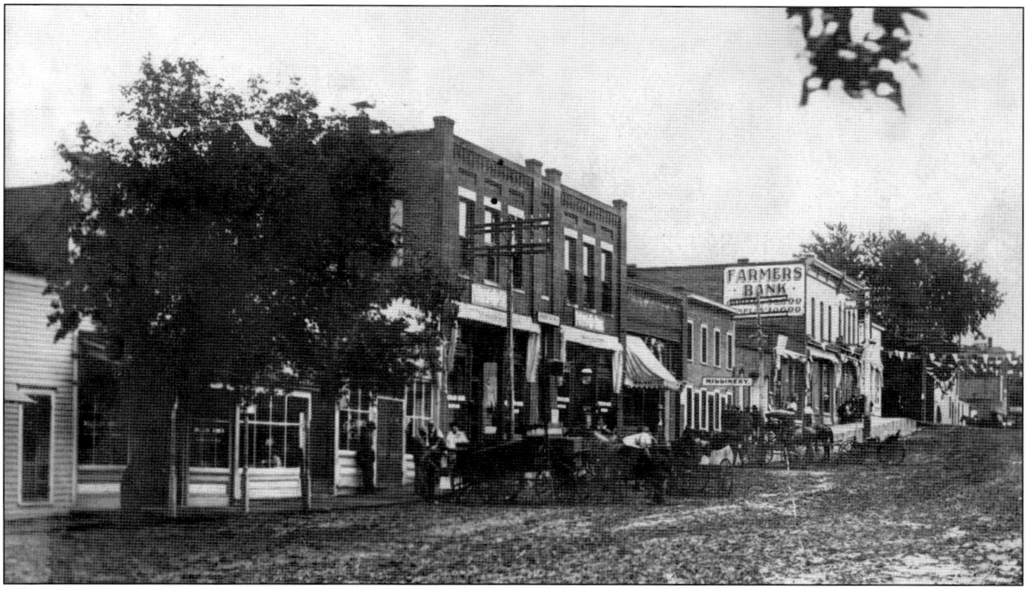

Due to fire danger, several of the wooden buildings in this photograph were later replaced by brick structures, many of which still stand today. Note that the sidewalk rises higher the farther west it travels. The raised sidewalk made it easier to load a tall horse-drawn wagon. This view looks west down Main Street in Tarkio. (Courtesy of the Atchison County Historical Society.)

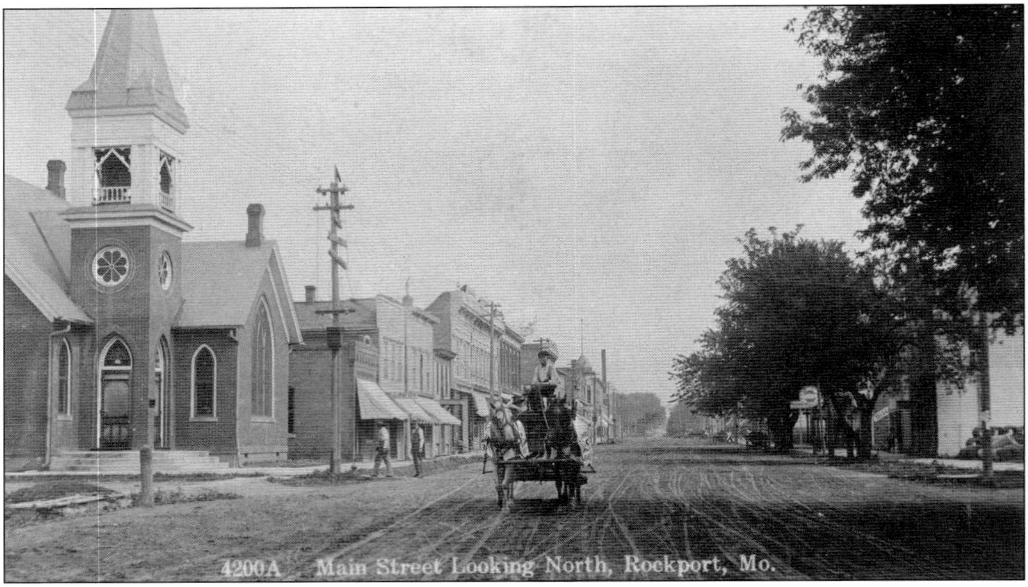

The church on the left, the South Methodist Episcopal Church, was razed in 1945. The South Methodist Church combined with the Methodist Church in 1934, and the lot was sold to M.O. McElhiney. McElhiney opened the Dairy Sweet at this location in 1957 and sold it to Charles Eddy that same year. This view of Rock Port looks north down Main Street. (Courtesy of Hon. Corey Herron.)

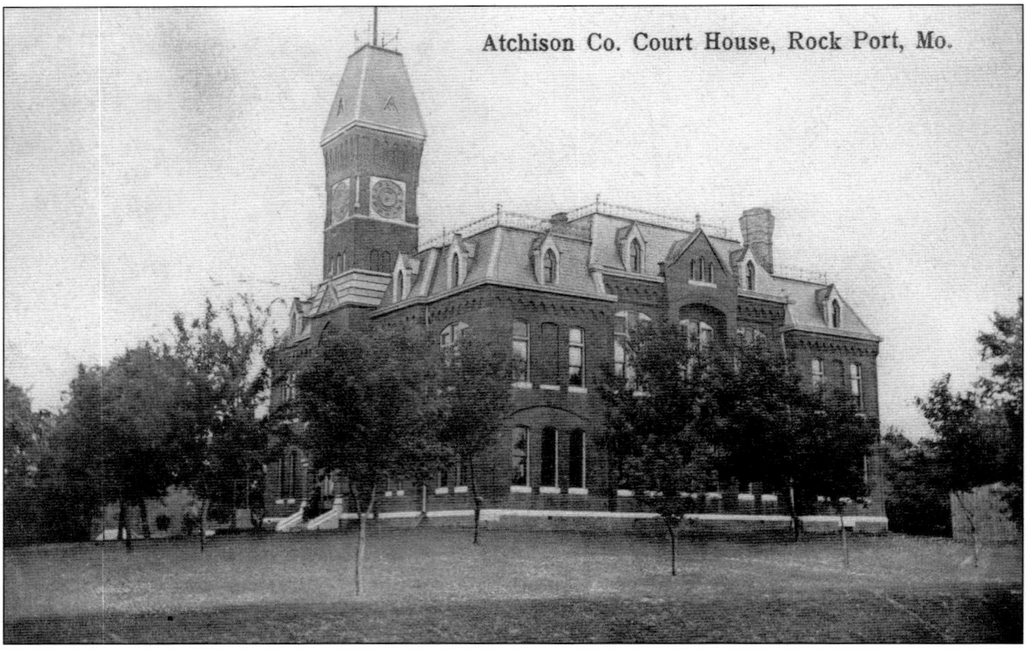

Tarkio wanted to be the county seat for Atchison County and even had a building ready, but Rock Port won out. On December 26, 1881, county representatives accepted plans from architects Eckels and Mann in St. Joseph, but residents refused to vote for the bonds twice in 1882. The court set money aside anyway, the building shell was constructed, and the interior was finished as money became available. The building was put into service on May 9, 1883. Note that there were no hands on the clock in the early years. (Courtesy of Hon. Corey Herron.)

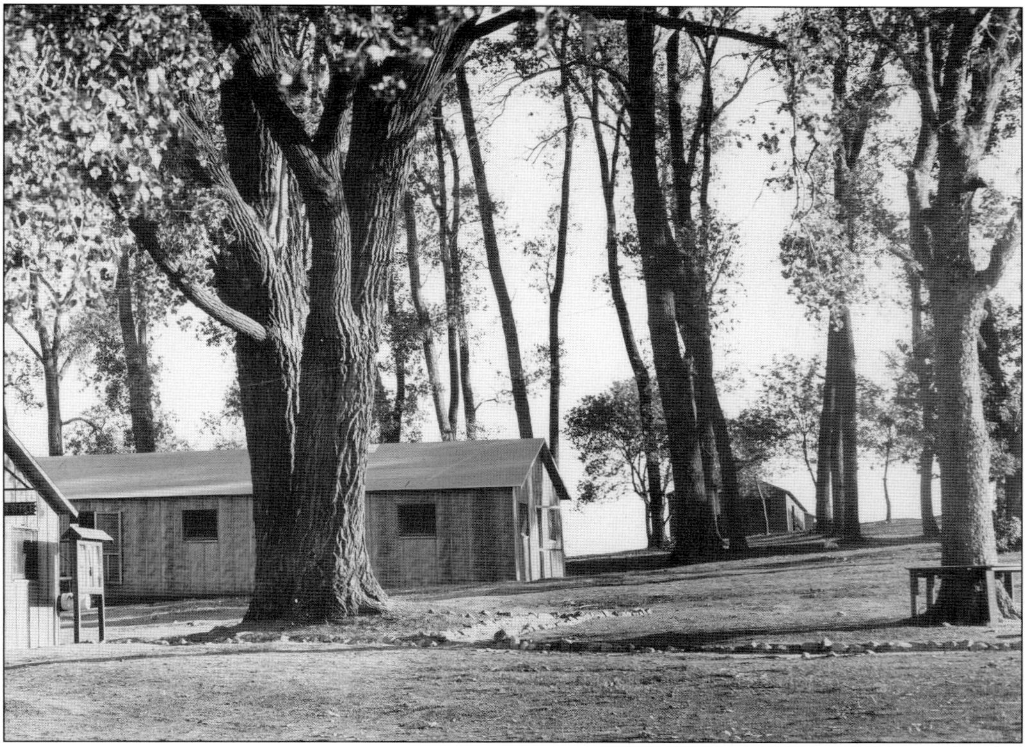

The CCC camp in Tarkio (pictured) was officially designated as Camp S.E.S.3, Company No. 1742. The officers were listed as Laurance E. Houlder, commanding officer, captain, CA-reserve; Peter A. Leuther, first lieutenant medical reserve; Fred E. Sims, first lieutenant, infantry reserve; and Vermund Ostergaard, educational adviser. (Courtesy of the Atchison County Historical Society.)

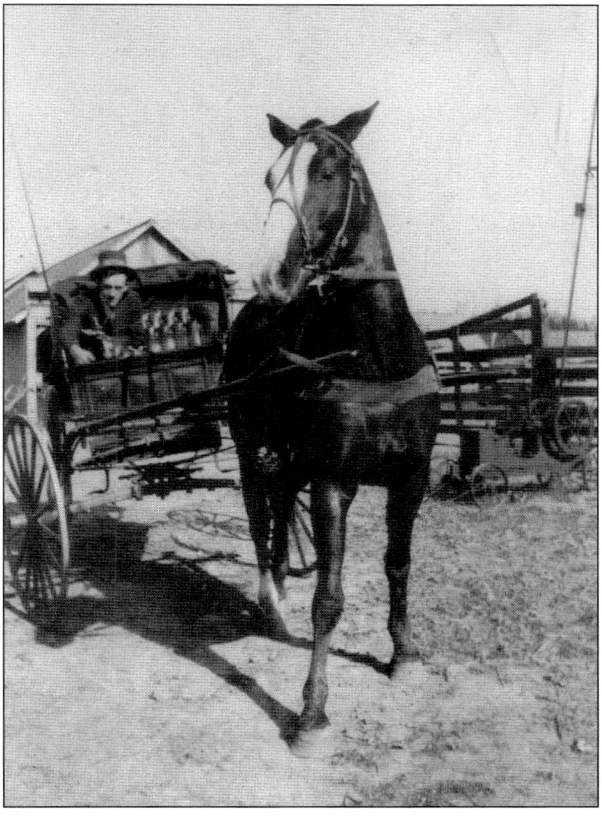

Horse and buggy did not require as much skill as riding on horseback, and until the mass production of automobiles made them more affordable, buggies could be bought for as little as $25 to $50. They were so popular that their use encouraged the graveling and grading of main rural roads and paving in smaller towns. This horse and buggy belonged to proud owner Herbert Cooper of Langdon. (Courtesy of Hon. Corey Herron.)

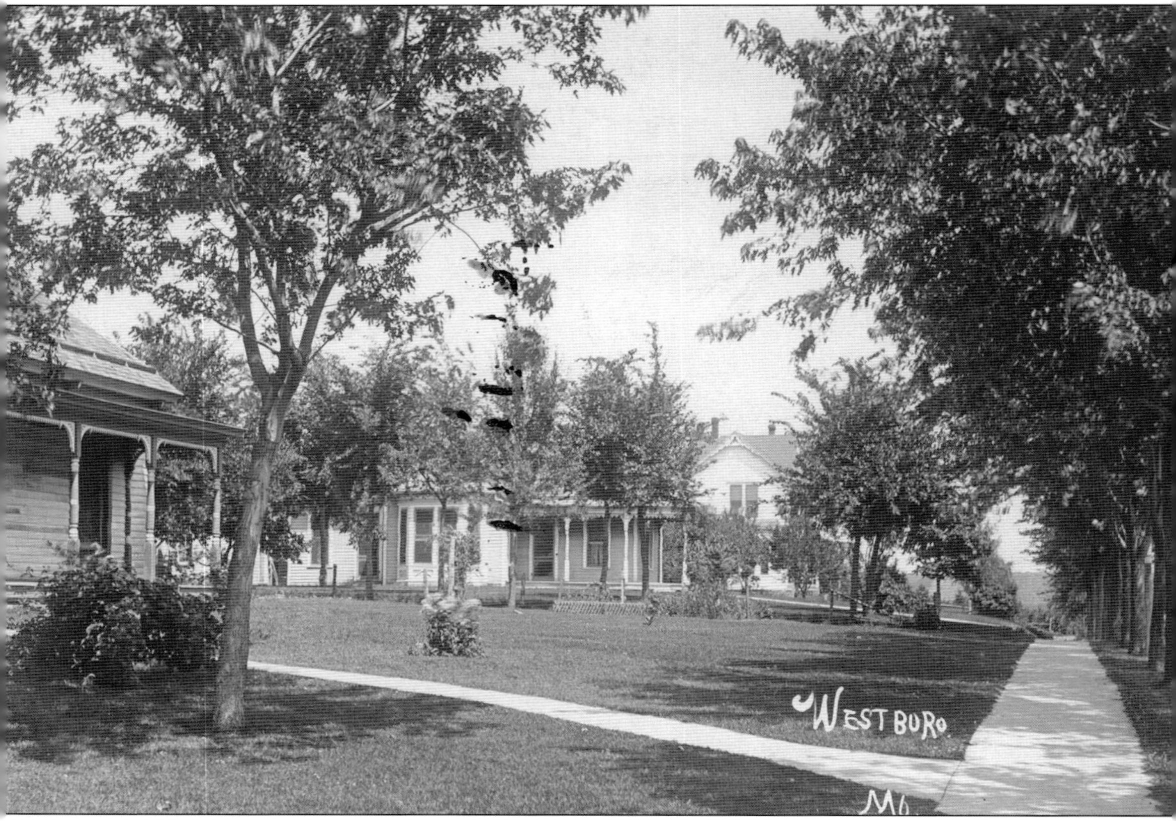

The village of Westboro was strategically located near a good water source and timber with which to build homes. The town was laid out on land owned by the president of the railroad, Charles E. Perkins, and offered for sale in December 1880. Very quickly, 50 lots sold for between $50 and $200. When the railroad chose its route, Westboro benefited because villages like Center Point were too far away from the line, prompting its residents to move to Westboro. (Courtesy of Hon. Corey Herron.)

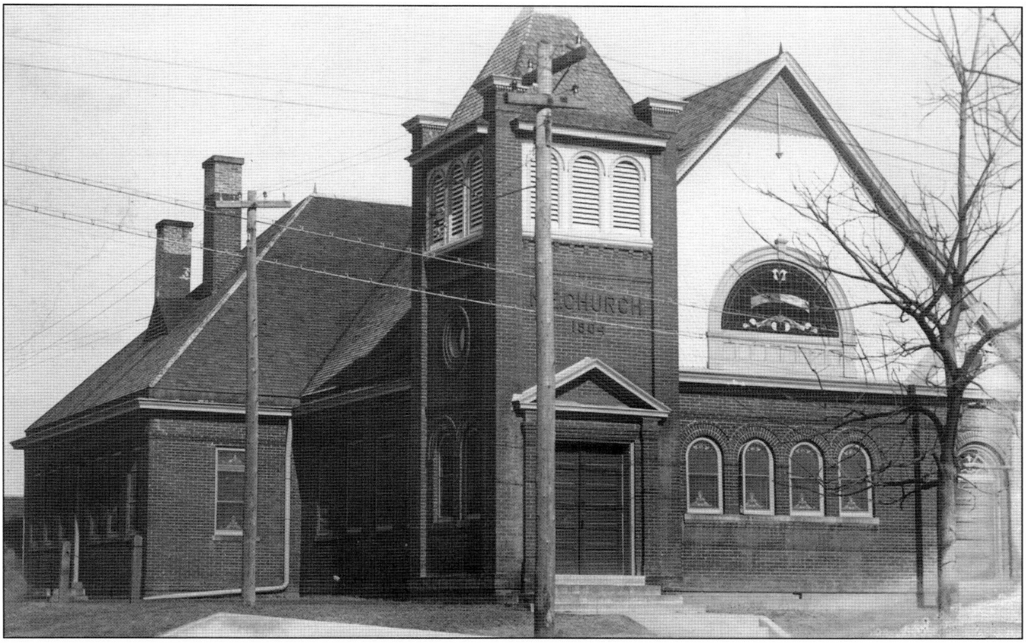

The Methodist Episcopal (M.E.) Church dates back to 1784, when Thomas Coke and Francis Asbury were the first bishops. In later years and through many mergers and divisions, the M.E. Church became the main component of the present-day United Methodist Church. The M.E. Church, South, also called the Southern Methodist Church, was the result of a split in the church on the issue of slavery. The split came about as a result of a conference held in Louisville, Kentucky, in 1844. The first M.E. Church was built in 1857, and in 1858 the South Methodist Church was constructed. Seen here is the Methodist Episcopal Church of Rock Port, with the date "1904" over the entrance. (Courtesy of Hon. Corey Herron.)

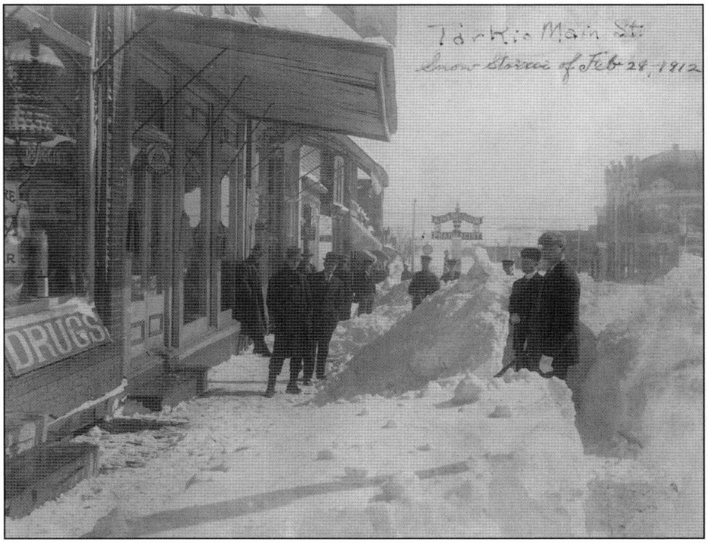

The tall building in the background on the right is the Tarkio Opera House, built with David Rankin's backing, that had a seating capacity of 864 people. There were also two highly decorated boxes on either side of the stage with the best views. With incandescent lamps for lighting, the building was known for its decorative frescoes. The opera house was torn down in the early 1970s. (Courtesy of the Atchison County Historical Society.)

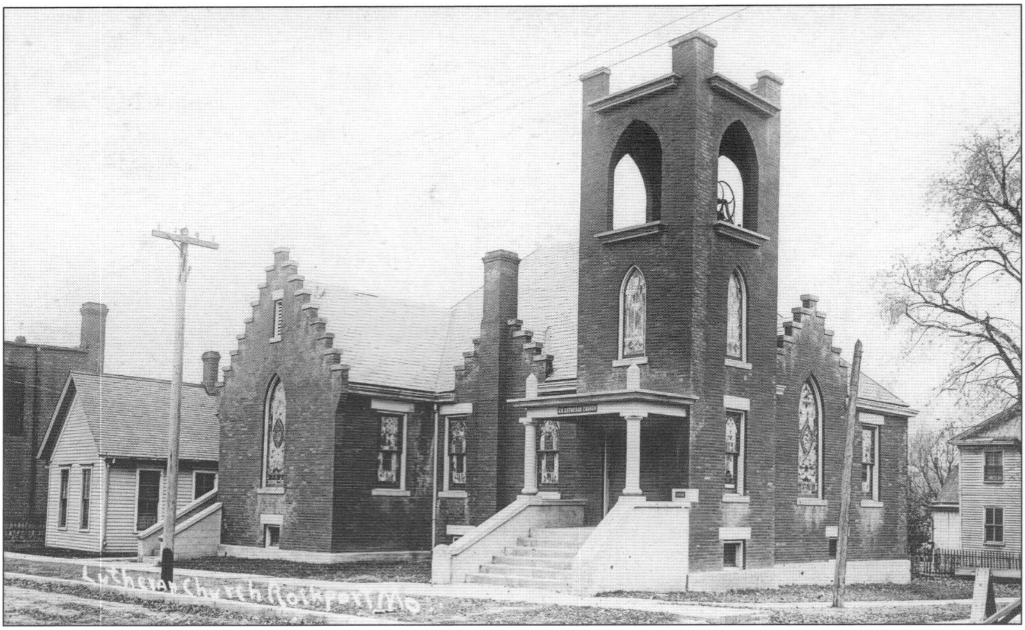

Conceived in 1858, the First Lutheran Church came about when the German Lutheran Church was organized. Originally built of logs in Rock Port, the first church was on Clay Street across from the present location of the courthouse. The second building was a frame structure built on the same site. This structure was torn down, and the post office is now located in its place. (Courtesy of Hon. Corey Herron.)

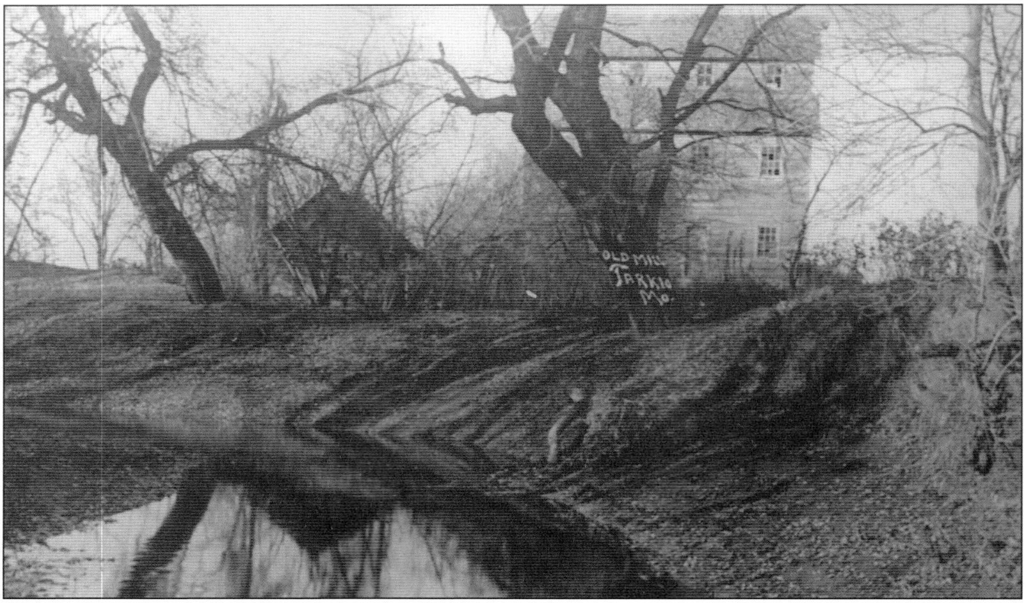

In the 1840s, Franklin Merrill, Henry Bush, John VanLeuven, E.N. Roberts, Richard Howell, Charles Fanning, James Murphy, and W.H. VanLeuven began building their homes near what is now Tarkio. Fanning is credited with building a gristmill on Tarkio River. Other mills were powered by water, livestock, or wind. Sometimes called corn mills, this referred to any mill that ground grain. In return, the miller was paid with a "miller's toll" in the earliest days: a portion of the ground grain in payment for his services. (Courtesy of the Atchison County Historical Society.)

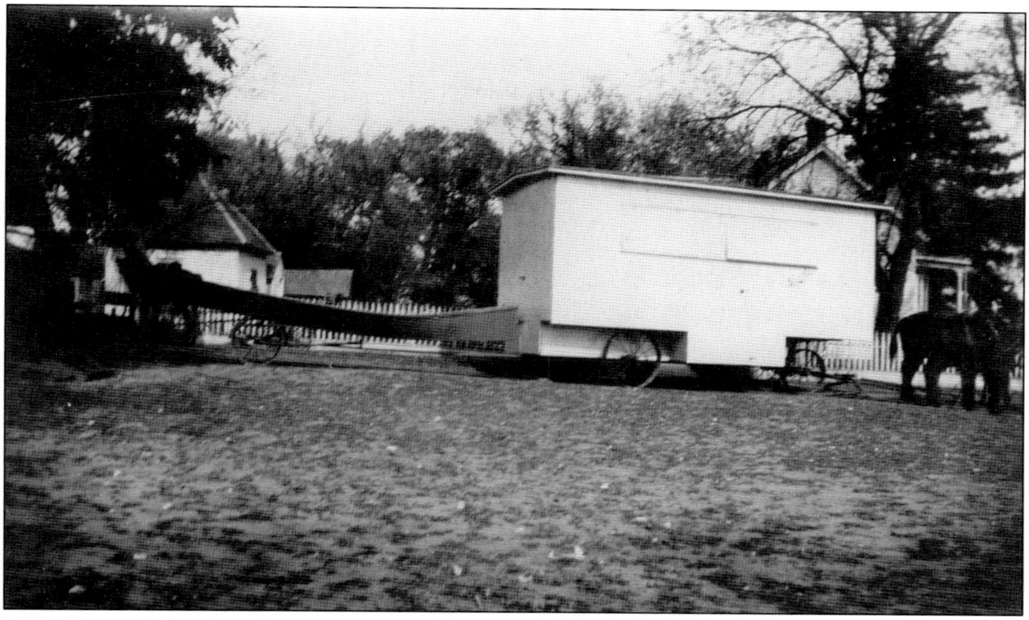

H.H. Harmes's famous "Campwagon" was used for hunting and fishing at Camp Kingfisher on the Missouri River. This wagon can still be seen today by appointment near the old town of Milton and is pictured here with one of Harmes's fishing boats. Today, visitors can view historical items and get a taste of what camping was like in the early 1900s. (Courtesy of Betty Wennihan.)

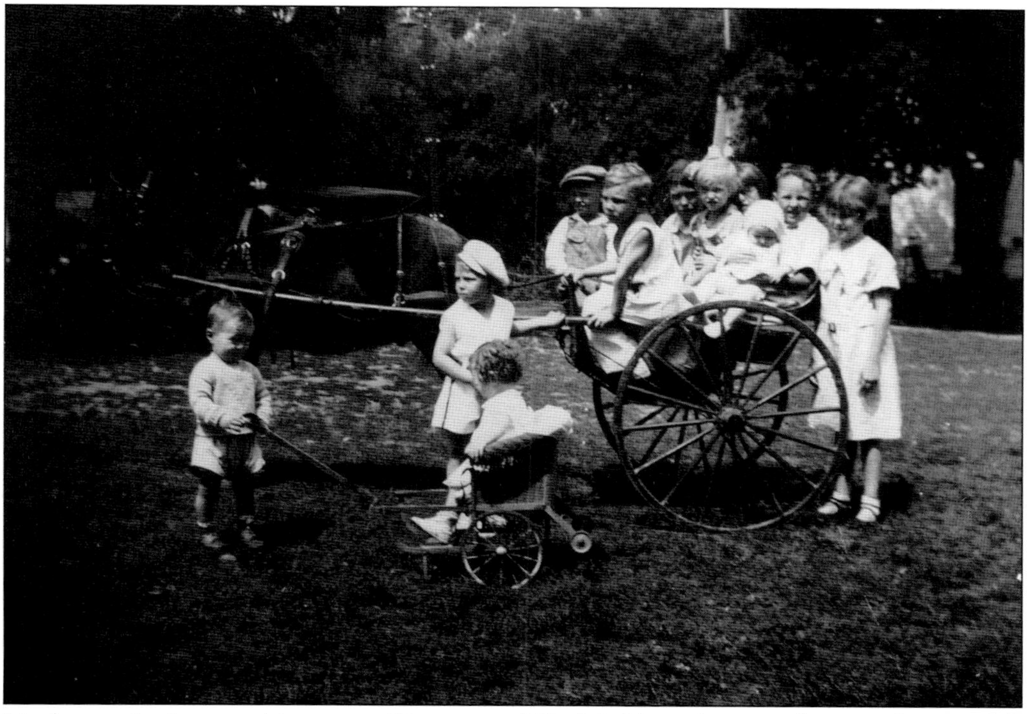

Much trust is given to this pony pulling a cart full of children. In most photographs, an adult is seen holding the horse's halter in case it bolted. These children are the offspring of H.H. and Maggie Harmes of Milton. (Courtesy of Betty Wennihan.)

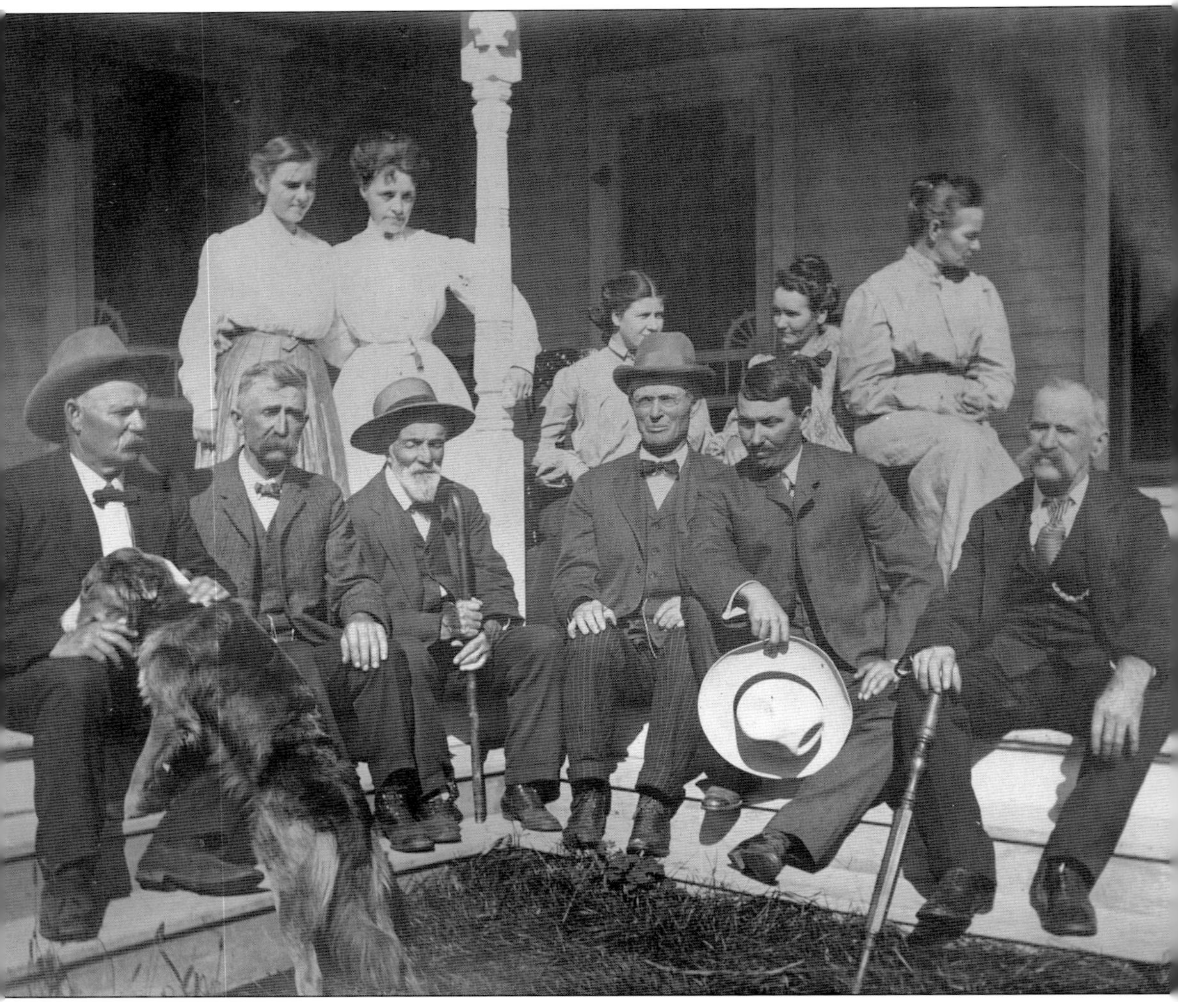

Sunday was a day of reverence and giving thanks to one's creator, usually followed by a large Sunday dinner with family and friends. Here, everyone posing looks to be having a happy time together except one woman who apparently did not like to have her photograph taken and looked down and away instead. (Courtesy of George and Patty Laur.)

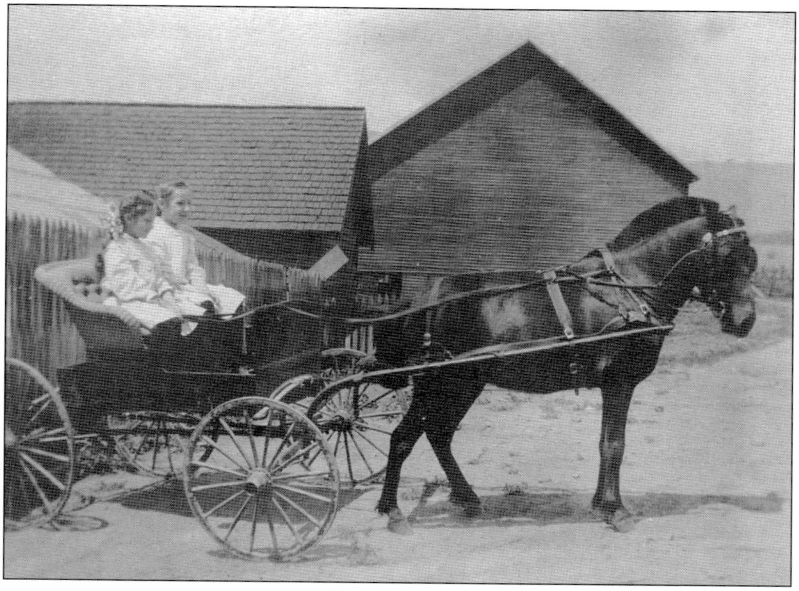

Merle (left) and Faye Seymour were daughters of Rufus G. Pebley (born 1867) and Ida G. Pebley (born 1868), who had seven children. Both Rufus and Ida are buried at Pleasant Ridge Cemetery near Fairfax. Here, Merle and Faye take a buggy ride in their Sunday best in the Fairfax area. (Courtesy of Betty Wennihan.)

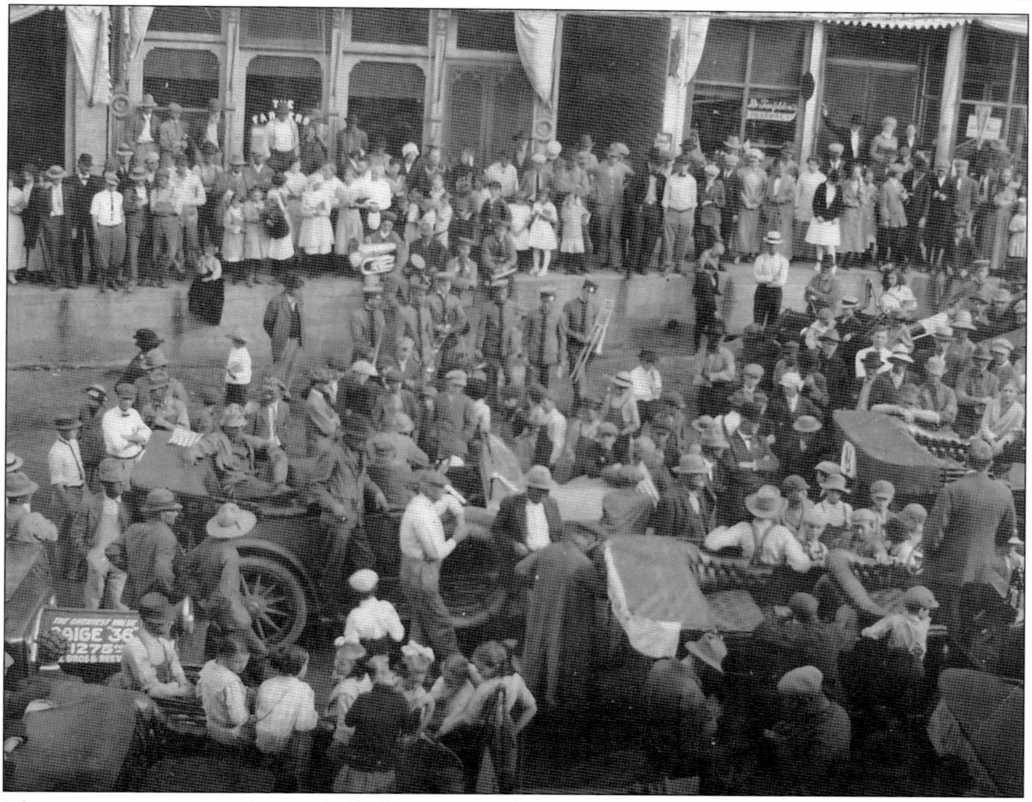

This street scene was taken right before the Fairfax parade, as everyone seems to be trying to find their correct place in front of Dr. Templeton's Pharmacy. After some difficulty fighting floodwaters at Phelps City, Dr. O.P. Templeton and his family moved to Main Street and Broadway in Fairfax in 1910. Dr. Templeton was known to wait on customers one at a time regardless of their social standing or financial means. And, if the World Series was on the radio, patients had to come back when the game was over or sit and listen to it with him. (Courtesy of Betty Wennihan.)

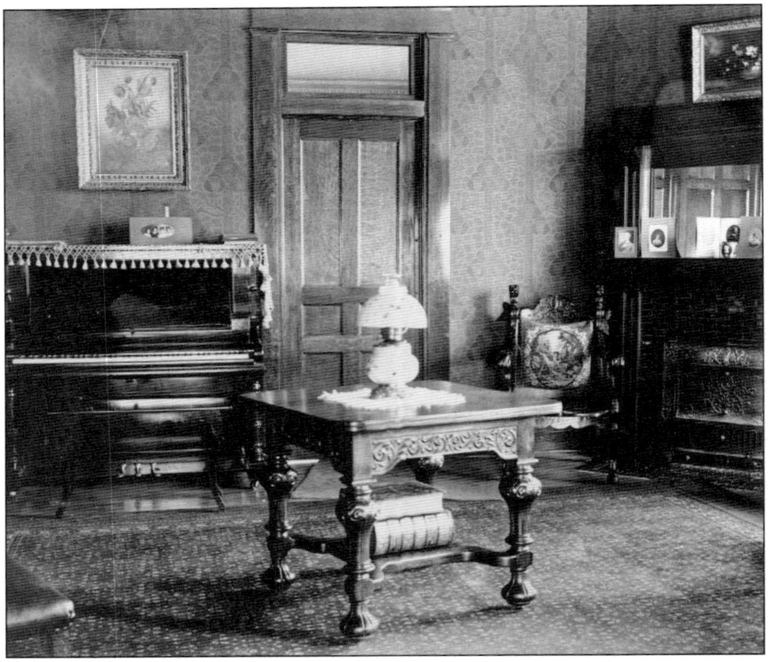

These two images are from the home of George Laur. This was not a typical farm home in the early 1900s, with a piano, a heavily carved wooden chair, and tables and dressers that reflect a successful life. The two large books under the table are probably family Bibles. In the days before electricity, television, or radio, a piano was invaluable for family entertainment. (Courtesy of George and Patty Laur.)

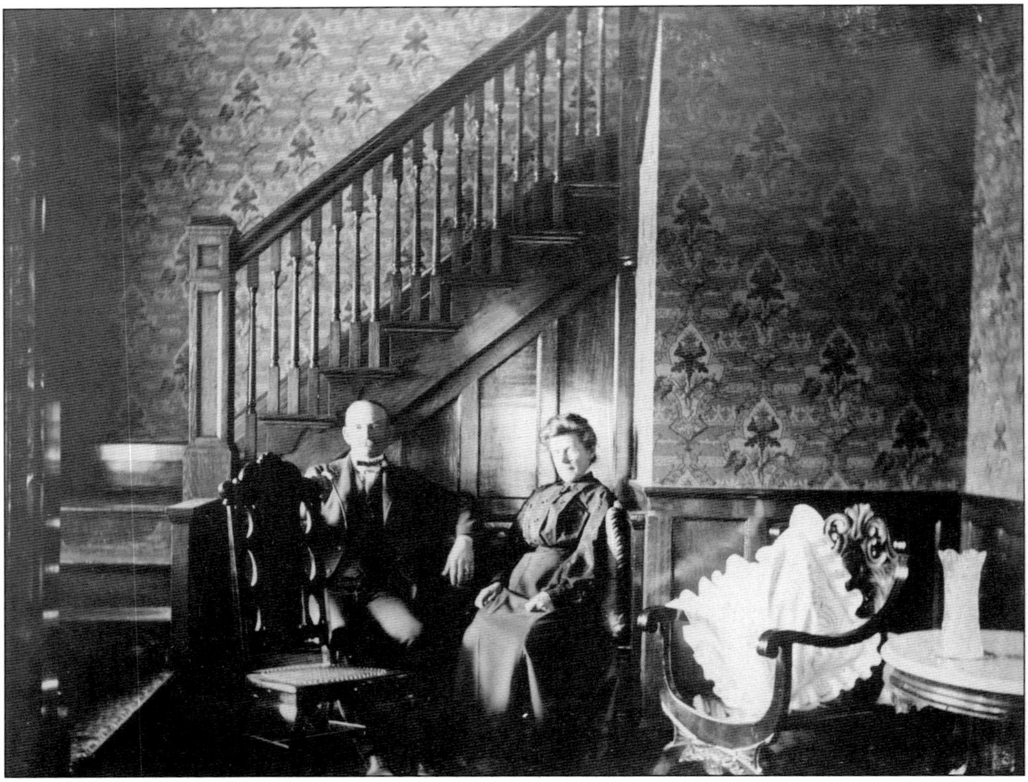

Mr. and Mrs. Edwin Rankin are seen here visiting at the home of George Laur near Westboro. The home was built by George and then passed on to his son Tom. Today, his grandson George lives in the home and keeps it looking as nice as when it was first built. (Courtesy of George and Patty Laur.)

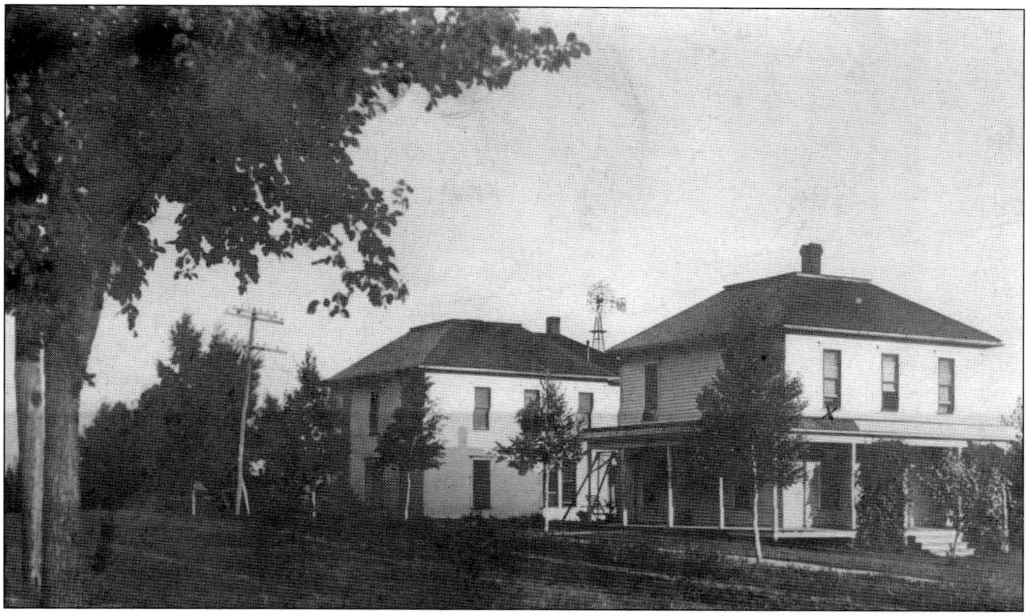

Westboro was incorporated on January 10, 1882. The earliest church in Westboro was not a church at all but actually the railroad depot, on loan from the depot agent, a Mr. Ringo. Later, Hazel Grove united with the Wesley Methodist Church of Walden Grove to form Westboro Methodist Episcopal Church. The home on the right was the parsonage of the Westboro United Methodist Church and still stands today. (Courtesy of Anna Belle Johnson.)

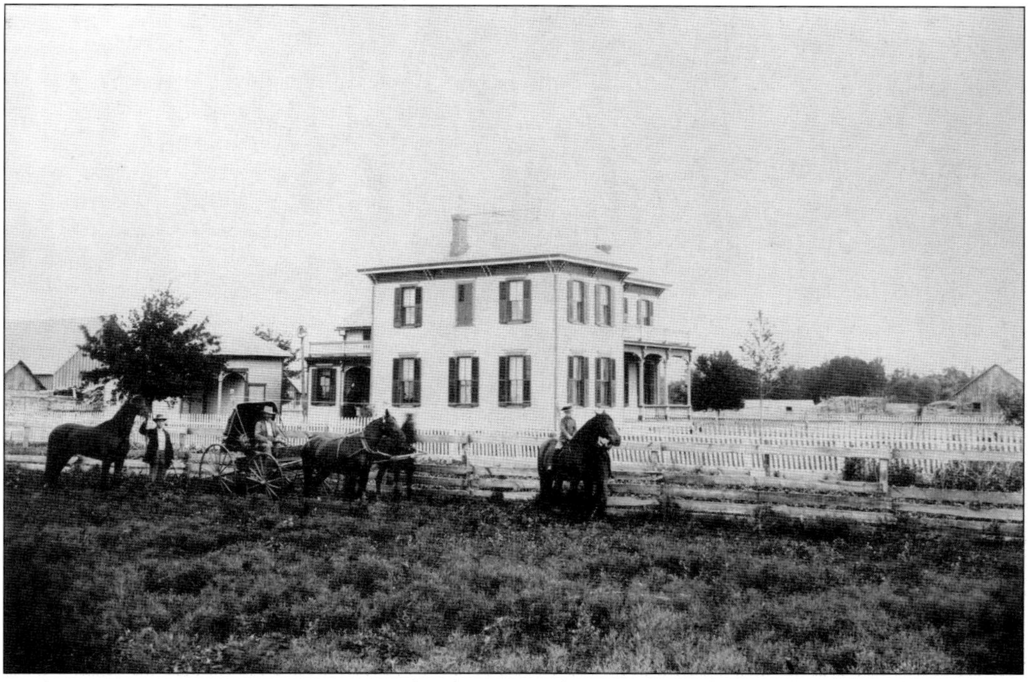

In this image, Harmon Harmes is in this buggy, Wike Harmes holds the horse on the left, and Willie Harmes is the young man on the horse on the right. Harmon Harmes lived from 1868 until 1940, living to be 71. His wife, Maggie, was born in 1871 and lived to be 79, passing away in 1951. This is their stately home near Milton. (Courtesy of Betty Wennihan.)

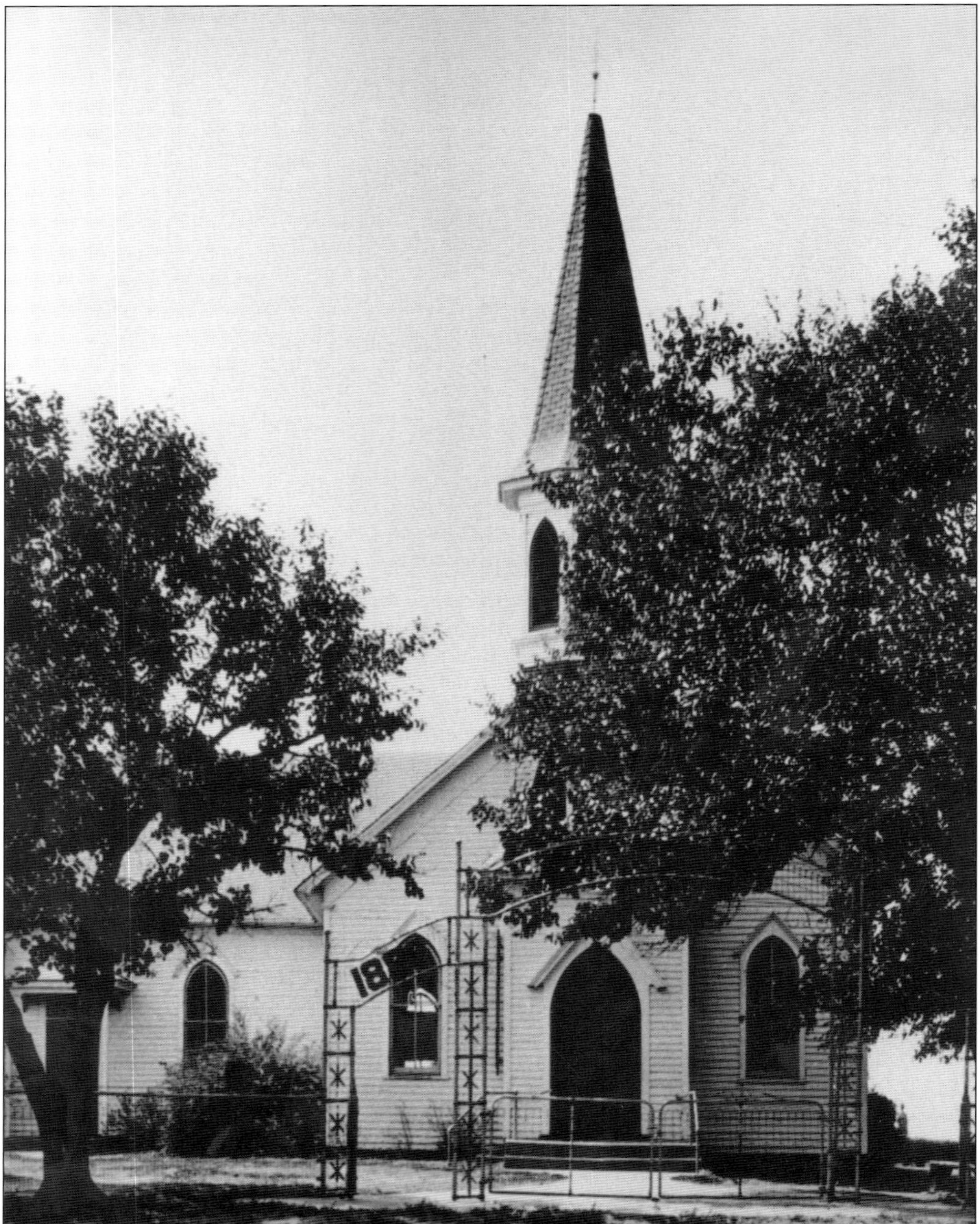

The first St. John's Lutheran Church was originally built in 1886 near the junction of State Highways B and F on five acres donated for the church and cemetery by Adam Layman. The church cost $1,465 to build and had a 53-foot spire. With World War I underway, the confirmation class of 1917 was the last to be taught in German, although a few entries in the 1917 treasurer's report were in English. (Courtesy of George and Patty Laur.)

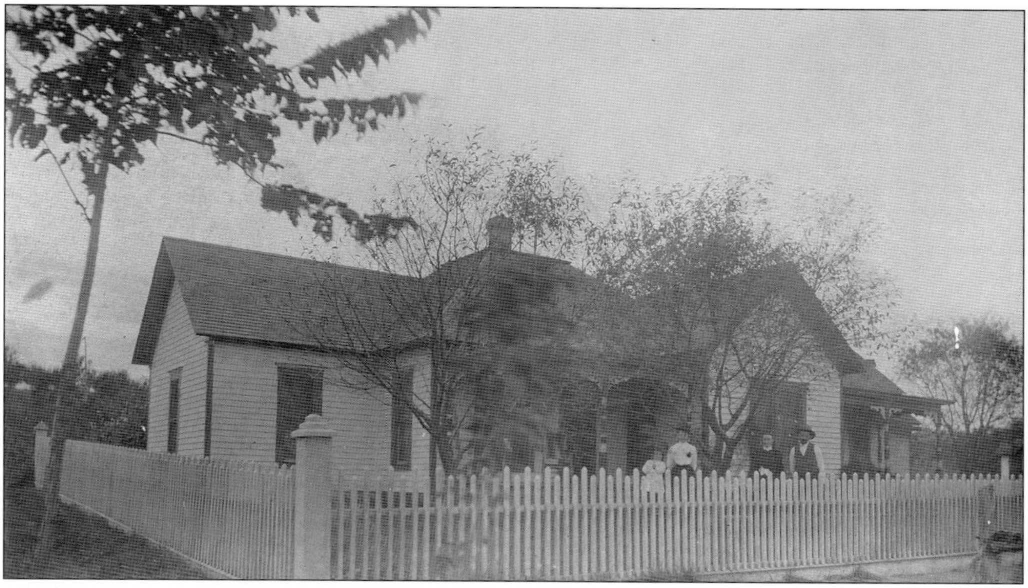

The home of Oscar and Emma Uttvits at the west end of Main Street is seen here around 1906. Standing in front of the house are, from left to right, daughters Laura and Ethel and Emma and Oscar. This home still stands in Westboro. Although Oscar began as a farmer, he later went into the hardware business and was very successful. (Courtesy of Marcia L. Frede.)

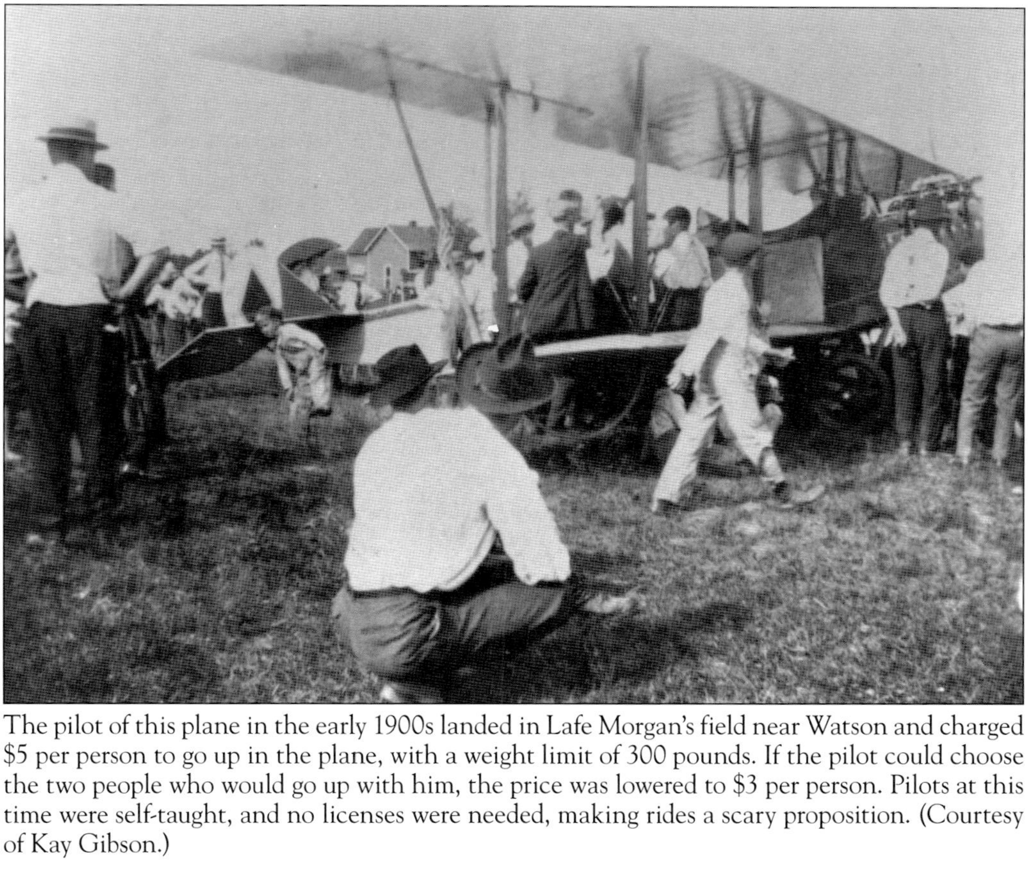

The pilot of this plane in the early 1900s landed in Lafe Morgan's field near Watson and charged $5 per person to go up in the plane, with a weight limit of 300 pounds. If the pilot could choose the two people who would go up with him, the price was lowered to $3 per person. Pilots at this time were self-taught, and no licenses were needed, making rides a scary proposition. (Courtesy of Kay Gibson.)

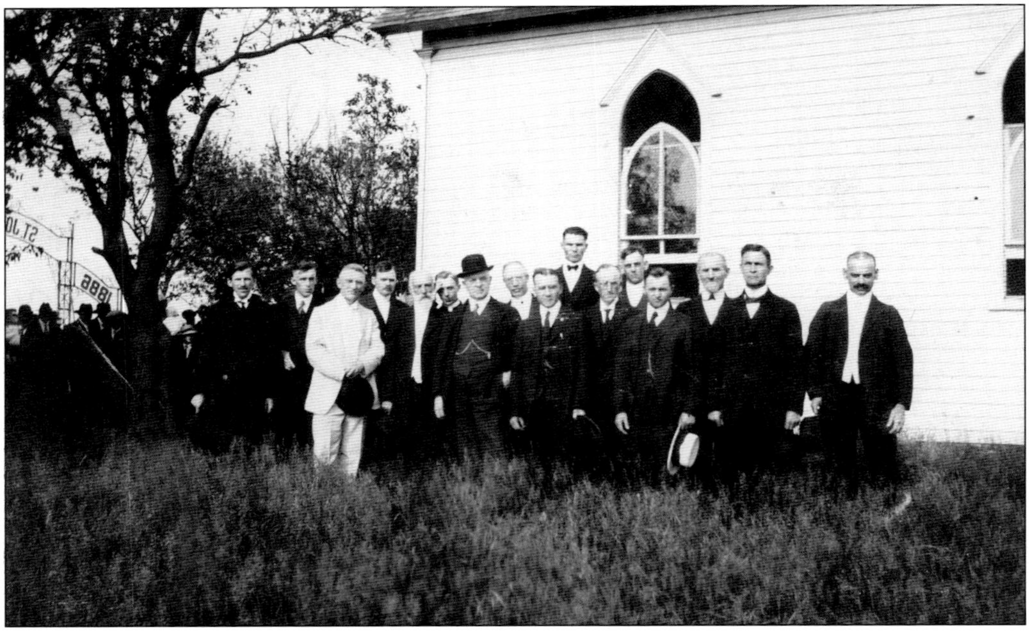

A minister's convention was held in 1926 or 1927 at St. John's Lutheran Church near the Farmer's City Store. F.W. Nolte was the pastor at St. John's at this time and is seen above among a group of men posing for the camera. St. John's was a progressive church that invested $1,120 for the installation and upkeep of the Berlin electrical system, which was built by locals between 1919 and 1921. The system was then sold back to the light company and was one of the first utilities in the area to serve a rural community. The image below is of St. John's Parsonage and Cemetery. (Courtesy of George and Patty Laur.)

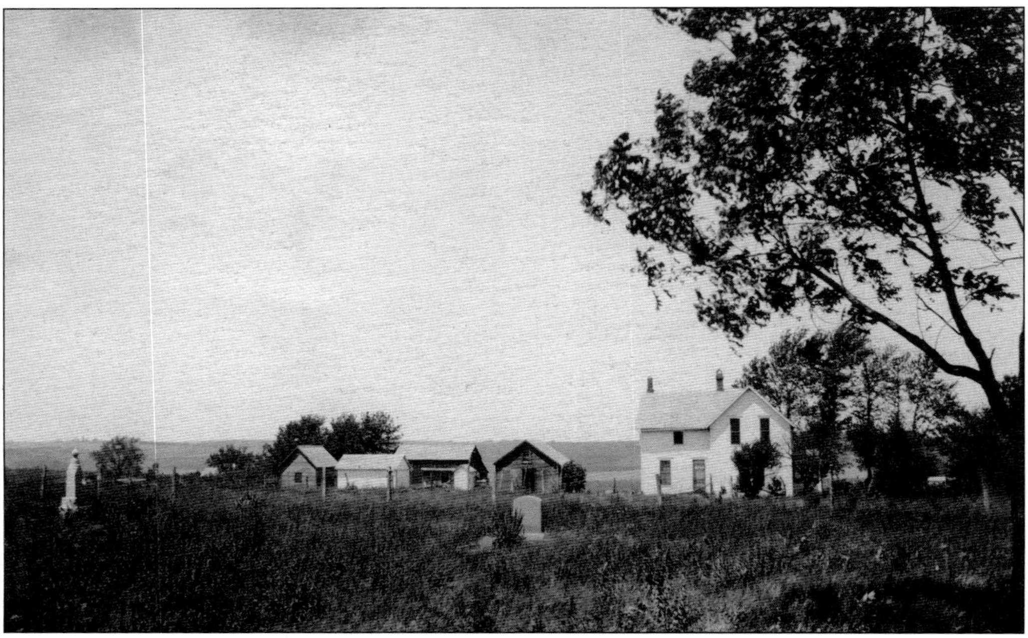

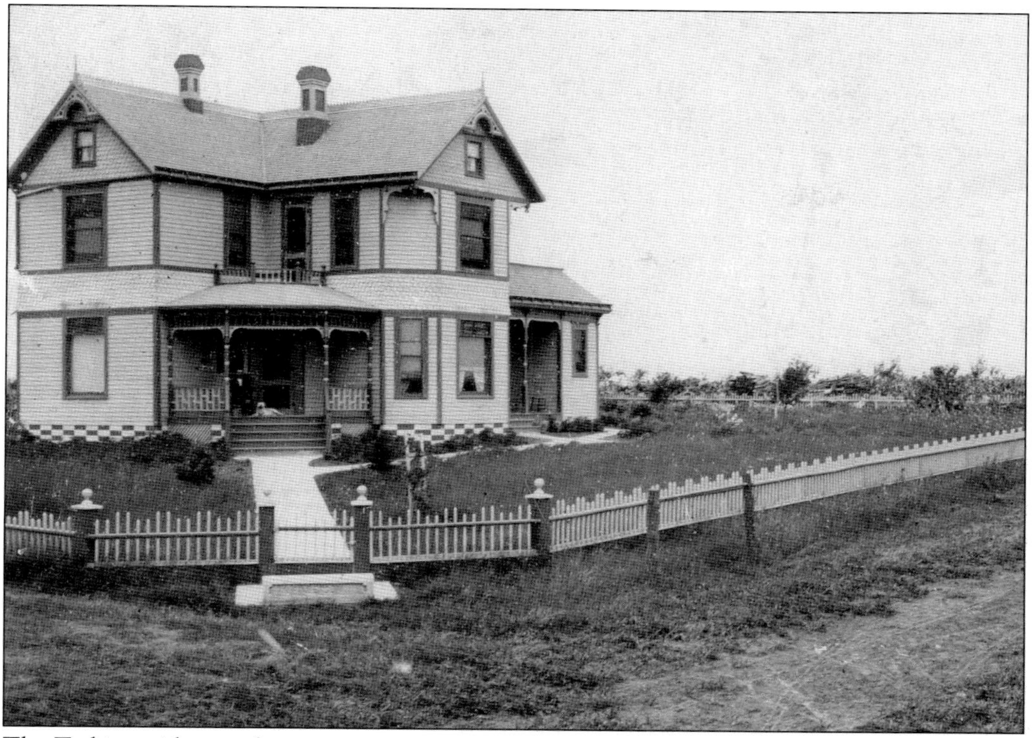

The Tarkio residence of H. Anderson is seen here with its paved sidewalks, stained-glass windows, double chimneys, and picket fence. Fences began to be used in the early 1900s to keep animals, especially cows, out of owners' yards. (Courtesy of Pat Fisher.)

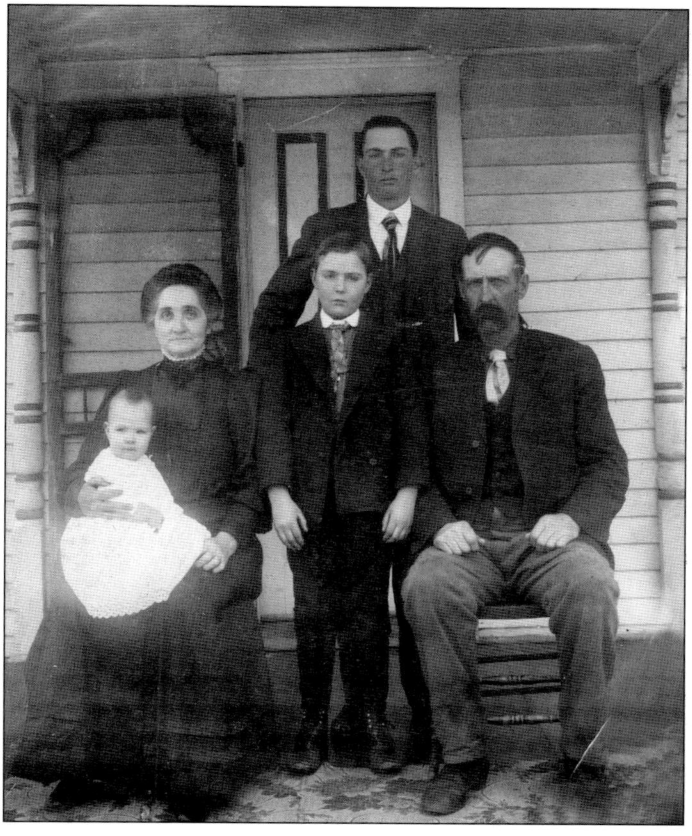

The McDaniel family, who lived near Fairfax a little west of English Grove Cemetery, is seen here on the front porch. They are, from left to right, Emma Katherine (holding baby Mildred), Otto, Fred, and Vernile McDaniel. Mildred is the mother of Maxine Staples, who currently resides on the eastern edge of Atchison County. (Courtesy of Maxine Staples.)

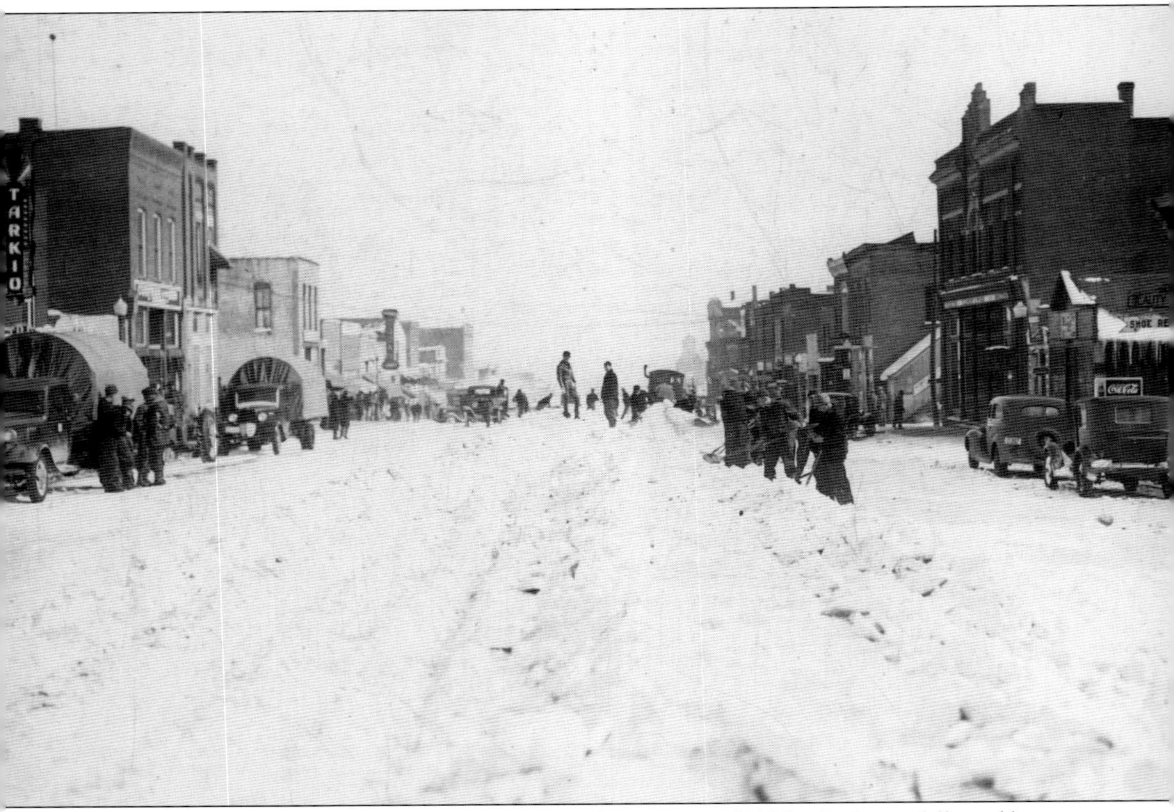

There were many record highs documented in the summer of 1936, which was followed by a severe winter that included this snowstorm on Main Street in Tarkio. The back of this photograph states that 38 inches of snow fell, making roads impassable. (Courtesy of the Atchison County Historical Society.)

While children of the Great Depression never knew any other way of life, adults had experienced the change from the Roaring Twenties to an economy with 25-percent unemployment, many closed banks, and a severe drop in agricultural prices—about 60 percent. When banks closed, many lost their life savings. A happy Maxine Staples is seen here in her baby buggy in 1930. (Courtesy of Maxine Staples.)

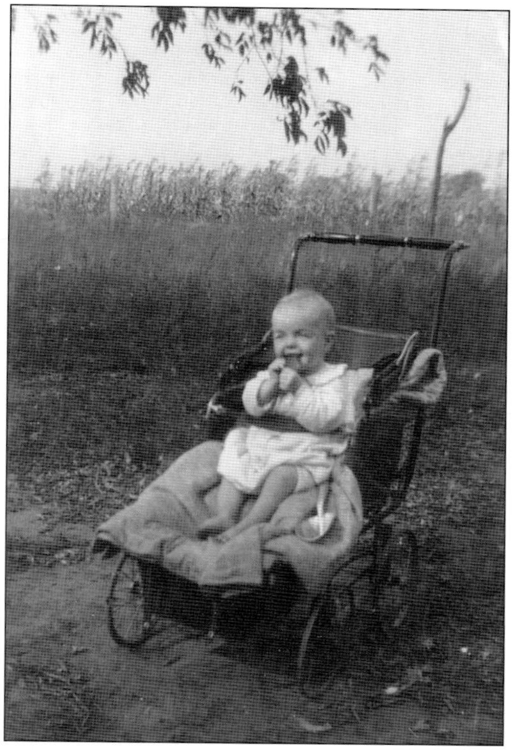

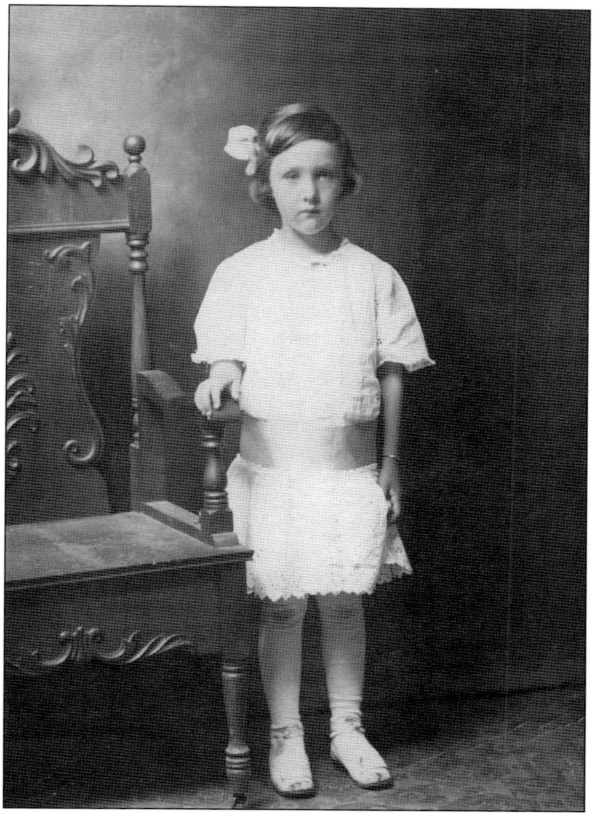

This young lady, Mildred McDaniel, looks melancholy because she was in trouble with her parents. She fell down and stained her stockings on the way to the photographer's studio. She had been so excited to put on her prettiest dress and go to the studio that she started running and tripped. (Courtesy of Maxine Staples.)

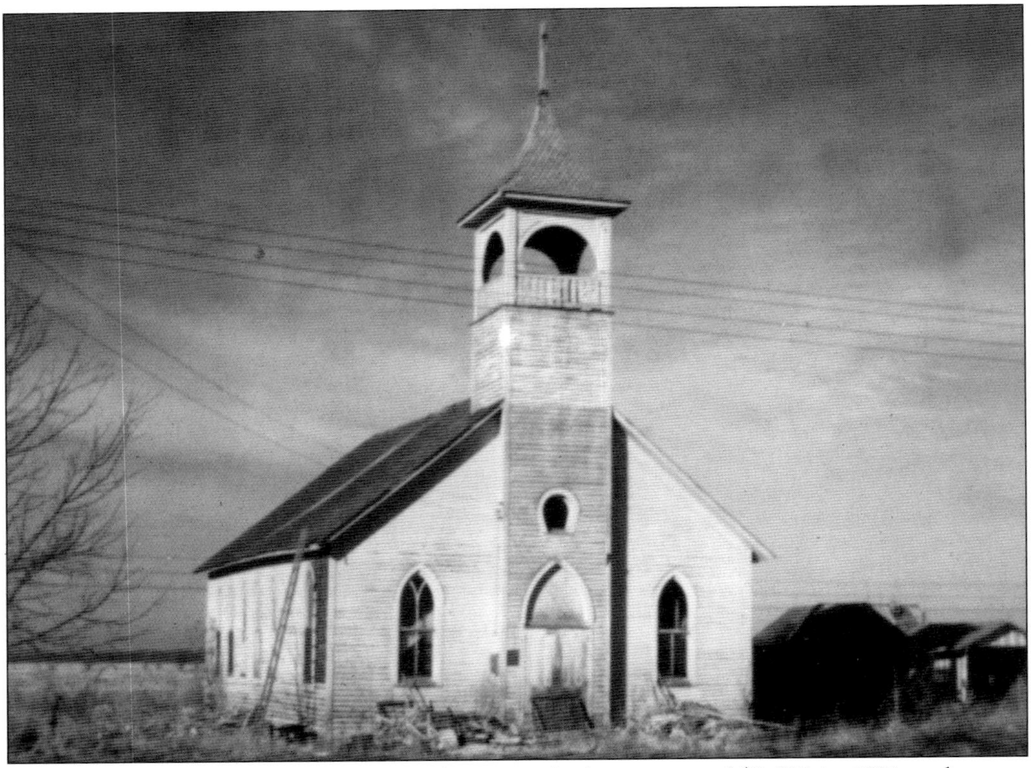

The Catholic Church of Watson, seen here, was built at a cost of $2,500 in 1891 and at one time was used as a school. After it closed, its members were forced to attend Catholic services in Hamburg, Iowa, or Tarkio, Missouri. (Courtesy of Kay Gibson.)

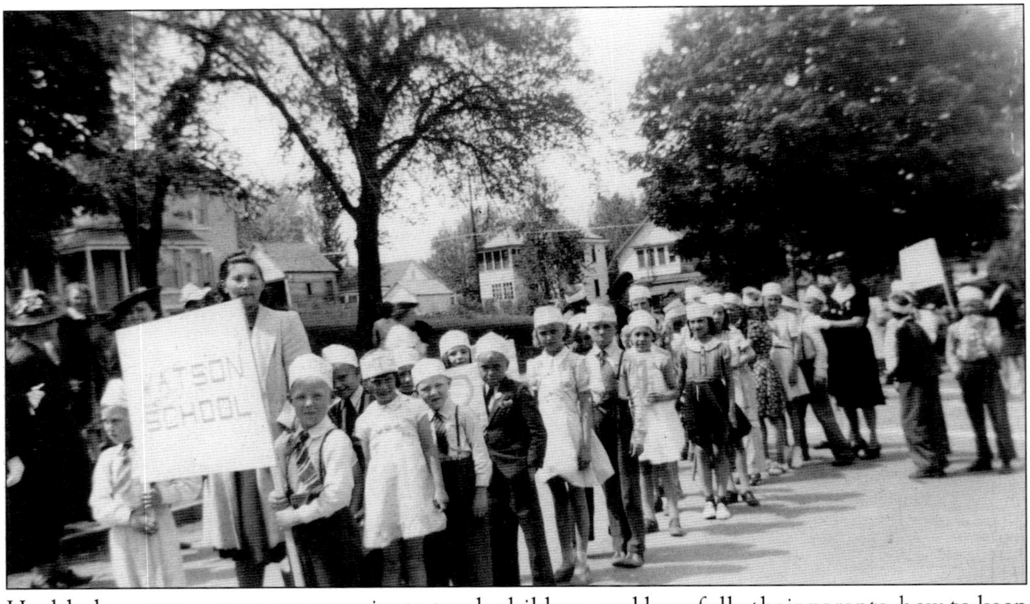

Health days were a great opportunity to teach children, and hopefully their parents, how to keep themselves healthy. This photograph shows a Health Day parade in Tarkio attended by Watson School District students. (Courtesy of Kay Gibson.)

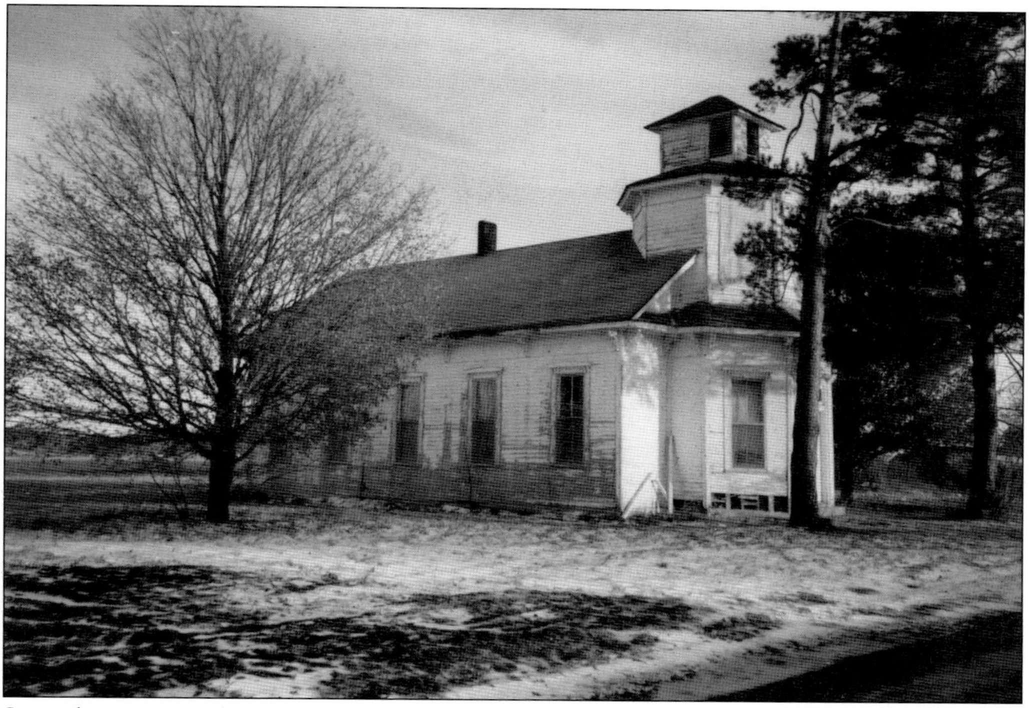

Started in Sonora, the Cumberland Presbyterian Church originally met in a schoolhouse. The church in Watson, seen here, was built in 1869 at a cost of $3,000 with a seating capacity of 500, and membership grew to 175 by 1882. Dr. I.B. Jones was superintendent of the church and oversaw its construction. It later merged with a Methodist church to keep religion flourishing. (Courtesy of Kay Gibson.)

This is the Missionary Baptist Church in Watson, which still stands but is no longer used as a church. The tall steeple was eventually shortened because upkeep was too expensive. (Courtesy of Kay Gibson.)

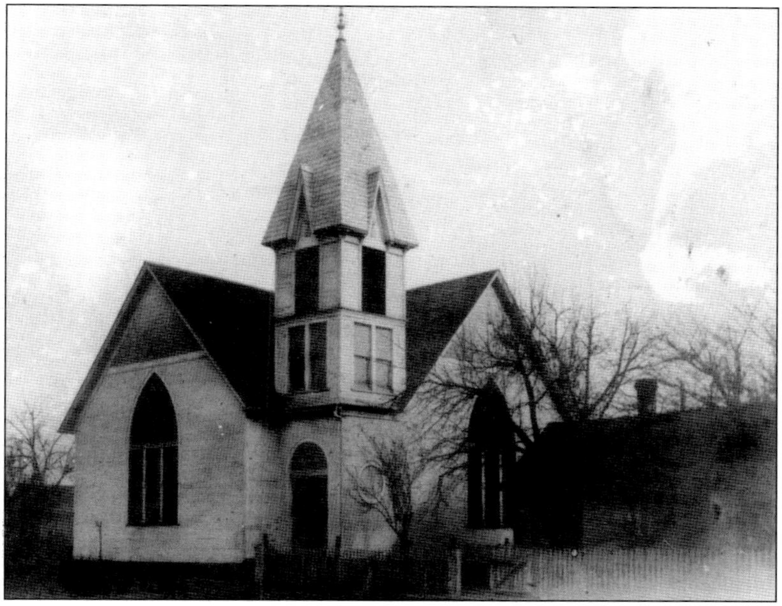

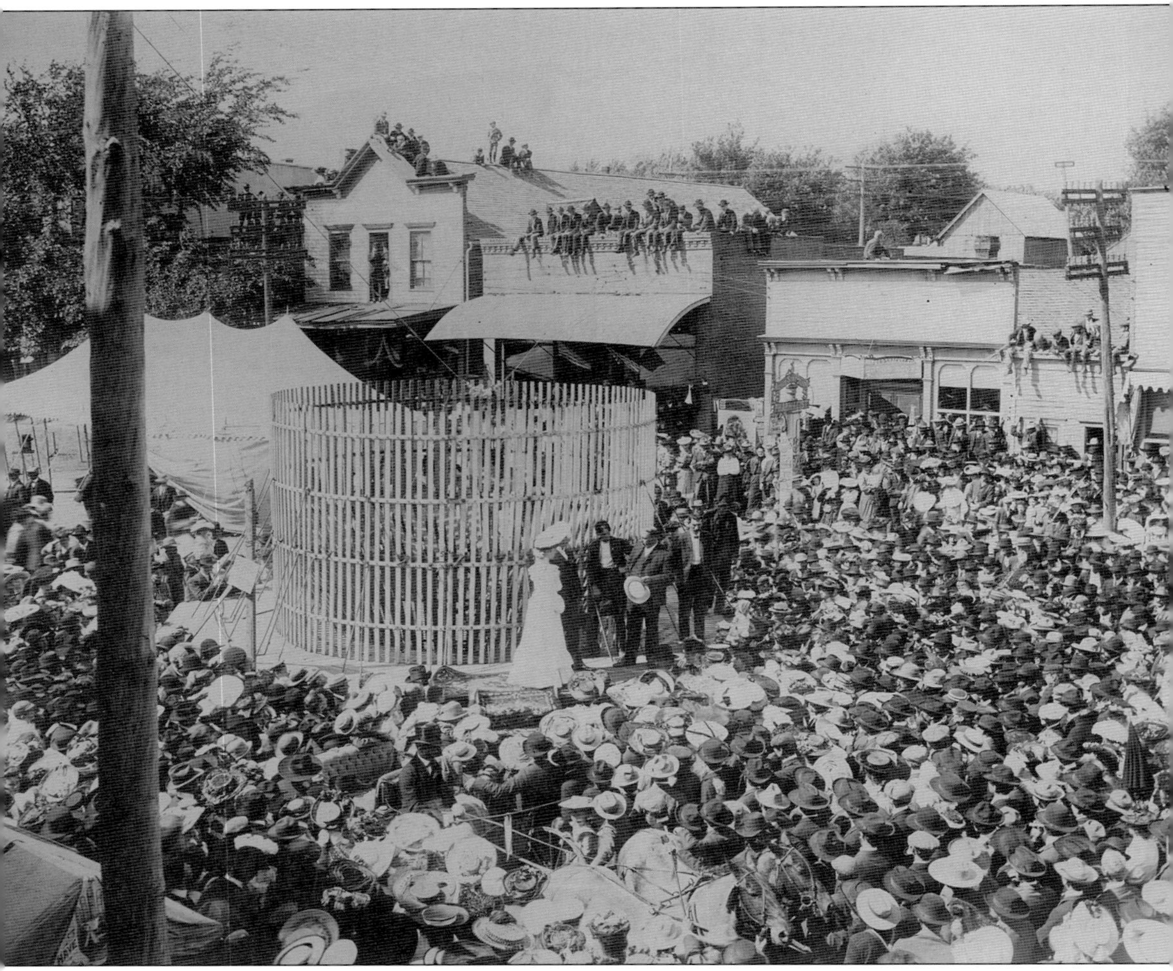

In August 1904, Elizabeth Henshaw married Francis Nuckolls, and they invited everyone in Tarkio to their outdoor wedding. The Nuckolls family came from Virginia and made their mark on the area, with the Nuckolls Addition in Rock Port named after them as one example. Stephen F. Nuckolls helped lay out the town of Nebraska City and in later years moved west and had Nuckolls County, Nebraska, named for him. In 1855 and 1856, another pioneer, Columbus Nuckolls, helped survey the area of Fremont County, Iowa, into what would become Hamburg, Iowa. (Courtesy of the Atchison County Historical Society.)

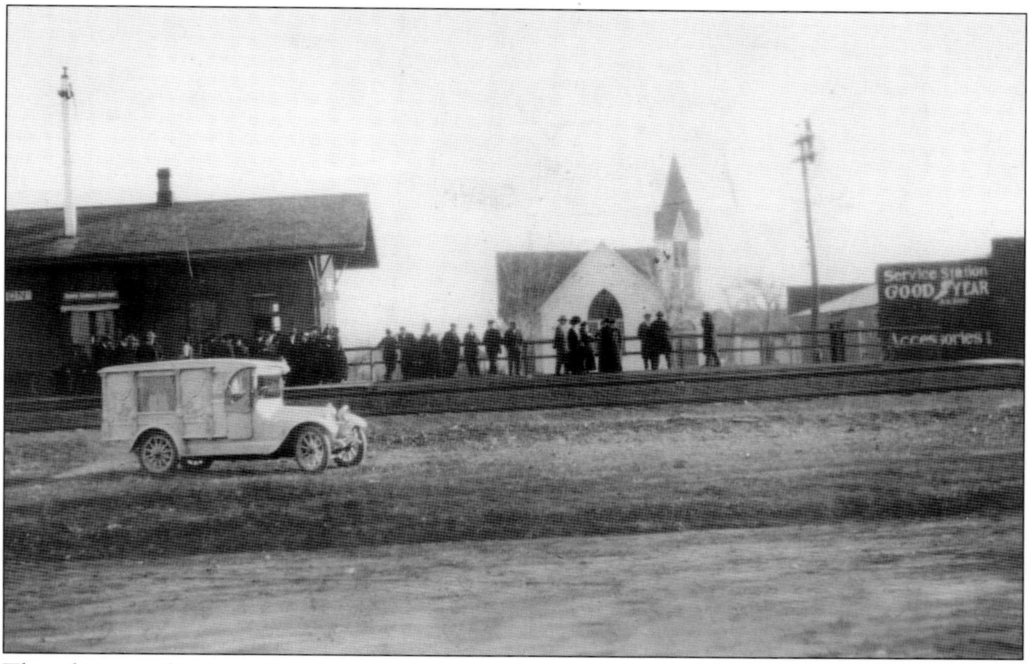

This photograph captures quite an event in northwest Missouri: the first motor-driven hearse to come to Watson and meet the train to pick up the deceased. The church behind the hearse is the Missionary Baptist Church. (Courtesy of Kay Gibson.)

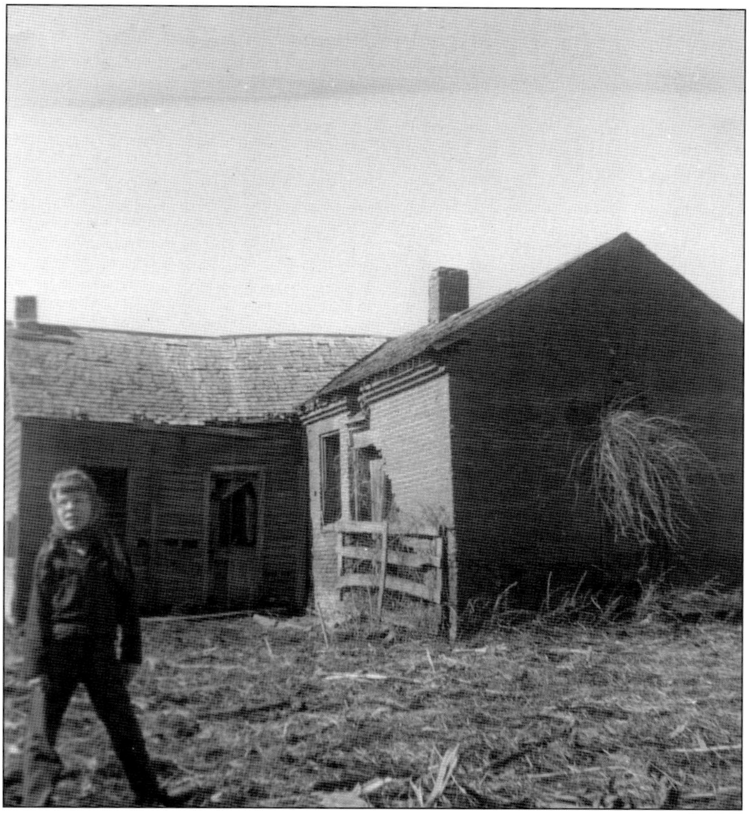

Sonora, one of the first towns in Atchison County, was on the Missouri River. Today, only a few foundations remain. Kay Gibson is seen here in front of the last house to be torn down. When the railroad went through nearby Watson, it meant the end for Sonora. The once-bustling town supplied wood and other necessities to steamboats that docked there. Frequent flooding was also a factor in its demise. (Courtesy of Kay Gibson.)

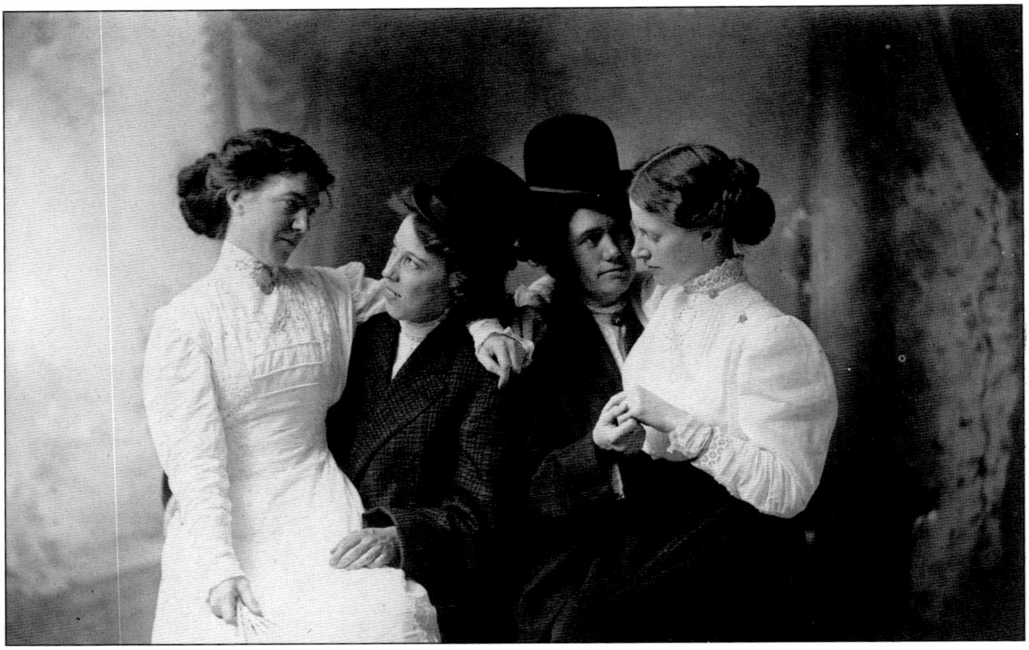

In a time when Victorian-era morals were still common, the parents and friends of these women might have been shocked by this photograph. Clowning around for the photographer, these four ladies dressed up as couples. (Courtesy of the Atchison County Historical Society.)

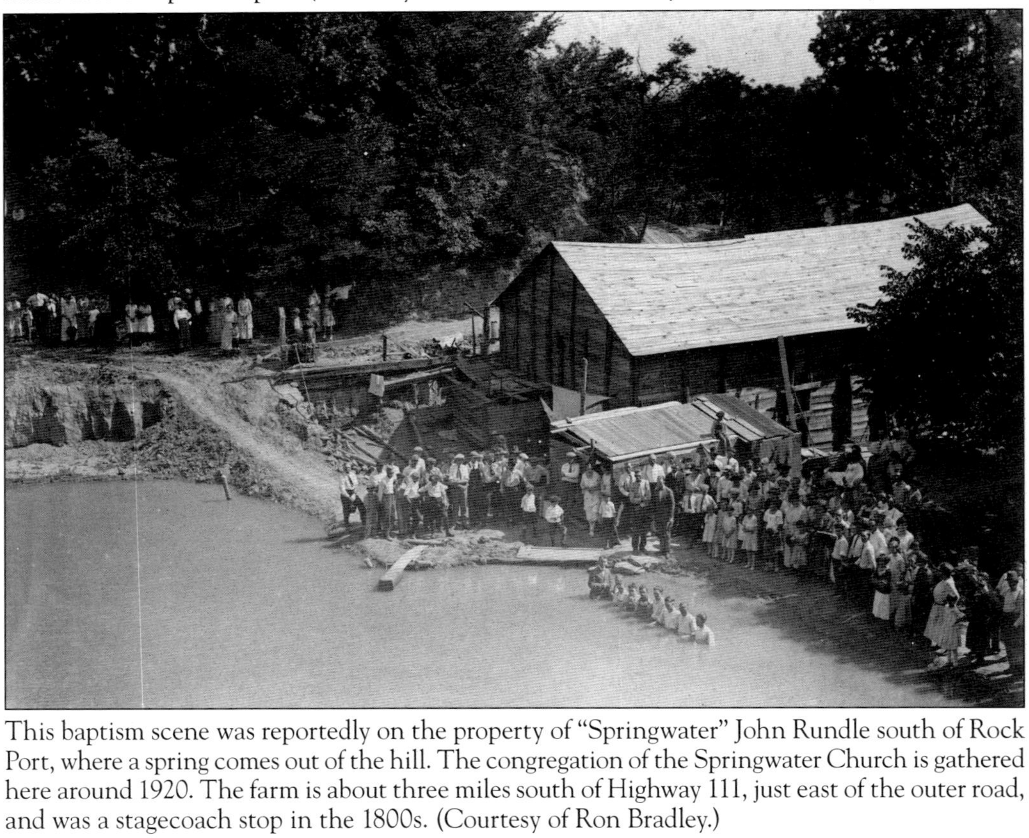

This baptism scene was reportedly on the property of "Springwater" John Rundle south of Rock Port, where a spring comes out of the hill. The congregation of the Springwater Church is gathered here around 1920. The farm is about three miles south of Highway 111, just east of the outer road, and was a stagecoach stop in the 1800s. (Courtesy of Ron Bradley.)

Six

Relaxation

One story goes that when an old woman was asked what families in the 1930s did for fun or entertainment, she replied, "Nothing, we just worked." While it is true that there was much more work in those days, there was also at least some time for rest and relaxation. There were dances, festivals, outdoor weddings, and many picnics served under the shade of oak trees. What these people lacked monetarily they made up in friendship, creativity, and goodwill.

A popular activity of the era was the Chautauqua, a national phenomenon that began in southwest New York on Chautauqua Lake in the late 1800s. Culture and entertainment were offered for the whole family in the form of singing, lectures, preachers, teachers, musicians, and politicians. By the height of the movement's popularity in the 1920s, there were many permanent Chautauquas within a short distance of cities with good rail service; however, in a short time, many Chautauqua circuits sprang up and circulated all over the country. While many Chautauquas resembled summer school and were organized to educate, some had nondenominational religious leanings and others were blatantly church-oriented.

In addition to the Chautauqua, organizations for women and men abounded. For the men, there were the Masons and Shriners, the American Legion, Boy Scouts, and the Lions Club, among many others. For the ladies, there was the American Legion Auxiliary, Atchison County Democratic (or Republican) Women, Girl Scouts, Business and Professional Women's League, the Order of Eastern Star, communities garden clubs, and many sororities. All of these organizations gathered for friendship and camaraderie, but their serious sides usually involved doing good for those less fortunate.

BOATING AND FISHING.

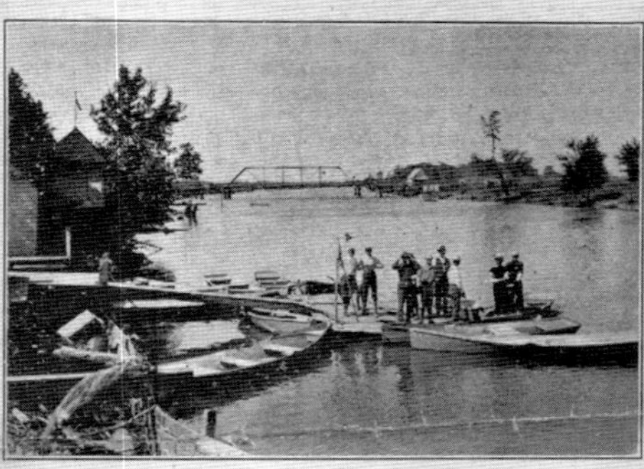

"The Langdon" offers special attractions for pleasure parties. Fine lawn and shade trees. Plenty of good boats, minnows and fishing tackle always on hand.

Address,

R. A. DITTMAR, Proprietor,

LANGDON, MO.

THE LANGDON

FAMOUS FISHING RESORT

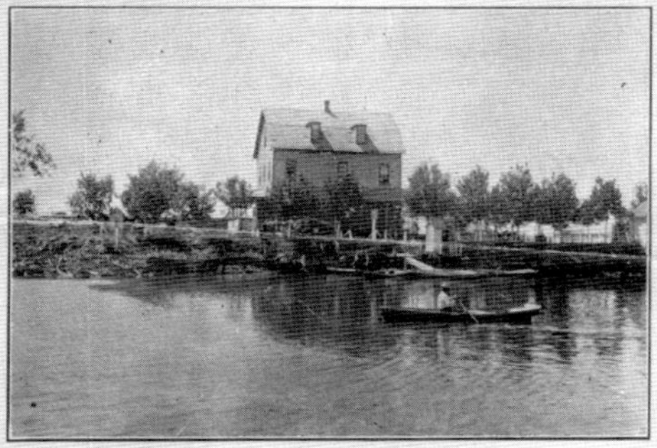

FIRST-CLASS ACCOMMODATIONS.

SPECIAL RATES FOR FISHERMEN.

For Terms and Information Address,

R. A. DITTMAR, Proprietor,

LANGDON, MO.

For swimming, fishing, or spending a relaxing weekend in the shade, the Langdon Resort was the place to be around 1900. The railroad was close by, with both north-south and east-west connections, making it ideal for out-of-town guests and locals alike. The Missouri Conservation Department stocked the river with many types of fish even though it was only a short distance downstream to the Missouri River. (Both, courtesy of Hon. Corey Herron.)

GAME FISH ABOUND.

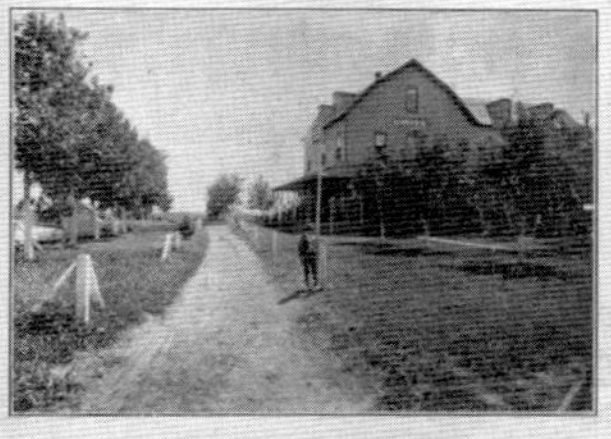

"The Langdon" is beautifuly situated at Langdon, Mo., on the Nishnabotna river, midway between St. Joseph and Council Bluffs on the Main line of the Burlington, is the best as well as the most accessible fishing resort in the middle West. The Nishnabotna river is kept fully stocked with Black Bass, Crappy and Pike by the Missouri State Fish Commission.

A GOOD TABLE.

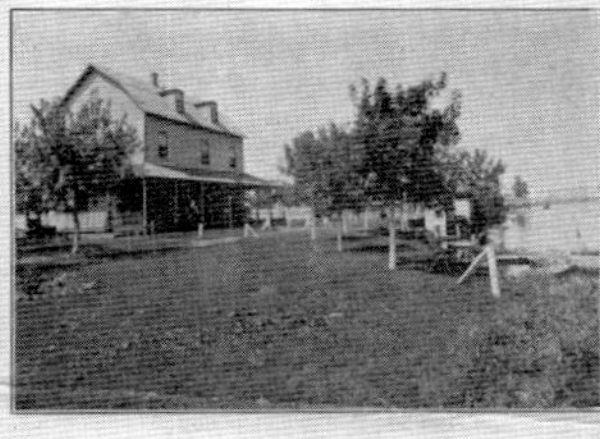

The Burlington Route through trains from St. Paul to Kansas City, and from Omaha to St. Louis, stop at "The Langdon" for meals, which is sufficient evidence of the quality of the fare provided. The accommodations are first-class in every respect. And the proprietor is noted for his efficiency in providing for the comfort of his guests.

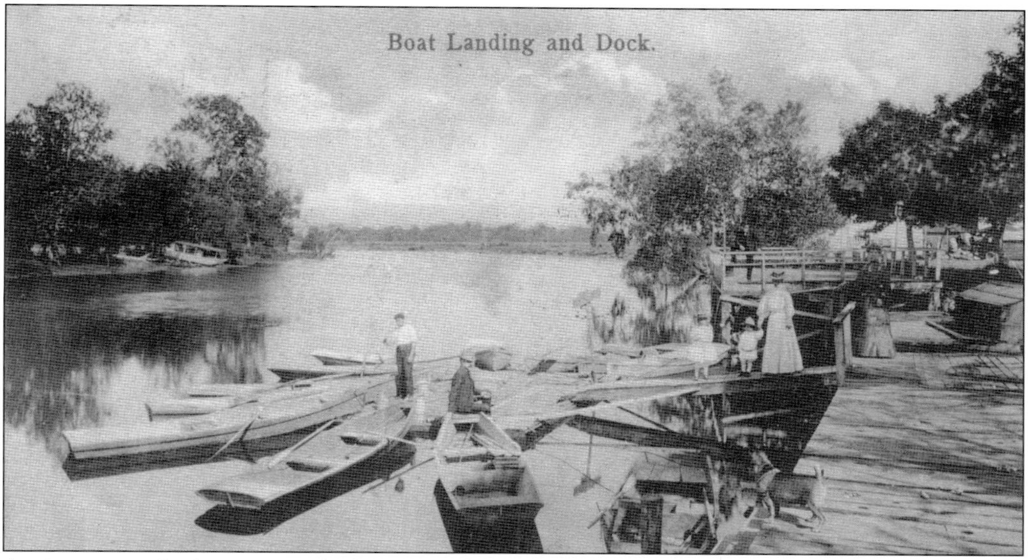

As Americans had more time for leisure in the early 1900s, Langdon Resort was a welcome respite for people from Kansas, Nebraska, Iowa, and Missouri, who could come to the resort and enjoy fishing, swimming, boating, and being pampered at the hotel and restaurant. The Langdon Resort is seen here when J.C. Stone was the proprietor. (Courtesy of Hon. Corey Herron.)

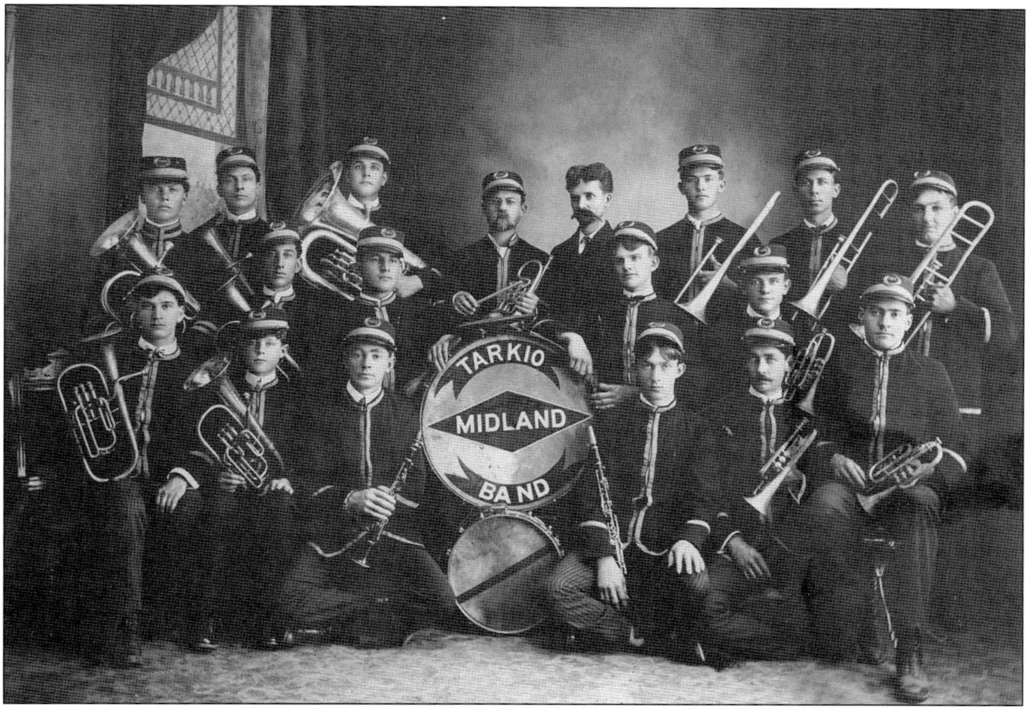

The Tarkio Midland Band represented Tarkio and Midland Manufacturing Co., which made two-bottom plows and employed about 140 people. Tarkio Manufacturing was another enterprise of David Rankin and supplied many farmers with modern equipment to help them cut down on the amount of labor needed in farming. Rankin was a true believer in reducing the costs of production and was quoted as saying that anyone in business has that as their goal. The two-bottom plow helped the farmer be more profitable. (Courtesy of the Atchison County Historical Society.)

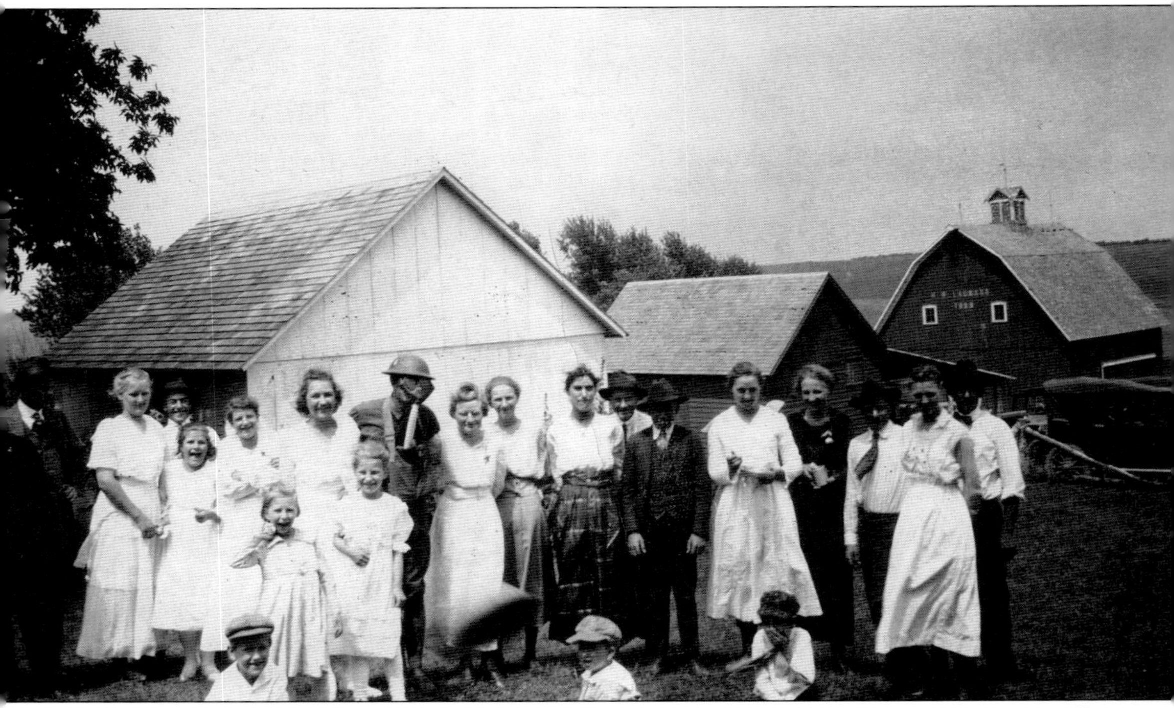

These family and friends get together around the time of World War I on the farm of H.W. "Billy" Laumann. Laumann was born in 1858 in Hanford, Germany, and married Marie Louisa Kemper in 1884; they had five children. Laumann paid $12.50 per acre for 120 acres of land just north of St. John's Lutheran Church. Note that the barn displays, "H.W. Laumann, 1883." (Courtesy of Phil and Meta Hull.)

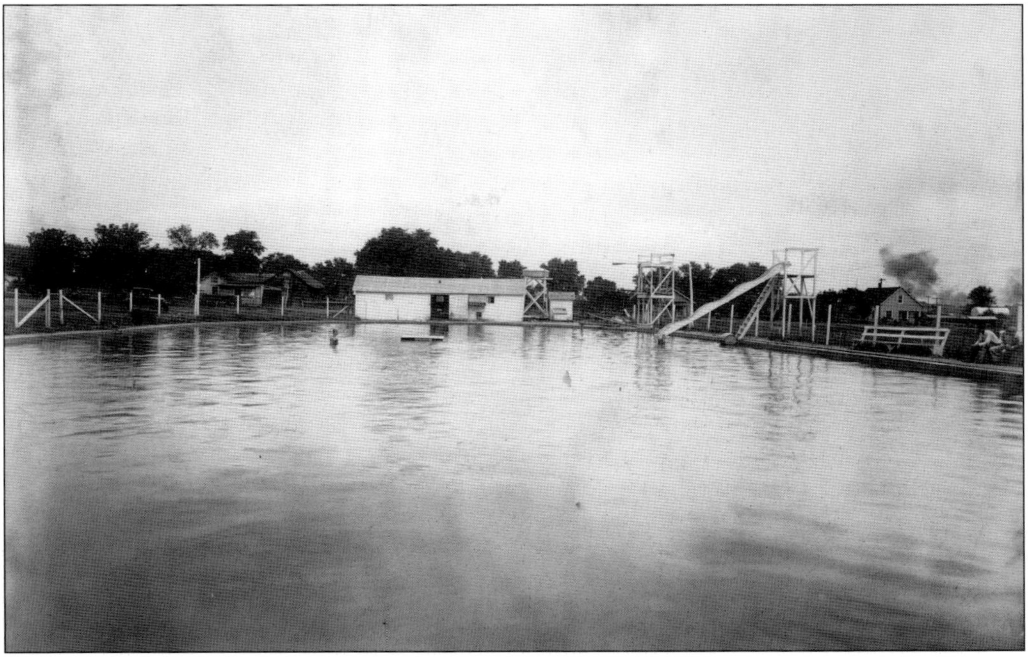

The first swimming pool in Tarkio, seen here around 1900, was quite popular with local residents, as people did not travel very far from home in those days and few had air-conditioning. The pool was located north of the present-day rodeo grounds. (Courtesy of the Atchison County Historical Society.)

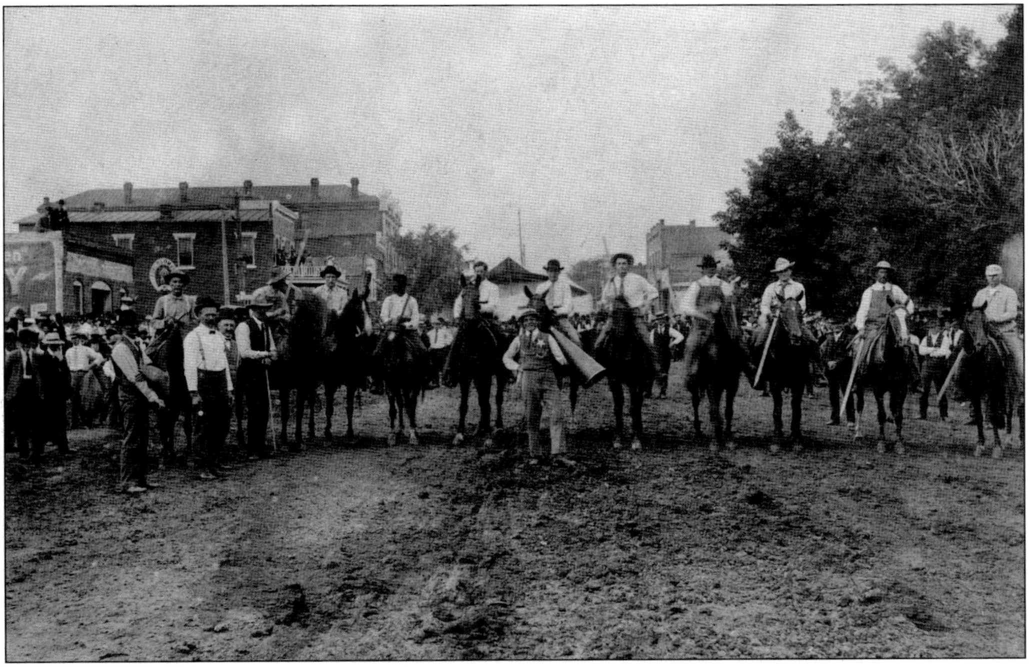

Before a horse race in Tarkio around 1900, the judge of it holds a megaphone and wears a star on his chest. The riders are not smiling, however, as a contest with their prized horses was serious business. Only one rider used a riding crop, while most used a long piece of wood to spur their horses along. (Courtesy of the Atchison County Historical Society.)

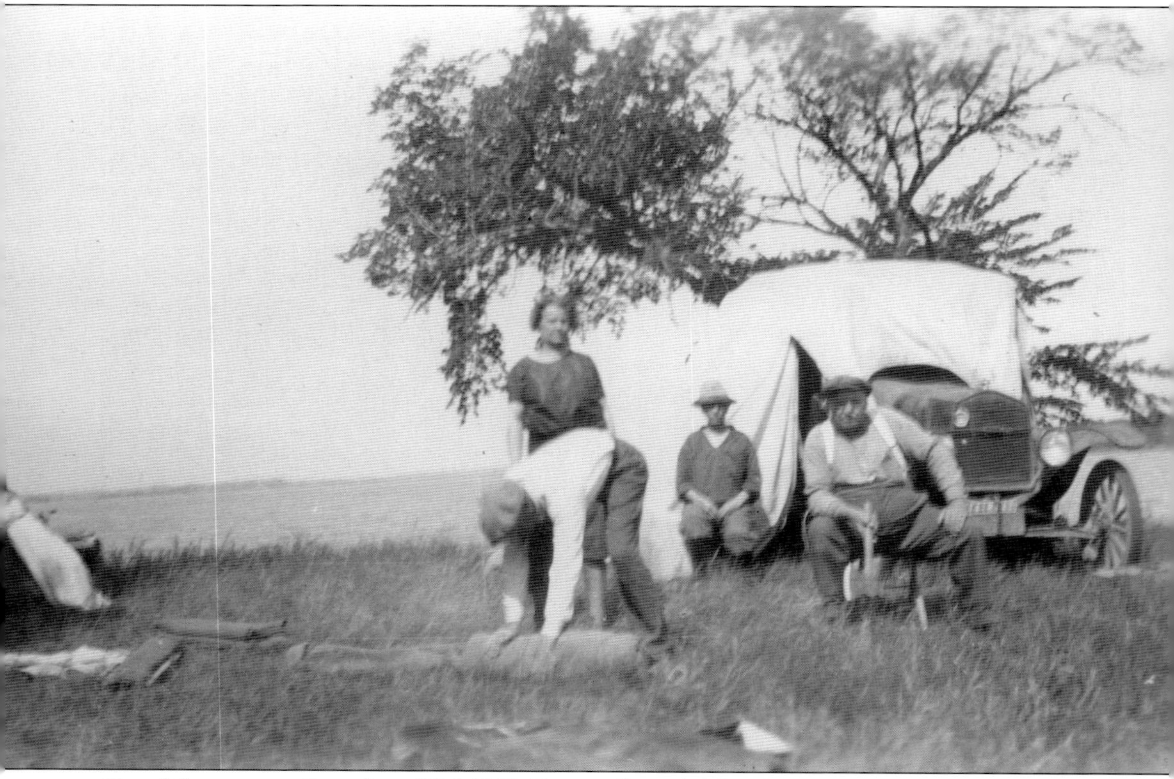

On a fishing trip to Canada in 1925, H.H. Harmes (far right), his daughter Mary (sitting, background), and their best friends, L.R. (leaning forward in foreground) and Pearl Scott (standing behind L.R.), break camp. A trip to Canada in the 1920s was a major undertaking—and one that few would attempt—as roads were still mostly dirt and gravel. Although not fancy, the tarp over the car provided privacy and protection from the elements. (Courtesy of Betty Wennihan.)

Mary Harmes is seen with her catch on a fishing trip to Canada in 1925. Mary and her sisters, the children of H.H. Harmes, were not given middle names, just letters, much like future president Harry S. Truman, whose middle initial did not stand for anything. (Courtesy of Betty Wennihan.)

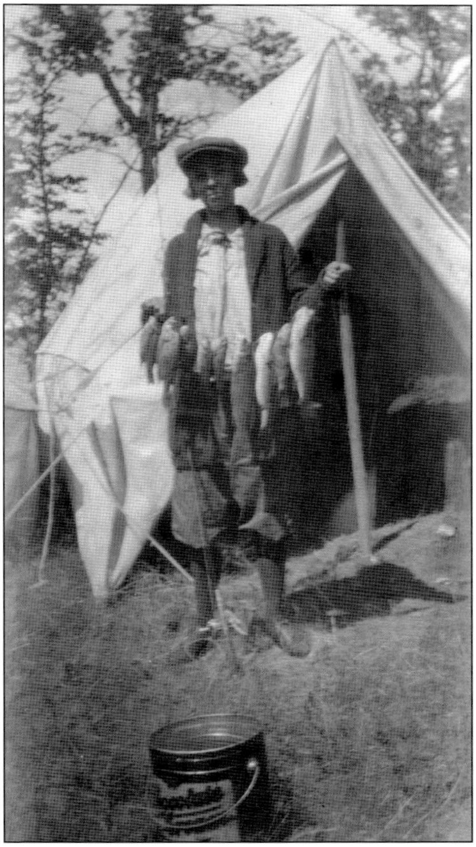

This horse, King, seen around 1925, was very aggressive and would bite those who got too close. Both the owner, H.H. Harmes of English Grove, and the horse look very proud in this photograph. (Courtesy of Betty Wennihan.)

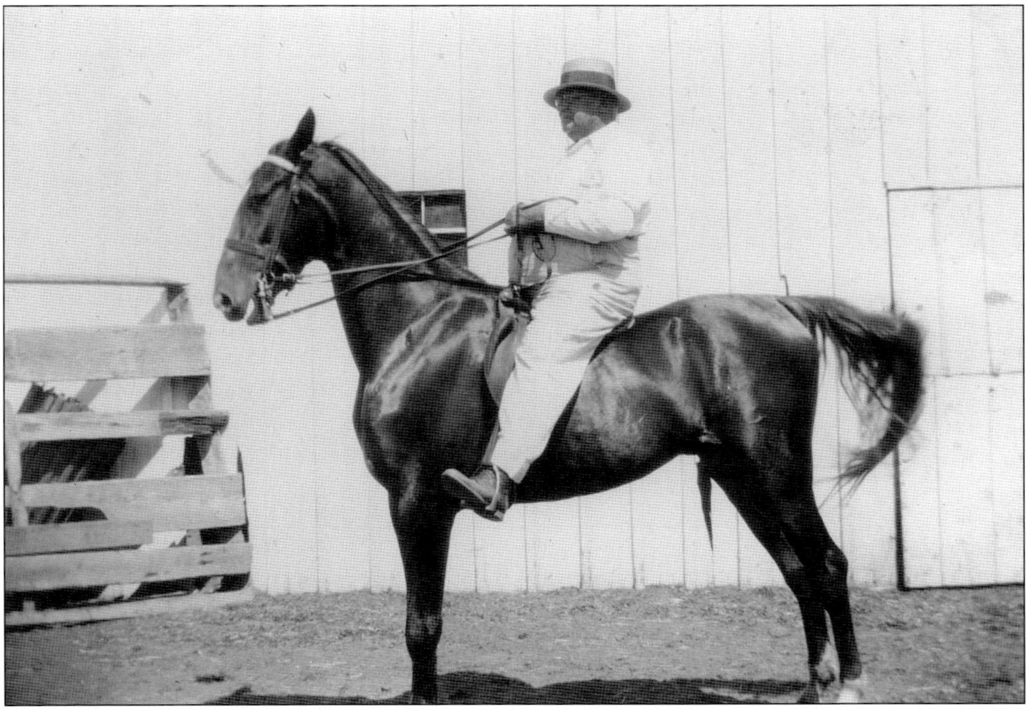

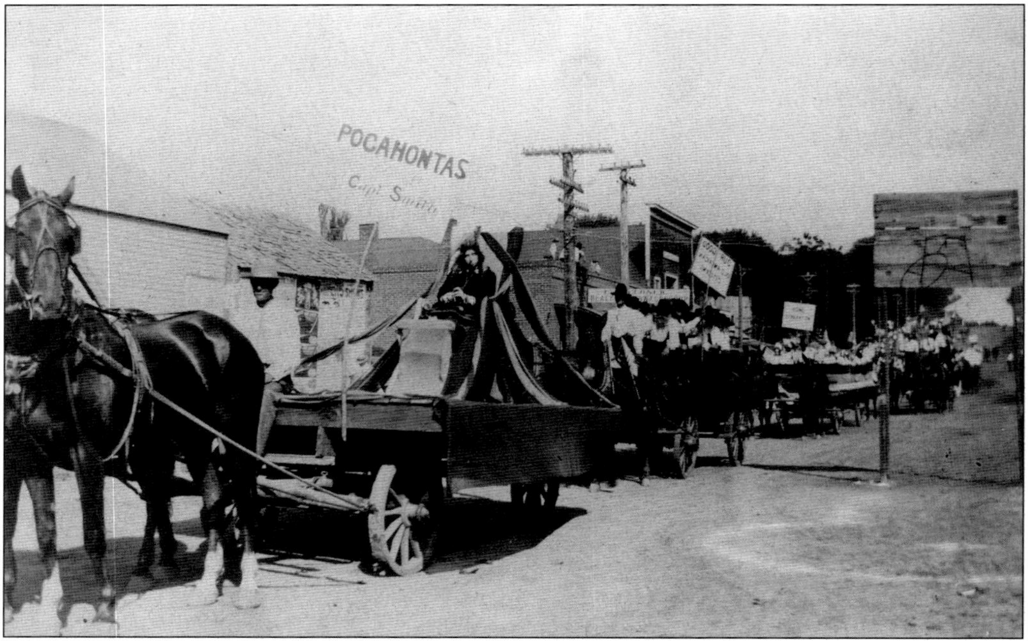

The 1910 Fairfax parade saw Flossie Price, who later married Merve Mann, chosen to represent Pocahontas. The Fairfax celebration has been going on for many years and involves almost all the residents of Fairfax and many from the surrounding communities. Today, food, crafts, and games are enjoyed, and churches and civic groups such as the Masons, Kiwanis, and the Optimists all set up booths. (Courtesy of Betty Wennihan.)

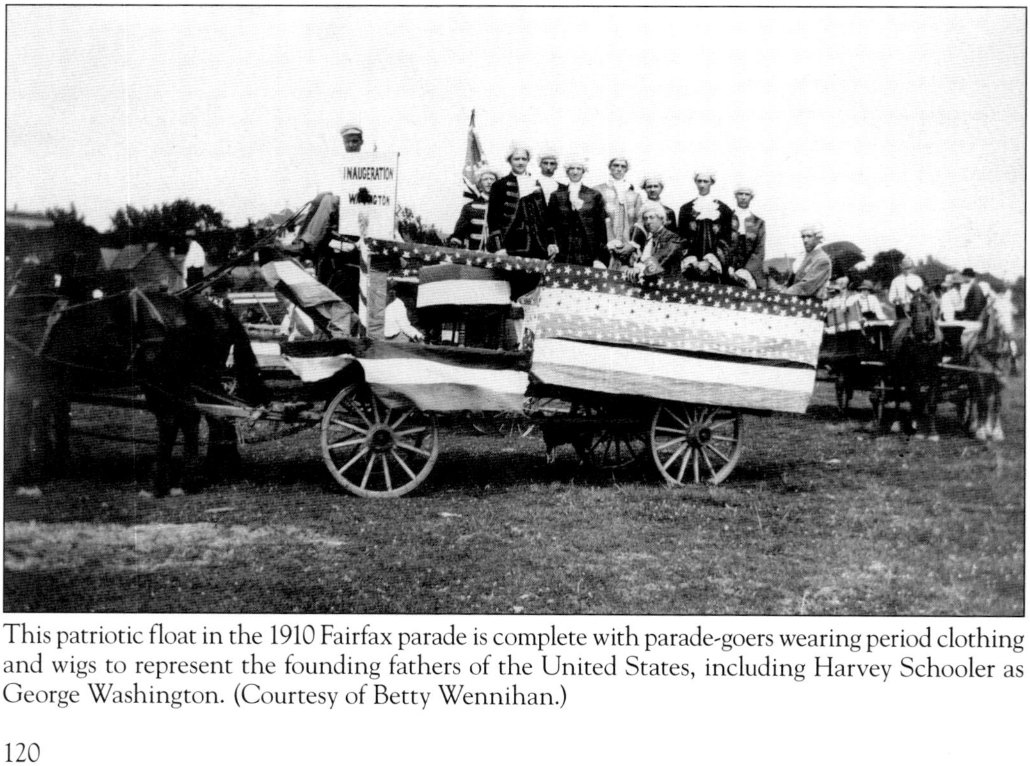

This patriotic float in the 1910 Fairfax parade is complete with parade-goers wearing period clothing and wigs to represent the founding fathers of the United States, including Harvey Schooler as George Washington. (Courtesy of Betty Wennihan.)

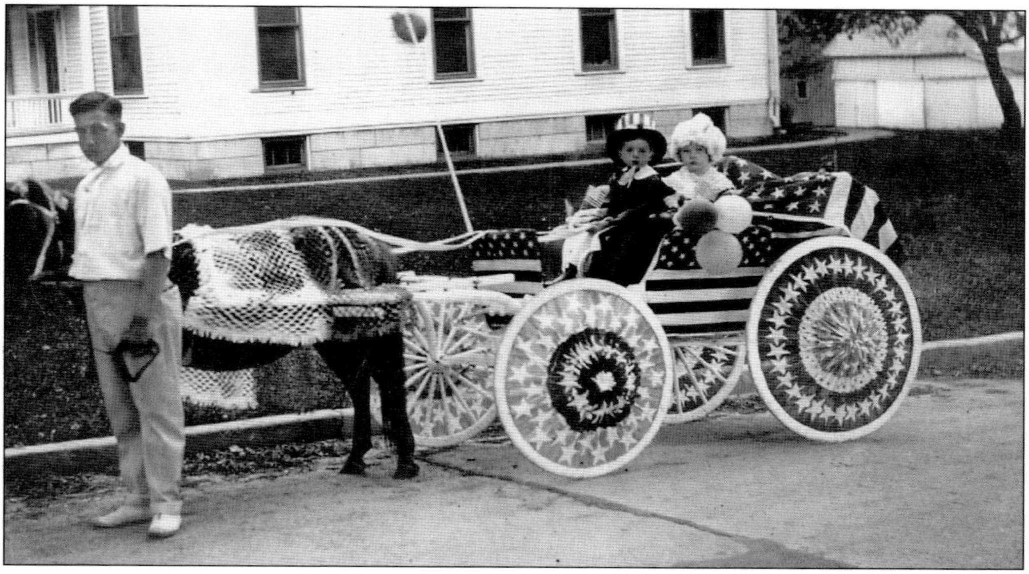

The two children in this buggy, cousins Robert A. "Bob" Rankin and Grace Elizabeth Giffen, pose as Uncle Sam and Betsy Ross for the 1916 Fourth of July parade. Rankin attended Tarkio College and graduated in 1935. He and his wife, Florence Shaw Lorimer, were married and lived in Colorado for seven years before moving back to Tarkio. Rankin was very active in the community and the state and was on state and national livestock boards. They had one daughter, Sarah, who was born in 1938 and later married William Elam. (Courtesy of the Atchison County Historical Society.)

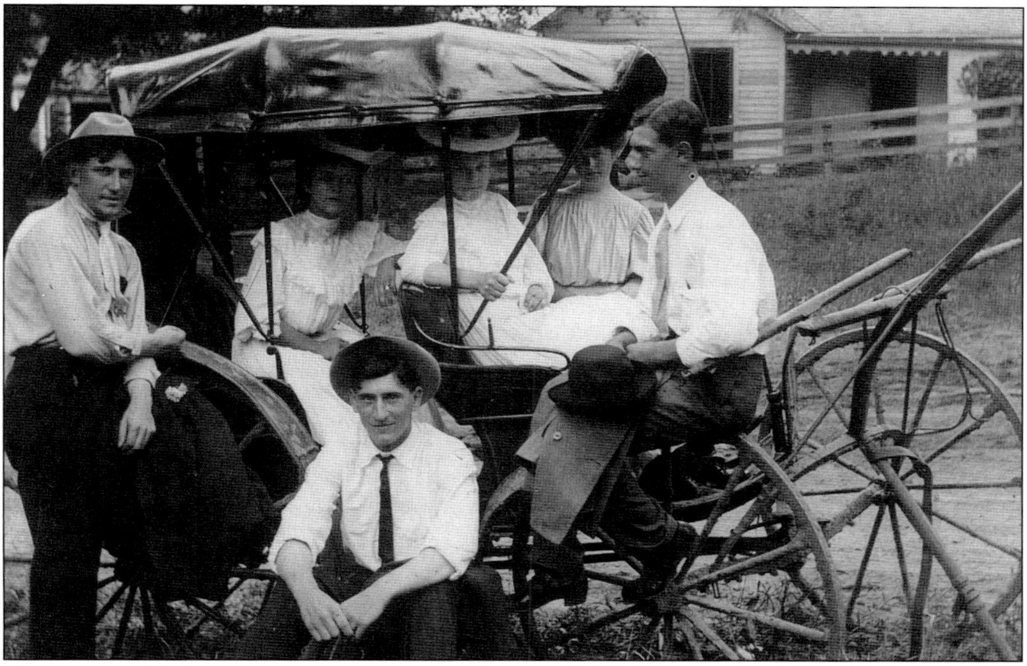

These young adults are about to attend the Fairfax parade in 1906, with the women wearing hats and long dresses and the men wearing ties. Many people could afford a two-wheeled buggy by this time, while the more well-off could afford a four-wheel buggy. (Courtesy of Betty Wennihan.)

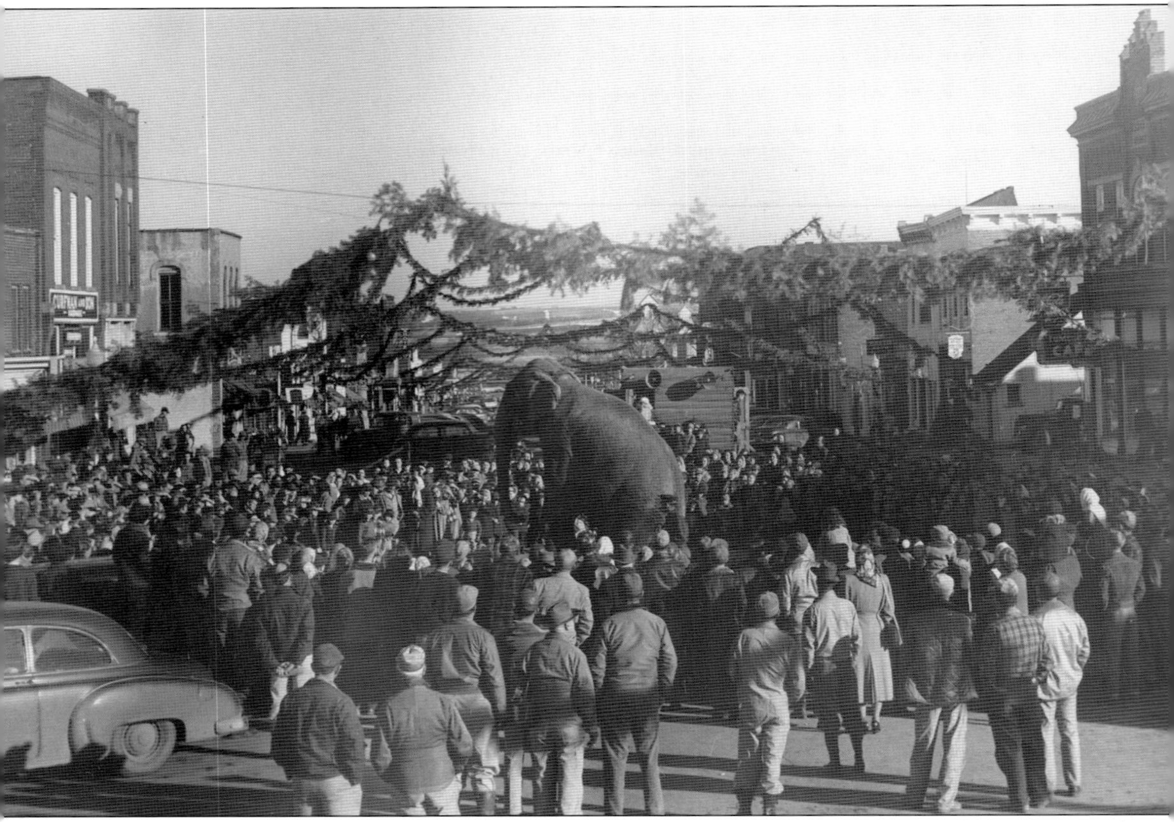

At Christmastime in Tarkio, Santa and an elephant came to celebrate in front of Curfman's and Sons Hardware (left) on Main Street. Curfman's was well known in Tarkio for 94 of city's first 100 years. The store was established in 1881, and owner Amon Albert Curfman was a town trustee. His son Ardery took over the business, raised cattle, and was a landowner in the area. (Courtesy of the Atchison County Historical Society.)

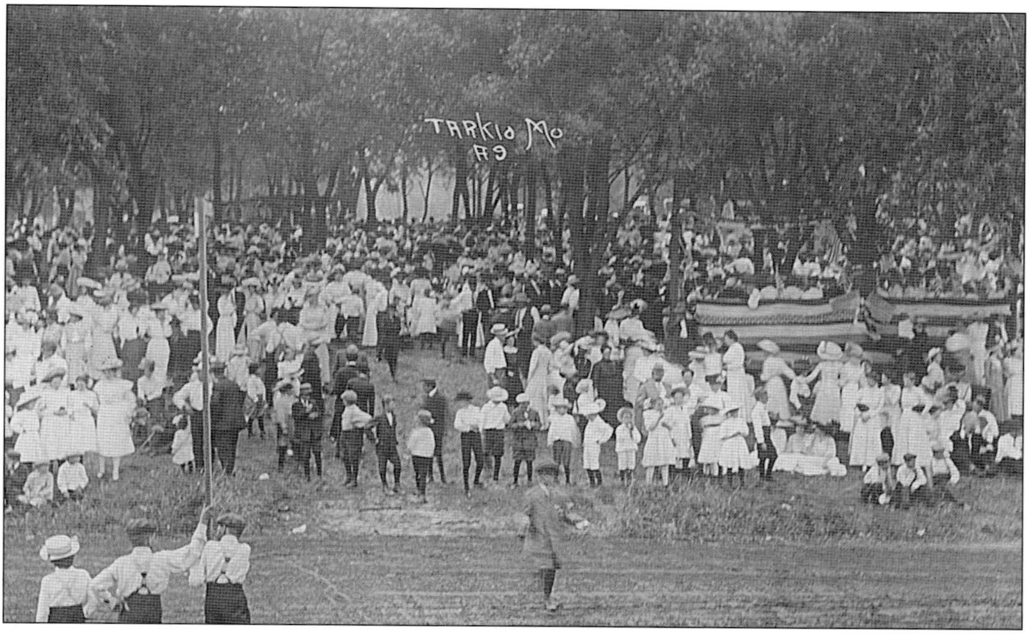

This Chautauqua was held in Tarkio in 1917 in the north city park, with horseless carriages in the background. The Chautauqua was a chance for people throughout the United States to experience lectures, the arts, religious speakers, and music over a period of three to seven days. It was also a chance to see neighbors and catch up on local news in a shady, cool place. (Both, courtesy of the Atchison County Historical Society.)

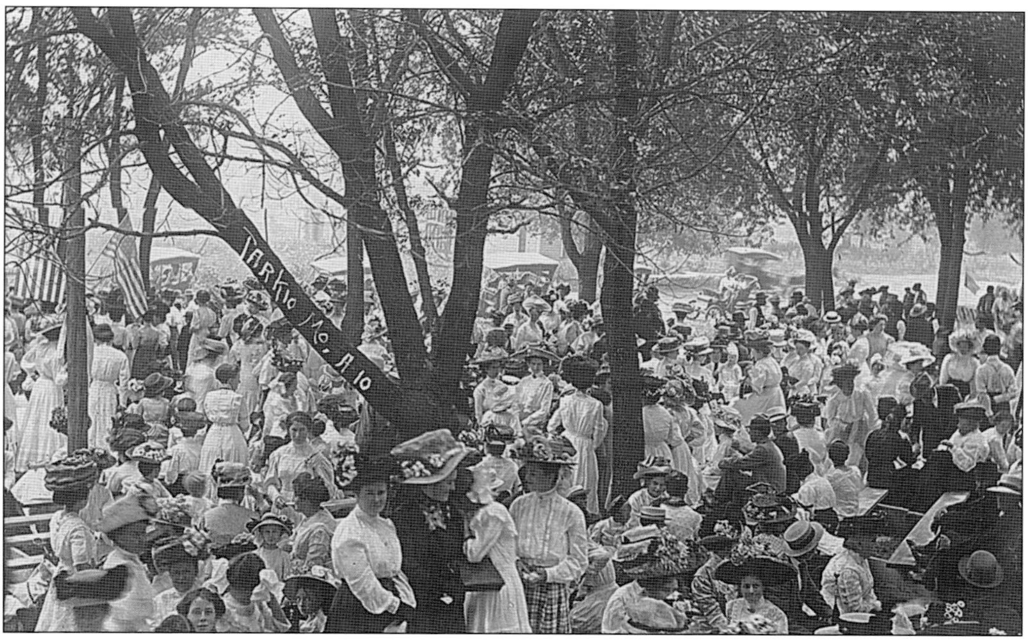

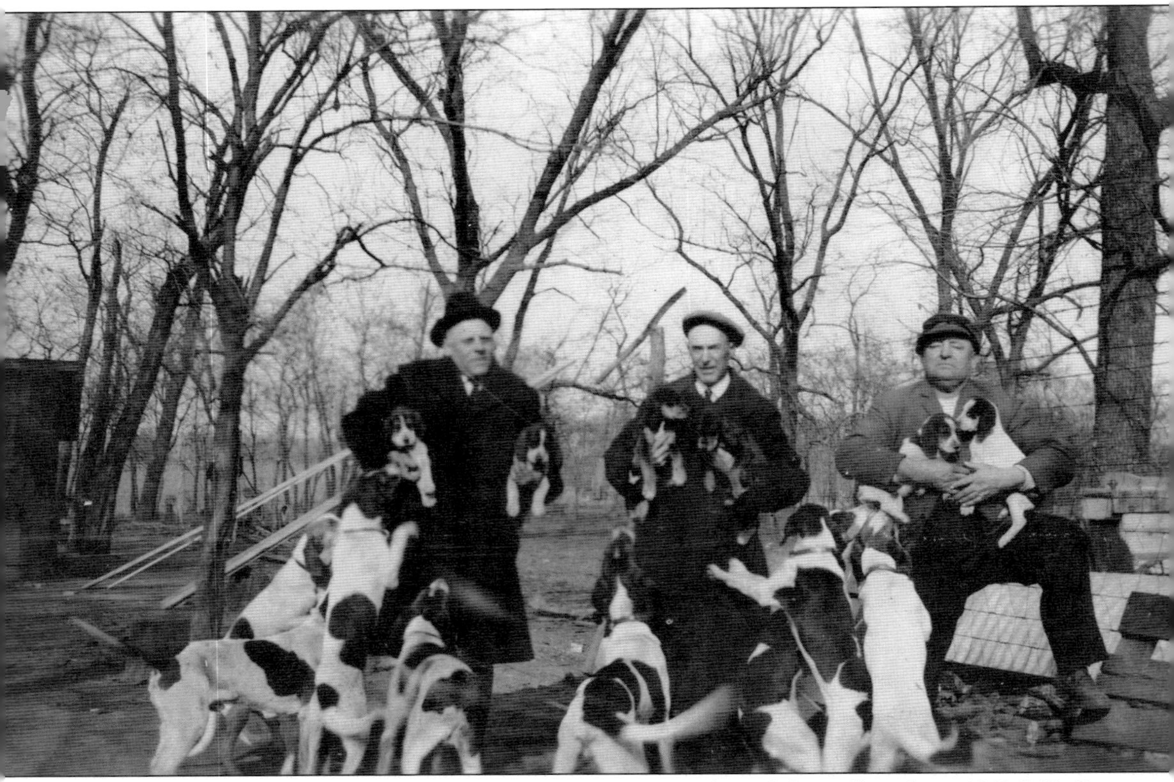

Hunting with dogs was a popular sport for common people and the well-to-do in 1919. L.R. Scott is in the center, and Harmon Henry Harmes is on the right near the Missouri River on Harmes's land. Also shown are Butcher, Red, Effie, and the rest of the foxhounds. Harmes and his friends enjoyed hunting and fishing along the river. He called his land on the Missouri River "Camp Kingfisher." (Courtesy of Betty Wennihan.)

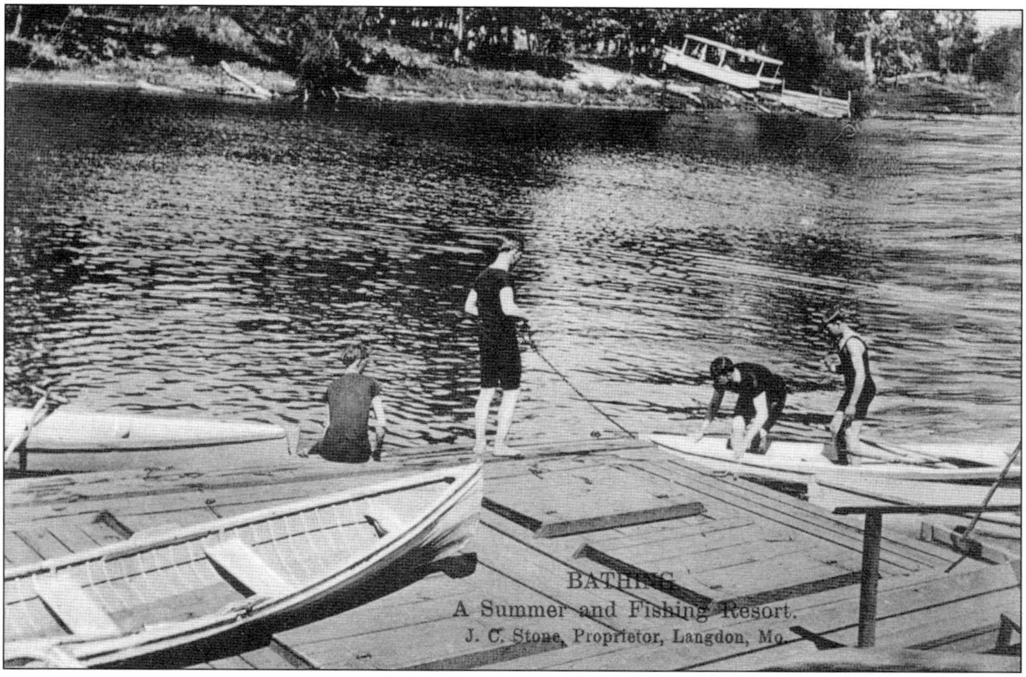

In 1909, at the time of this postcard, J.C. Stone was the proprietor of the resort at Langdon on the Nishnabotna River near where it meets the Missouri River. In these early days, the large lakes that many people vacation on today had not been dammed up yet. An added benefit was the train service that served Langdon and brought people in from miles around. (Courtesy of Hon. Corey Herron.)

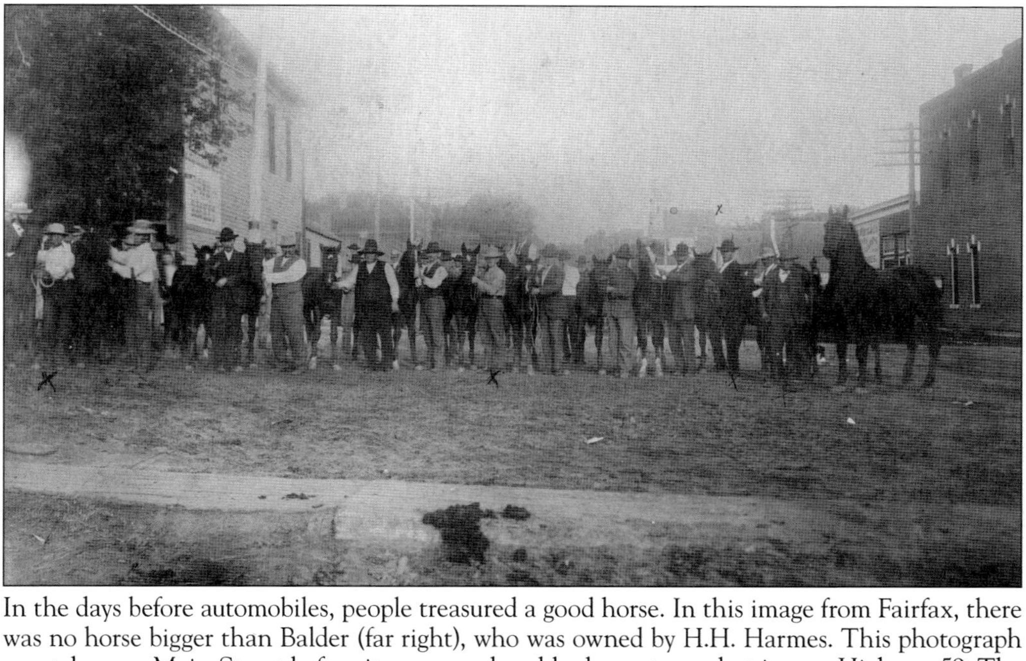

In the days before automobiles, people treasured a good horse. In this image from Fairfax, there was no horse bigger than Balder (far right), who was owned by H.H. Harmes. This photograph was taken on Main Street before it was paved and looks east on what is now Highway 59. The brick building on the right was White Mercantile, where Wake Up N Save opened a new business in 2012. (Courtesy of Betty Wennihan.)

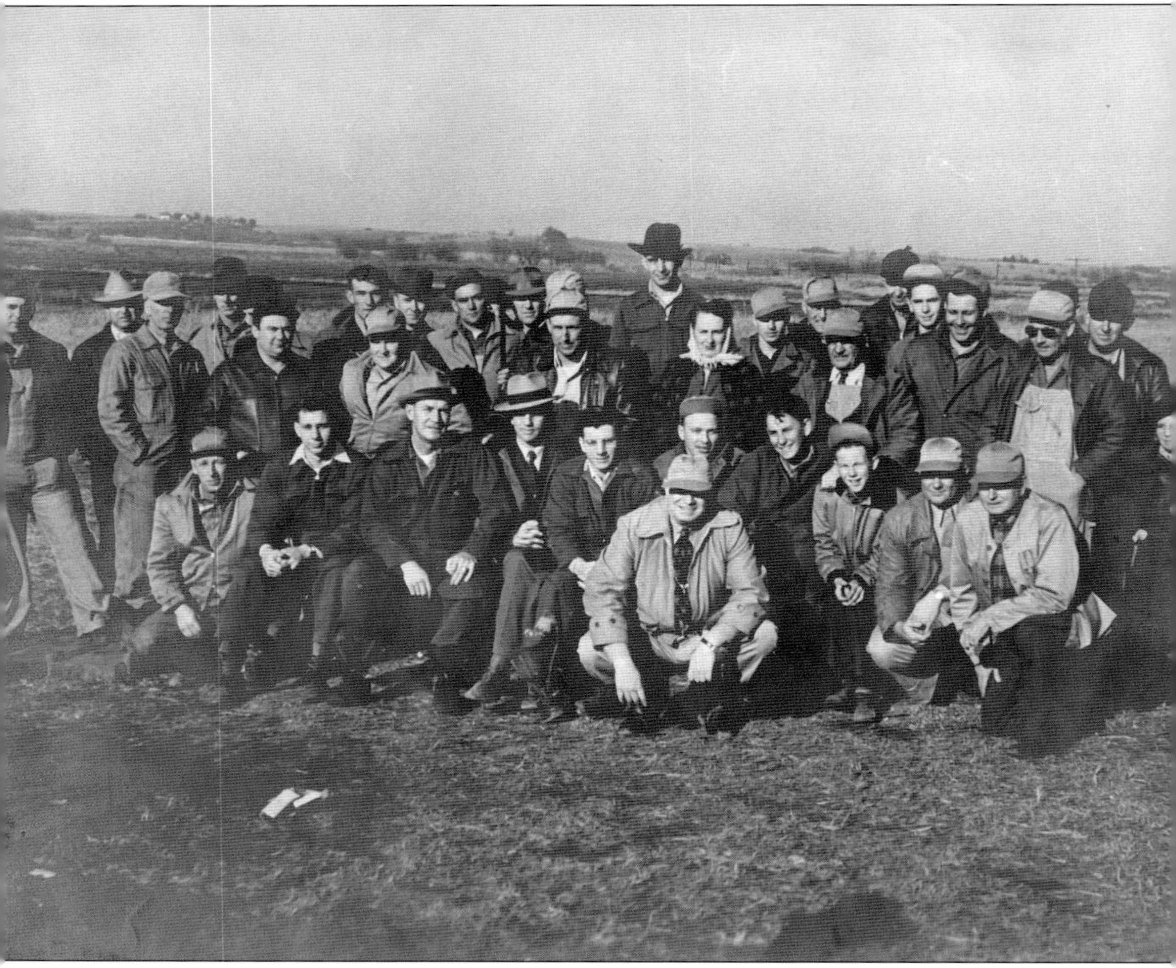

The Tarkio Gun Club, seen here, was on the Leland White farm near the junction of Highway 136 and R Avenue. White was a graduate of Tarkio College in 1920, and he and his father, David Foster White, were successful businessmen in Tarkio. David White purchased the farm in 1905, and Leland later left his business and went into farming. Leland's mother, Mary Alice Sutherland, was born in 1893 in Tarkio. (Courtesy of the Atchison County Historical Society.)

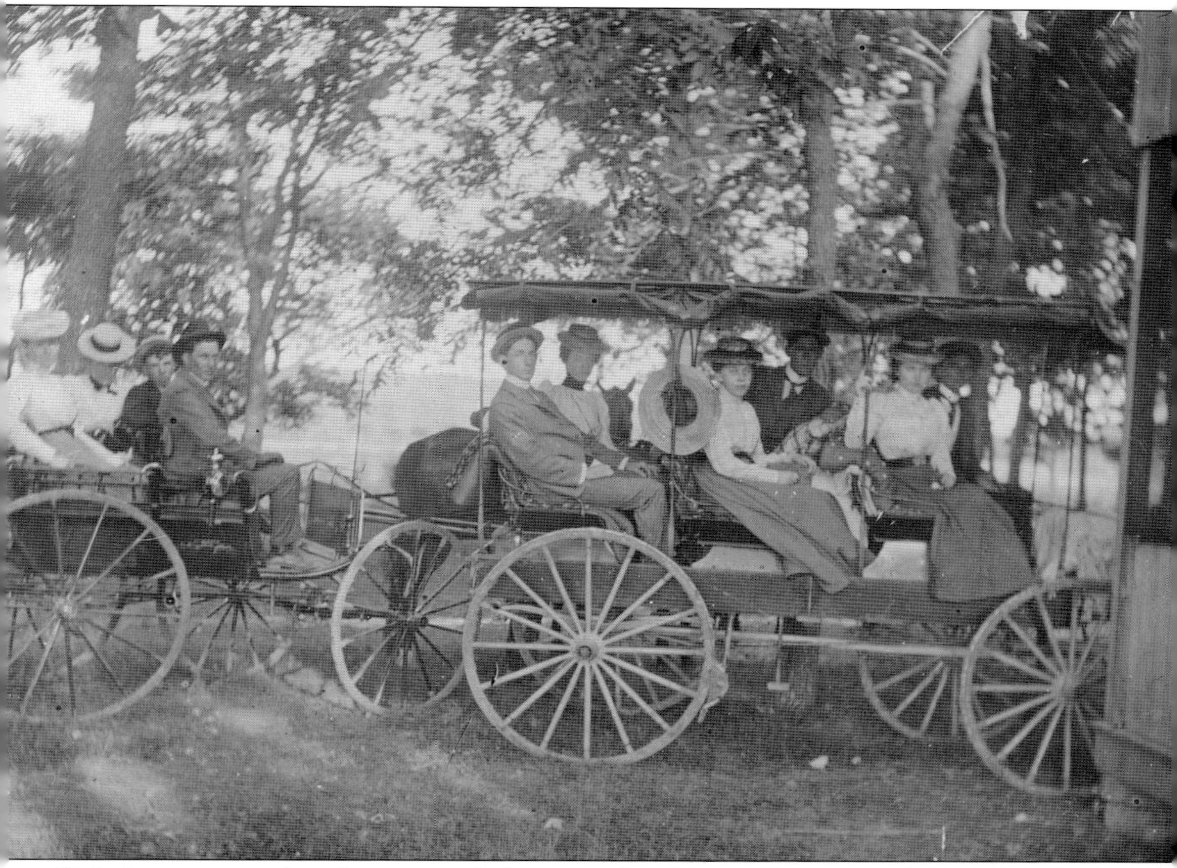

With the exception of two first names, the last names listed among this group include Stevenson, Rankin, Stevenson, Lynn, Coe, Tom Laur (of Westboro), and Coe; one of the Coe girls is Mayme Coe. The Stevenson name referred to here is related to the successful Stevenson family of Tarkio that owned the Tarkio Valley Bank. Brothers Robert M. Stevenson and John P. Stevenson established the bank, and George Joseph Stevenson came later to help with the business. George Joseph was also president of Stevenson Farm Loan Company and was a member of the Missouri Bankers Association and a state bank examiner. (Courtesy of George and Patty Laur.)

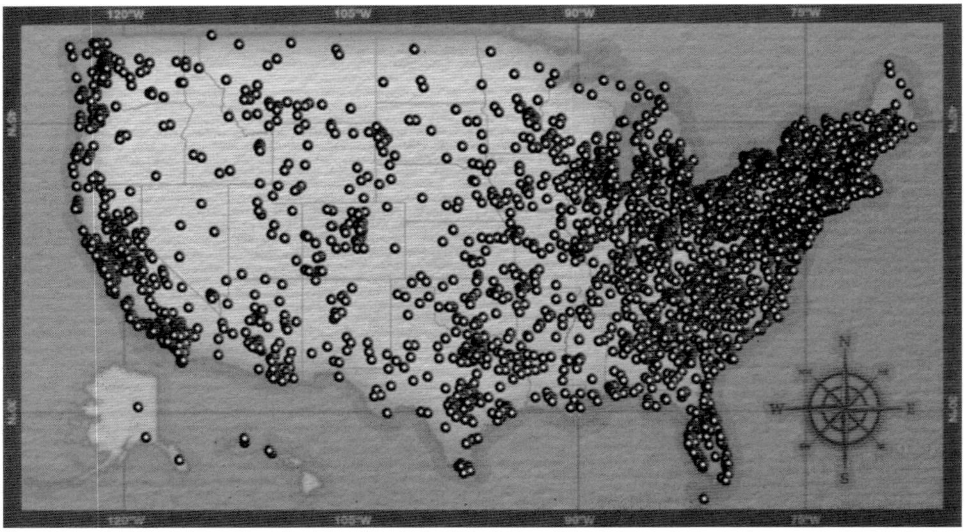